Contested Places

Contested Places

Edited by
Anne Magnussen, Peter Seeberg,
Kirstine Sinclair and Nils Arne Sørensen

UNIVERSITY PRESS OF SOUTHERN DENMARK 2013

© The authors and University Press of Southern Denmark 2013

University of Southern Denmark Studies in History and Social Sciences vol. 469

Printed by Narayana Press
Cover Photo: Martin Rheinheimer

ISBN 978 87 7674 748 0

Printed with grantly support from:

Faculty of Humanity, University of Southern Denmark

University Press of Southern Denmark
Campusvej 55
DK-5230 Odense M
www.universitypress.dk

Distribution in the United States and Canada:
International Specialized Book Services
5804 NE Hassalo Street
Portland, OR 97213-3644 USA
www.isbs.com

Distribution in the United Kingdom:
Gazelle
White Cross Mills
Hightown
Lancaster
LA1 4 XS
U.K.
www.gazellebookservices.co.uk

Contents

Contested Places, Introduction   7
Anne Magnussen & Kirstine Sinclair

INTERSECTIONS

Palestine in Western Travel Literature Narratives
with a Focus on the 19th Century   23
Peter Seeberg & Rune Andersen

Dominion and Transportation – Constantinople as Contested Place   51
Christian Høgel

Detroit's River Rouge as Contested Space   69
David E. Nye

London Lived and Intersected: Anti-Israeli Gaza
War Demonstrations in London in 2009   93
Kirstine Sinclair

BORDERS AS PLACE

Delineating Slovenia: Establishing and Bordering a National Sphere   115
Peter Thaler

Belonging on the Border. Mexican American Strategies
at *El Primer Congreso Nacionalista*, Texas 1911   135
Anne Magnussen

Schleswig as a Contested Place   155
Michael Bregnsbo and Kurt Villads Jensen

Enclaves as Contested Places   179
Per Grau Møller

MEMORY SITES

The Ground Zero Mosque: A Clash Over (Civil) Religion and Freedom   195
Jørn Brøndal

The Battle at Thermopylae and the Myth of Greek Unity   217
Jesper Majbom Madsen

In the Haven of Eternity? A Churchyard as a Contested Place   239
Martin Rheinheimer

A Violently Contested Void – No Man's Land during the First World War   265
Bjarne Søndergaard Bendtsen

Contributors   287

Contested Places, Introduction

Anne Magnussen & Kirstine Sinclair

This volume consists of 12 very different studies. From an analysis of a cemetery in western Denmark over the study of border conflicts in Slovenia to the analysis of the conflicting memories of Thermopylae. All the studies have one thing in common, though: they focus on contested places from a historical perspective.

Historians have been studying contested places since the foundation of history as an academic discipline. It could even be argued that the greater part of traditional history is exactly this: the study of contested places. Most studies of empires, ancient civilisations and cultures, of nation states, wars and diplomatic relations involve conflicts about territory in one way or another. However, it is only within the last 10-15 years that place has been integrated in historical studies as a theoretical and analytical concept. This development has been heavily inspired from outside the historical discipline, from cultural geography.

With this volume we wish to contribute to an increased theoretical and methodological consciousness of place as a concept and as an analytical tool or lens within historical studies. Below we offer a short introduction to the major phases in the development of the theoretical framework behind the study of contested places; however, the main focus of the volume is not theoretical, but rather on examples of how a focus on place can be translated into concrete questions and analytical strategies suitable for studies on a Master of Arts level and within courses touching on history, culture and identity.

In using analyses of contested places as examples of historical studies, we hope to inspire new understandings of, for instance, territorial, cultural, and national interconnectedness; of the limits of perceptions of culture connected to place (thinking inside and outside national boxes);

and of the phenomenon of globalisation, both in an historical and a contemporary perspective. Looking at historical phenomena and periods of time through the perspective of place adds to our understanding of the past, but it also works the other way around, as a consciously historical sensitivity to the study of how place contributes to the understanding of a given place.

The Institute of History at the University of Southern Denmark includes spatiality as part of its research profile, which distinguishes it from other Danish history research departments. The studies included in the volume are the result of a co-operation among the Institute's researchers, representing different periods of time and diverse areas, from American and Middle Eastern studies to Danish and Classical studies. The co-operation continues, but it has already resulted in mutually inspiring discussions highlighting place as an extremely fruitful perspective for interconnecting traditionally separate areas and studies. It is this ability to connect and inspire that we want to help develop further with students in university courses, and we offer the contributions in the present volume as a point of departure for further discussions.

To suit the purpose of a university course based on historical questions and place, the chapters of the volume are divided into three parts with regard to analytical foci rather than to theoretical, geographical or historical aspects. These are *Places as Intersections, Borders as Places* and *Memory Sites*. The three categories differ when it comes to designing a specific study, not least regarding their conceptual framework.

Theoretical Framework and Developments

Before the 1960s, the study of place was largely focusing on ideographic differences between regions. That is to say, places were studied in opposition to each other with attention paid to how the geography of one region would be different to, for instance, the geography of a neighbouring region. Regional geographical studies were based on an understanding of place as geography – as something that could be placed on a map and described in its entirety and uniqueness. Thus, every place was seen as unique due to geographical characteristics if not merely due to the fact that no two places are located in the same physical spot. Cresswell has given a thorough account of this approach and mentions work by Herbertson (1905), Fleure (1919) and Hartshorne (1939) as examples.[1]

Later, regional geography was supplemented by humanistic geography focusing on subjectivity and experience rather than spatial science. With his books published in 1974 (*Topophilia*) and 1977 (*Space and Place*), Yi Fu-Tuan quickly became one of the most widely read humanistic geographers. One of Tuan's main arguments was that individuals turn space into place through endowment of values and through activities: "[…] if we think of space as that which allows movement, then place is pause".[2]

According to Tuan, the human individual, body and mind, is connected to the outside world through the use of senses and mobility, through experience in other words. Humans learn to know the world through sensing it and moving around in it. This is how we learn to understand our own capabilities and the limits of our reach, just as this is how we learn about distance and the basic laws of physics. For a baby the world is no bigger than the distance from its mouth to its food source, most commonly the mother. As it grows older and starts to move around, territory is conquered, knowledge of the world expands and thus the world itself expands for the child.[3]

Following the focus on people in places came an understanding of places as results of social constructions and power relations. This development matched a more general trend towards structuralism in humanistic research in the 1980s. At the heart of this thinking is the understanding that place is not natural but rather the results of human power and power relations. Place is considered as being constructed in two respects in this thinking: both in terms of meaning and in terms of materiality.[4] To say that a place's meaning is constructed means ascribing knowledge and values from the surroundings. For instance, to say that the meaning of a neighbourhood in London such as Tottenham marked by the riots in the summer of 2011 has to do with the forces of

---

1. Tim Cresswell: *Place. A short introduction*, Oxford 2004, p. 16-17.
2. Yi-Fu Tuan. *Space and Place: The Perspective of Experience*, Minneapolis, MN 1977, p. 6
3. Tuan: *Space and Place*, pp. 19-33.
4. Cresswell: *Place*, p. 30.

capitalism or social structures, unemployment and a general dissatisfaction with the British state and society is to ascribe meaning based on knowledge of a particular historical, social and societal conflict to the place. In the same way, claiming that Tottenham is also a construction in terms of how it is materialised, the lay-out of the streets, the housing blocks, the parks, etc. also expresses an understanding of place as man-made as opposed to natural. Humans designed and built these housing schemes, and life in such schemes takes certain specific forms and invites to certain categories of problems and conflicts. Harvey is one of the prominent representatives of this line of thinking,[5] and the main question he is interested in when studying place is: "[B]y what social process(es) is place constructed?"[6]

Also developing from Tuan and similarly minded cultural geographers was an emphasis on people in places and on "geography as the study of the Earth as the home of people",[7] which has resulted in place studied in connection with culture and practice (post-structuralism, phenomenology). Here, it is argued that place is so much more than social constructions. Place should be studied as the basis for human existence and activities. As Malpas phrases it: "[...] place is not founded *on* subjectivity, but is rather that *on which* subjectivity is founded". That is to say, place is understood as something natural and something constructed or resulting from human activity simultaneously. The two, the natural and the man-made, are seen as interacting. Some have developed this into the argument that people only become part of places through performance and that places are best understood as events.[8] Others inspired by this thinking have argued that places are losing their meaning in the globalised world and that all places are becoming one – that everything is *in flux* and that this is the end of place.[9] This again has lead to studies of so-called non-places, places that

---

5. David Harvey: *Justice, Nature and the Geography of Difference*, Oxford 1996.
6. Harvey: *Justice, Nature*, p. 261.
7. Cresswell: *Place*, p. 24.
8. See, for instance, David Seamon: "Body-Subject, Time-Space Routines, and Place-Ballets" in A. Buttimer and D. Seamon (eds.) *The Human Experience of Space and Place*, London 1980, pp. 148-65.
9. Cresswell: Place, pp. 43-49.

have functions but can be everywhere and nowhere – places without any kind of uniqueness such as airports or supermarkets.[10]

Belonging to the group of post-structuralist cultural geographers is the widely read Doreen Massey, who claims that place is about connections, interrelations and intersections. Massey argues that places are connected according to patterns of human behaviour and activities and that these always go beyond market forces, state borders. This means that any place is defined by human activities and that no place has a single identity. She suggests that we think of place not as static or something we can fence in, describe and define, but as something intrinsically incomplete: place as process. In the following, we shall take a closer look at one of Massey's central concepts: "intersections" which we use in the present context as one of the category headlines for our contributions.

Places as Intersections

With her concept "intersections" Doreen Massey has developed a way of studying places that does not have its point of departure in the beginning and end of a place, between place as natural or man-made, or in the dichotomy between inside/outside place. She introduces a new perspective to the study of place with an outset that is fundamentally different from the focus on place as pause represented by Tuan, and on power and conflict, represented by Harvey described above. A new generation of cultural geographers are inspired by this way of thinking, apart from Massey most notably Tim Cresswell, but here, we will focus on Massey's key concepts related to place as intersections, as she is very much a driving force for recent conceptual developments.

In this volume, we understand intersections as often contesting trajectories making up a place. Examples of this are concurrent political representations of the same place or shifting dominant narratives about what a given place is. Another example would be how the same place

---

10. Marc Augé: *Non-Places: Introduction to an Anthropology of Supermodernity*, London and New York 1995.

can be used for different activities showing sympathies and antipathies in connection with the same event or conflict.

Thus, when thinking about place as intersections, the idea that places are natural and have natural boundaries is rejected and a focus on processes and movement through place is introduced. People moving through places with individual stories, preferences, convictions and networks have different stories to tell about the same place – they add different meanings to this place regardless of what type of place it is. All places – big city boulevards, class rooms and cemeteries – should be regarded as open due to people's movement through them. Furthermore, the interaction between people in any given place and the interaction between places both contribute to the creation of a place. As Massey explains: "Conceiving of space as a slice through time, as representation, as a closed system and so forth are all ways of taming it. They enable us to ignore its real import: the coeval multiplicity of other trajectories and the necessary outwardlookingness of a spatialised subjectivity".[11] Thus, place is constituted through interrelations and interactions and is always under construction. Place, according to this perspective, is never closed or finished.[12] A place's uniqueness lies in the interactions between people in this place, how the world is represented in a unique way through these people's connections and activities here and not in the place itself.[13]

An example from the present volume about how different times produce different representations of the same geographical area is given by **Peter Seeberg and Rune Andersen** in their chapter about travel literature on Jerusalem. What they find is that throughout the 19th century, descriptions of Jerusalem have changed according to political and religious outlook and common perceptions of what kind of a place Jerusalem was, with the result that what is ultimately described in this travel literature is not a geographical area or a travel destination as much as it is a mythical destination – "a topological metaphor in the traveler's memory". Jerusalem is created in narratives. Similarly, **Christian Høgel** finds in his study of Constantinople that prevailing narratives about the

---

11. Doreen Massey: *For Space*, London 2005, p. 59.
12. Massey: *For Space*, p. 9.
13. Cresswell: *Place*, p. 74.

city's long history have portrayed the city as not just a contested place but a place which saw its importance and role change dramatically according to what empire it belonged to. However, when one looks closely at the city's geographical importance in connecting two continents and wealth due to sea and land trade, it becomes clear that the city's role and influence has been largely the same and has changed so much less than what shifting rulers would like their peers, populations and antagonists to think. Thus, people's stories about the city have changed more than the importance of the city itself.

David Nye takes us to a factory plant in the United States in his contribution. The point of departure in his chapter is the fact that in writing about the United States, it is very common to find descriptions of changes being made in what was once empty spaces; descriptions of the dichotomy between unutilized space and civilization and progress. However, through analyses of the site that became the most famous factory plant in American history, Henry Ford's River Rough plant, Nye argues that it is much more rewarding to move beyond the common dichotomy and look at such a place as the result of intersecting uses, understandings and meanings – as a place that is constantly being revised and reconstructed.

In the last contribution looking at places as intersections, **Kirstine Sinclair** has set out to find "outwardlookingness of spatialised subjectivities" in contemporary London. In her chapter, she analyses anti-Gaza-war demonstrations in London in the winter of 2008-09 and shows how the same message was delivered using the same medium – political activism in the shape of demonstrations – but different symbols and destinations in the city. January 2009 saw demonstrations in parks marked by peace symbols and demonstrations marked by banners with aggressive slogans in front of embassies. Against this background, the chapter discusses what stories about the conflict are being told, who the audiences are, and narratives of London are produced.

Borders as Places

At one time or another, (almost) any border between two nation states has been a contested place. A national border is where two political entities meet in geographical space, and as dominance over territory comes with control over resources and people, it is no surprise that a border region typically has a history of conflict.

What makes borders especially conflictive – and interesting to study – is that all kinds of questions relating to culture, identity, ethnicity, social structures, etc. criss-cross them continuously. With reference to the theoretical development within the field, studying the border as a place – only – defined by a juxtaposition of two parts would miss out on important points and on the very features that make a border a contested place. Furthermore, the many factors involved in a border region and the ways in which they interact change over time, making it fruitful to study borders – implicitly or explicitly – as intersections and processes in accordance with the new developments within cultural geography as described above.

However, it is equally clear that from the perspective of the individuals, communities and institutions involved, binary thinking is very much at work in the conflicts about borders as places. Nationalist and ethnic conflicts and debates about who belongs are commonplace in border regions. In this sense, thinking in oppositions is a crucial component in an analysis of a border region as intersection and process.

Many nation-state borders have been described and understood as *natural* or as implicitly timeless.[14] There has therefore been a tendency in historical studies to define the subject of study as that of the nation state, as an autonomous entity, without focusing explicitly on the historicity and complexity of its borders. Therefore, studying borders as intersections and processes may draw inspiration from the growing field of transnational studies. As a transnational perspective focuses on the interaction and dynamics between nation states, it agrees with place studies as discussed here on the basic questioning of the nation state

---

14. See, for example, Massey: *For Space*, pp. 64-65.

as autonomous. Transnational studies can in this way help specify and conceptualise studies of borders as contested places.[15]

Peter Thaler's chapter about Slovenia is a study of the efforts to construct a national border, that of Slovenia, primarily in the first half of the 20th century. As a place it could be argued to be contested relating to different ideas of the role of language, of history, and of provincial or ethnic identities. Different attitudes among the involved provinces were also in play.

In **Anne Magnussen**'s chapter on Texas, the focus is on an ethnic community that is by definition transnational, the Mexican Americans, at the beginning of the 20th century. The analysis shows that the Mexican American community fundamentally questions the juxtaposition of two nation states, as they activate historical, legal and socio-economic factors in their efforts to belong in the border region.

As processes, border regions change over time, and in historical studies, it is therefore obvious to think beyond the nation state when studying border regions. Many of the same concepts and strategies used to study borders between nation states can be used also when studying borders between kingdoms, empires, regional autonomies, counties and so on. Defining borders as processes furthermore invites studying borders over long stretches of time, involving changes in power and territorial dominance over centuries. This is what **Michael Bregnsbo and Kurt Villads Jensen** do in their chapter on the Danish/German border region.

Bregnsbo and Jensen's study of borders beyond the nation state draws attention to the many other types of borders – regional or local – that can be studied using the same conceptual framework and strategies as described above. An example of this is **Per Grau Møller**'s study of enclaves in Schleswig from the 16th to the 19th century. The contested nature of these enclaves was based on judicial and economic as well as political differences. Not least the judicial distinction concerning whether the peasants belonged to the kingdom or to the duchy continued to be in play throughout the centuries.

---

15. For further reading on transnational studies, we recommend Akira Iriye & Pierre-Yves Saunier (eds.): *The Palgrave Dictionary of Transnational History*, Basingstoke 2009, or in Danish: Nils Arne Sørensen "Den Transnationale Vending" in *Historisk Tidsskrift*, No. 1, 2009.

All the studies in this section depart from a delimitation of a region which is merely a juxtaposition of two territories that are opposed to each other at least according to one parameter, that of maintaining or gaining more power. The questions posed when studying borders as contested places are therefore typical. What exactly is contested and why? Which factors are in play that turn it into something more complex than political power over territory? How does the border region and its contested characteristics change over time?

Memory Sites

Memory is an integral part of the understanding of place as meaningful. Individuals, communities, institutions activate time in the way they define a place. They do this by attributing a certain history to a place, a history that defines the relationship between them and the particular place for present but also future purposes.[16] The history of a place is therefore decisive for questions concerning belonging, rights and power, and getting to define that history is typically in the interest of several groups and therefore often conflictive. Studies of place and memory are therefore often studies of contested places.

In their discussions of memory and place, cultural geographers such as Doreen Massey, Yi-Fu Tuan and Gillian Rose include memory and the significance of the past as an important factor in the construction of a particular place. In the words of Doreen Massey, "[...] the claims and counter-claims about the present character of a place depend in almost all cases on particular, rival, interpretations of its past" (Massey 1995, 185). In questions and conflicts of identity and belonging to a particular place, how the past of a place is interpreted is crucial, and the potential for conflict is obvious. Borders as contested places as described above

---

16. Cresswell and Hoskins: "Place, Persistence, and Practice: Evaluating Historical Significance at Angel Island, San Francisco, and Maxwell Street", In *Annals of the Ass. of American Geographers* 2008, 98 (2): 392-413; David Glassberg: *Sense of History. The Place of the Past in American Life*. Amherst 2001; Doreen Massey: "Places and Their Pasts". In *History Workshop Journal* 1995 (39): 182-192.

often involve an historical component, and the communities or institutions that get to define a place's past has a considerable power in defining its future, too, in terms of identity, power and belonging.

The field of memory studies has expanded immensely during the last 30 years, and when discussing the significance the past has in the definition of a place, it is impossible not to mention the work *Les Lieux de Memoire* by Pierre Nora from the 1980s.[17] Nora's work has had a crucial significance for the development of studies of monuments, museums, film, etc. in history departments all over Europe. Analysing memory sites has become a fruitful way of studying – mostly national – identities. Nora's definition of place (*lieu*) differs to some extent from the cultural geographers' referred to above. On the one hand, it is broader, as it opens for defining a film, a novel, a biography as a memory site. On the other hand, it is also more limited, as the study of *lieux de memoire* in Nora's sense focuses primarily on the symbolic meaning of a site relating specifically to national projects and identities. Still, Nora's work, as well as succeeding studies of *lieux de memoire*, can very well inspire new questions about memory and place.

Ground Zero in New York exemplifies a *lieu de memoire* also in Nora's sense of the term. From **Jørn Brøndal**'s analysis it is apparent that the contested nature of the place involves two competing conceptions of how to define a common US identity based on different interpretations of history. The example also shows to what extent debates or conflicts about a place's past influence present and future activities and identities. In this case, it relates to the acceptance of different religions, particularly Islam.

Even though many studies of memory and place refer to conflicts involving nation states or national identities, it is of course possible to study memory related to other types of places, bigger or smaller, or from other periods of time, than the nation state. This is the case in **Jesper Majbom**'s study of Thermopylae, in which the national Greek dimension is in play, but so is the more general idea of conflicts between civilisations. In his chapter, Majbom follows the myth about the confrontation at thermopylae and studies how the memory of it changes over time.

---

17. Pierre Nora: "Between Memory and History: Les Lieux de Memoire", in *Representations 26*, Spring 1989, The Regents of the University of California, p. 7-24.

Whereas the study of Thermopylae refers to a broader level than that of a nation state, and relates to a pre-national period of time, **Martin Rheinheimer**'s study of the Amrum cemetery works on a smaller scale, looking at the contested nature of the cemetery, especially as its function changes over time. The cemetery changes from being a crucial marker of local socio-economic status to a tourist attraction, and especially in the periods of change, the contested nature of the place becomes explicit.

Bjarne Søndergaard Bendtsen's contribution discusses the meaning and importance of no man's land as it is used both etymologically and metaphorically in literature and popular culture at the time of the First World War. His study finishes the group of contributions on memory sites by arguing that the concept of no man's land, however widely used it became in the early 20th century onwards, never carried the same meaning for veterans of the war and the general populations in countries affected by the war. To soldiers and veterans, a no man's land would be a narrow patch of territory between enemy lines, whereas no man's land to the wider population would become a metaphor for a place determined by its arid and unconquerable nature.

Concluding remarks and suggestions

As has probably been apparent, the three categories of foci interact in different ways, and it is seldom possible to distinguish clearly between them. Most of them involve an element of memory, one way or another, and in all three categories, it would be useful also to include a focus on intersections. Furthermore, the dichotomies that are active in the study of borders are often in play in the other categories as well. A good example of how these categories are theoretical rather than empirical is seen in the analysis of Ground Zero. Albeit somewhat artificial to categorise empirical case studies as we have done in the current volume, we have chosen to do so in order to emphasise the importance of the research questions posed. Thus, it is the dominant puzzle in the research questions that determines what category a chapter has been placed in. Hopefully, the categorisation can in and of itself be the subject of student and classroom discussions.

The chapters in this volume can be supplemented with other case studies within history, but also other disciplines. In a Danish context, Anne-Marie Mai recently published the monograph "Where the literature takes place".[18] This work also emphasises how an interest in place and space has been increasing recently, also in fields other than history.

Finally, we would like to recommend further reading of the theoretical works that form the backbone of this edited volume. Especially, we would like to recommend the work by Cresswell as a good starting point and also work by Tuan, Massey et al. Please find full references in the bibliography.

---

18. In Danish: *Hvor litteraturen finder sted*, København 2010.

INTERSECTIONS

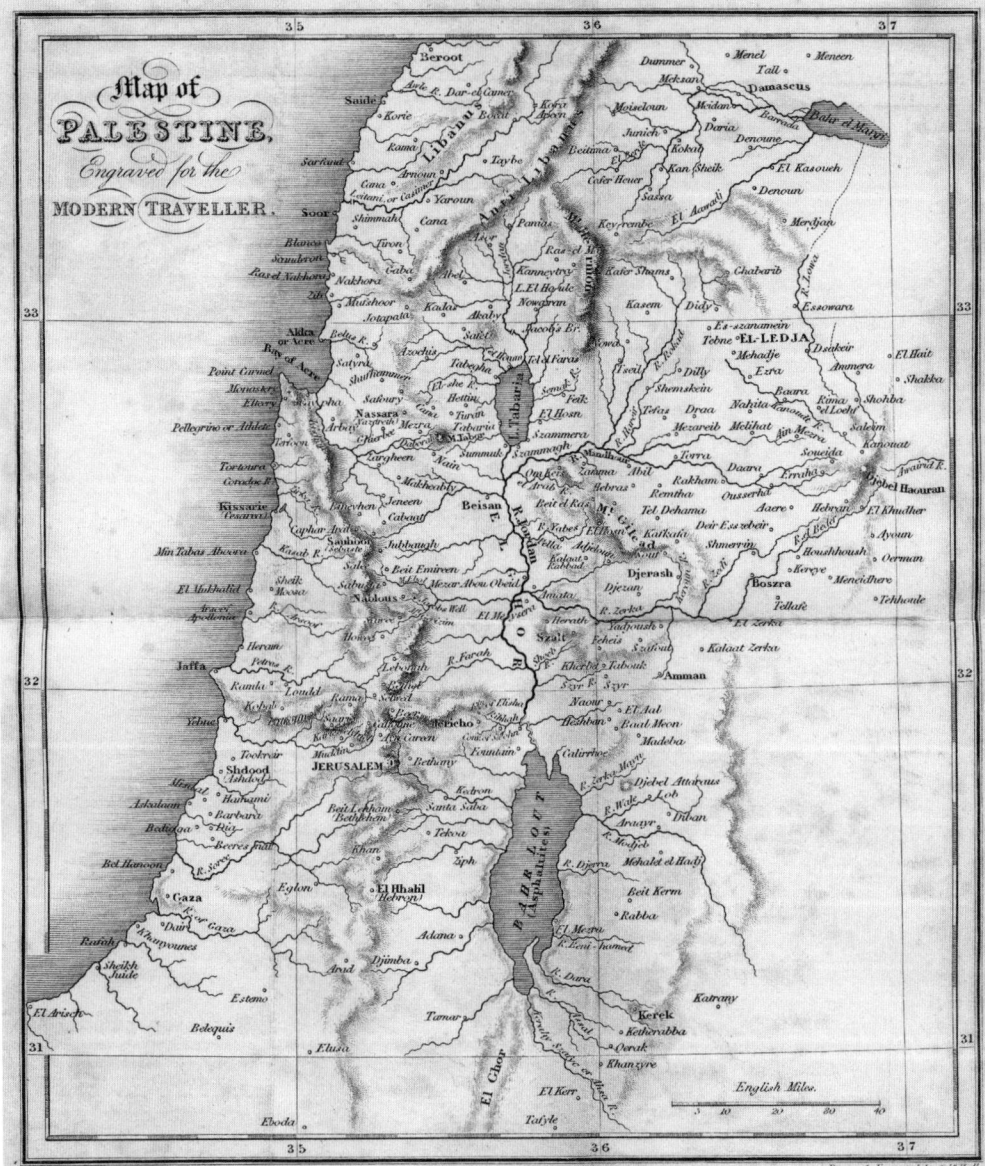

Palestine in Western Travel Literature Narratives with a Focus on the 19th Century

Peter Seeberg & Rune Andersen

"This most interesting of countries is a small canton of Syria, included within the limits of the Turkish empire, and governed by the pashas of Acre and Damascus"
(Josiah Conder: *The Modern Traveler*, 1831)

Palestine was from the beginning of the 16th century to the end of World War 1 exposed to four hundred years of Ottoman rule. The Ottoman hegemony in the Arab World was for centuries uncontested, but a gradual weakening of the Ottoman Empire led to the creation of strong local rule, which sometimes more or less cut the connection to the Porte and led to an occasional reconquering of parts of Ottoman lands. The empire was in the first half of the 19th century under attack from an expansive Egypt, which even threatened the Porte itself. The Sultanate in Istanbul was saved by European intervention and after the Ottoman restoration in the early 1840s the sanjak of Jerusalem, as described by Butrus Abu-Manneh, began to enjoy a special status among the Palestinian sanjaks.

Palestine appears as a conflict-ridden place, which in this chapter is analyzed by looking at contemporary travel literature. Under Ottoman rule the area became subject to complex contradictions related to the conflict between Egypt and the Porte and fraught relations between Palestine and the administrative system of the Ottoman Empire, where Palestine was exposed to local or regional institutional changes in the sanjak structures. Taking its point of departure in travel literature it is the idea to examine the notion of Palestine, as it emerges in selected travelogues, topographical descriptions and guide books with an emphasis on the 19th century.

It is not the intention to use the material as sources to the history of Palestine. Rather it is the ambition to analyze the texts in their historical context as expressions of Western thought regarding Palestine as contested place, as contemporary narratives which demonstrate perceptions of struggles over place as these are interpreted by Western travelers from the 19th century. Also the chapter will not reveal "colonialist misunderstandings"[1] of the Orient, but attempts to contribute to research on Western-Middle Eastern encounters with a focus on the contemporary political culture. The travelogues, topographical descriptions and guide books can in this perspective shed light on contradictions and paradoxes in both static societal structures and dynamic societal changes occurring in Palestine as a contested place – with an ambition of contributing to the historiography focusing on place taking the construction of a Palestinian history as point of departure.

Place, hegemony and identity

> "The Entente Powers are determined that the Arab race shall be given full opportunity of once again forming a nation in the world (…) Great Britain and her Allies will pursue a policy with this ultimate unity in view. So far as Palestine is concerned we are determined that no people shall be subject to another…"
> ('Hogarth's Message', January 1918)

The Balfour Declaration of 1917 transformed the position of the Zionist movement vis-à-vis the Arabs in Palestine and created an umbrella under which they could pursue their goal of establishing a Jewish state in Palestine. Therefore the Arab leaders were angry and worried. As Avi Shlaim points out, Hogarth's Message is crucial for understanding the

---

1. See for instance Amos Nadan: "Colonial Misunderstanding of an Efficient Peasant Institution: Land Settlement and Musha Tenure in Mandate Palestine, 1921-47," in *Journal of the Economic and Social History of the Orient* 46, no. 3 (2003).

attitude of King Hussein's to the situation in the Middle East after the Balfour Declaration. With the promise Hussein "thought he had Britain's assurance that the settlement of the Jews in Palestine would not conflict with Arab independence in that country."[2] Hussein was hardly opposed to Jewish settlements in Palestine and having a guarantee that nothing would happen which might jeopardize the political and economic possibilities for the Arabs in Palestine, he remained silent for a while. Later, when he realized that the British refused to recognize Arab independence in Palestine, he felt betrayed, as Shlaim mentions, and accused them of breach of faith.

Palestine constitutes in this context a hierarchy of meaning. The area became conquered by the Ottomans from 1514 to 1517 and was a part of the empire until 1917. In the 19th century Acre[3] and later Jerusalem were the dominant cities in the area; Palestine was in a period even a province under direct rule by the Porte. Palestine was during the 19th century going through a process where its status as a subnational entity strengthened a local feeling of national coherence, but where external influences created de-nationalizing tendencies. First of all, of course, through the external influence from the Porte. Secondly because of the Egyptian invasion and retreat. Thirdly as a result of the British dominance, indirectly in connection with the reconstruction of Ottoman hegemony after the threat from Mohammad Ali and later when the alliance between the British armies and the Arab Revolt pushed the Ottomans back towards Anatolia. In 1918 king Hussein was greatly disturbed by the possible consequences of the Balfour Declaration, first of all of a new possible reality which he anticipated, namely a Palestine dominated by Jews.

Palestine as place can be defined by its nationalities and subnationalities, as it will be discussed below: a Palestinian in for instance 1850 was in possession of several identities, being a subject of the Sultan in Istanbul, an Arab Palestinian, a Muslim, an inhabitant in Jerusalem understood as a city and as a provincial center. Saskia Sassen points to such spatial

---

2. Avi Shlaim: *Israel and Palestine. Reappraisals, Revisions, Refutations*, London and New York 2009, p. 7.
3. See Thomas Philipp: *Acre. The Rise and Fall of a Palestinian City, 1730-1831*, New York 2002.

dimensions of identity, reflecting on subnationalities in relation to globalization.[4] This way of conceptualizing identity can, however, also be applied on changes of identity related *in casu* to the historical deroute of an empire. Identities related to place are exposed to destabilizing of hierarchies, as mentioned by Sassen.[5] They are also exposed to delocalization, when for instance the status as sanjak moves from Acre to Jerusalem, and furthermore to changes of local or regional scaling as when, on the eve of Muhammad Ali's invasion, the sanjaks of Jerusalem and Nablus were transferred to the control of the governor of Acre, Abdullah Pasha.[6] Place has its history, in this context related to a community being transformed and modernized.

Timothy Oakes discusses how place as theoretical concept have had a tendency of becoming devalued in modern social science as a result of its conflatedness with the concept of community – often thought of as a concept related to premodern realities: local communities, tribes etc. In traditional vs. modern dichotomy place might often be attached to the former. Oakes claims, however, that by analyzing intersections between much nineteenth- and twentieth-century literature and contemporary cultural geography, it is possible to argue that place should not be related to the traditional society, but rather to the paradoxes and contradictions of modernity (see later).[7] And modernity is not only national uniformity and spacial hegemony, but represents also resistance to unilinear progress. Place is not, as Oakes shows, a terrain of emancipatory subjectivity, this is beyond what place might deal with, but place can help explain historical dynamics and new developments, regardless if they have restorative utopia as nexus or not.

An enormous number of historical accounts – and an in the second half of the 20th century historically unparalleled media coverage of the small entity – make it obvious that Palestine is one of the most frequently debated places in history, especially in modern times. It is, however, im-

---

4. Saskia Sassen: "Globalization or Denationalization?," in *Review of International Political Economy* 10, no. 1 (2003).
5. Ibid., p. 5.
6. Ilan Pappé, ed.: *The Israel/Palestine Question*, London and New York 1999, p. 43.
7. Timothy Oakes: "Place and the Paradox of Modernity," in *Annals of the Association of American Geographers* 87, no. 3 (1997).

portant to determine the historical background for the notion of Palestine – and in attempting to do that to determine the relation between place and space when dealing with Palestine. History produces changing identities, as reflected on by Doreen Massey: [8] the Ottoman Empire experienced a decline and fall, and in Palestine local hierarchies were perpetuated or restructured. This chapter claims that we can deepen our understanding of this through the conceptualizations of spacial identity that we find in travel literature.

The notion of Palestine changes and this is reflected in several different perspectives. The spacial reconfigurations attached to the political development in the region emphasizes that Palestine as place can be understood as intersection – as a dynamic relation between the general center-periphery logic related to the relation between the center in Istanbul and the (Palestinian) province. This perspective, however, also has a dynamic dimension related to a regional-local contestation: Palestine as territorial place changes its institutional structures in a process which gradually produces new identity formations, and a Palestinian nationalism emerges which defines itself in ideological terms, but also in geographical terms. To speak with Tim Cresswell: "Place provides a template for practice – an unstable stage for performance. Thinking of place as performed and practiced can help us think of place in radically open and non-essentialized ways, where place is constantly struggled over and reimagined in practical ways. Place is the raw material for the creative production of identity rather than an a-priori label of identity. Place provides the conditions of possibility for creative social practice."[9]

The historical dimension attached to the theme of this chapter is represented in a dynamic and conflictual reality in the 19th century. This logic, however, is mobilized in new configurations in the 20th century, where the intersective perspective is underlined. The dramatic changes in Palestine related to the collapse of the Ottoman empire, the "triangular" interregnum of the mandate period and the dichotomous, yet

---

8. Doreen Massey: "Geographies of Responsibility," in *Geografiska Annaler* 86, no. 1 (2004).
9. Tim Cresswell: "Introduction. Theorizing Place," in *Mobilizing Place, Placing Mobility: The Politics of Representation in a Globalized World*, ed. Ginette Verstraete and Tim Cresswell, New York 2002, p. 25.

still dynamic, Israel-Palestine contradictions are interpreted in the travel literature, which in this chapter is taken as empirical point of departure.

Palestine under Ottoman rule

For centuries Palestine was a destination for travellers from the whole world. Many of them were pilgrims from all three monotheisms. Thomas Wright, a British academic, published in 1848 a collection of travel narratives covering a thousand years, starting with "The Travels of Bishop Arculf in the Holy Land" (700 A.D.) and ending with "A Journey from Aleppo to Jerusalem at Easter, A.D. 1697, by Henry Mandrell".[10] Ten years before that, in 1838, the American theologian Edward Robinson travelled to Palestine with the intention of following the route of the Israelites from Egypt to Palestine and identify the historical biblical sites.[11] According to Nabil Matar "the publication of his findings opened the door for the largest flood of travelers, missionaries, and millenarians in the modern period, all of whom viewed Palestine as a terra incognita to be discovered and possessed."[12] It is probably this overwhelming interest in Palestine which is the background for the fact that travel guides are produced as early as in the first half of the 19th century – and thereby later became a model for guide books for other destinations.

Place, geography and identity

An example of this, an early travel book covering Palestine, is Josiah Conder's "The Modern Traveller. A Description, Geographical, Histori-

---

10. See Thomas Wright, ed.: *Early Travels in Palestine Comprising the Narratives of Arculf, Willibald, Bernard, Sæwulf, Sigurd, Benjamin of Tudela, Sir John Maundeville, De La Brocquière, and Maundrell*, 1st ed., London 1848.
11. Nabil Matar: "Palestine," in *Literature of Travel and Exploration. An Encyclopedia*, ed. Jennifer Speake, London and New York 2003.
12. Ibid., p. 915.

cal, and Topographical of the Various Countries of the Globe. Palestine".[13] It has the character of a modern guide book, and, published in 1831, it contains a thorough description of Palestine, its boundaries and geography, political divisions, natural history, climate etc. It also has a number of chapters, which describes the different localities of the area, with descriptions of routes to and from, and detailed accounts of the buildings, monuments and sights. There is a map of Palestine, a glossary of Arabic words occurring in the geography of Palestine and an appendix with a description and a map with index numbers showing the sights of the old city. In the introduction Conder presents Palestine as a canton of Syria:

> "Palestine, the land of Israel, the kingdom of David and Solomon, the most favoured and the most guilty country under heaven; during between two and three thousand years, the only section of the earth where the worship of the true God was perpetuated, –
> "Over whose acres walked those blessed feet
> Which eighteen hundred years ago were nailed,
> For our advantage, to the bitter cross" –
> This most interesting of countries is a small canton of Syria, included within the limits of the Turkish empire, and governed by the pashas of Acre and Damascus."[14]

Conder describes how the country is very narrow, consisting of a slip "which does not exceed fifty miles",[15] stretching out between the Mediterranean and the Jordan River – in the north the "range of the Libanus and the Anti-Libanus forms a natural boundary" and in the south "it is pressed upon by the Syrian and Arabian deserts". This is obviously somewhat imprecise and in accordance with the reality that Palestine was "within the limits of the Turkish empire" and governed by pashas of Acre and Damascus. It was neither possible nor meaningful in detail to describe the borders of Palestine more precisely than the following:

---

13. Josiah Conder: *The Modern Traveller. A Description, Geographical, Historical, and Topographical of the Various Countries of the Globe. Palestine,* New (?) ed. London 1831.
14. Ibid., p. 1. The inserted quotation is from Shakespeare: Henry IV, Part 1, act 1, sc. 1.
15. Ibid., p. 2.

"Palestine is now distributed into pashalics. That of Acre or Akka extends from Djebail nearly to Jaffa; that of Gaza comprehends Jaffa and the adjacent plains; and these two being now united, all under the jurisdiction of the Pasha of Acre. Jerusalem, Hebron, Nablous, Tiberias, and, in fact, the greater part of Palestine, are included in the pashalic of Damascus, now held in conjunction with that of Aleppo, which renders the present pasha, in effect, the viceroy of Syria. Though both pashas continue to be dutiful subjects to the Grand Seignior in appearance, and annually transmit considerable sums to Constantinople to ensure the yearly renewal of their office, they are to be considered as tributaries, rather than subjects of the Porte."[16]

Palestine as place is thus firstly to be understood as a loosely defined area characterized by Turkish hegemony and as a physically defined territorial area. It is secondly, however, a territory in the sense that it also is defined by its local authorities and their mutual relations; land distributions related to the obligations, as tributaries, annually to "transmit considerable sums to Constantinople". Conder mentions that the population is very heterogeneous, consisting of "Turks, Syrians, Bedouin, Arabs, Jews, Latin, Greek, and Armenian Christians, Copts, and Druses." These differences are to be seen also in the physical features: "The Syrian physiognomy assumes, however, a cast of features characteristically different in the Aleppine, the Turkman, the native of Mount Libanus, the Damascene, the inhabitant of the sea-coast from Beirut to Acre, and the Bedouin." The Ottoman hegemony is expressed by the fact that "[T]he Turks, in Palestine, as elsewhere throughout the empire, occupy all the civil and military posts."[17]

The English Reverend J. A. Spencer, who visited Egypt and Palestine in the 1840s, also comments on the physical features of the people he met on his travels. It seems that he had expected to find people looking rather different from Europeans and was caught by surprise by what he actually found:

---

16. Ibid., p. 6.
17. Ibid., p. 7.

"The people of the villages, and in the fields, looked at us with curiosity, and some degree of sullenness, but they did not at all molest us, or refuse to answer any questions which we chose to ask; in general too, I was a little surprised at the light color of the inhabitants, who, with the exception of the effect of the sun upon those exposed in the fields, appeared to me as of much the same complexion as most of the people of our own country. This applies more particularly to the younger women and children, many of whom, I noticed, had very beautiful, sparkling, black eyes, and regular features, not infrequently of classic mould."[18]

To Spencer Palestine is unfamiliar, the Palestinians make strange noises and can apparently be somewhat scary, as observed while travelling from Jaffa to Jerusalem:

"...the drums were beaten, the castanets jingling, the women making that indescribable noise not unlike an ullaloo, the yellow and red flags flying, and the people in a state of some excitement. The cause of all this, we learned, was the departure of pilgrims to Neby Músa, or the tomb of the Prophet Moses, which, for convenience' sake, the Mohammadans have located on the west side of the Jordan (...) We were rather glad not to have come in contact with these pilgrims, for they are full of fanaticism, and on such occasions seem to consider it a merit to insult and abuse Christians."[19]

In Spencers narrative we find statements, where contradictions between the different religious groups in Palestine come to the fore. In his description it is especially the Muslims, who seem to be offensive towards people from other beliefs, as it can be seen in the quotation above. Spencer foresees that a solution might be found to the inappropriate situation. In a sense Spencer in the midst of the nineteenth century is anticipating the conflicts of the twentieth century, by pointing to a likely clash with the Muslims. Palestine is here seen, by the English clergyman, as a contested

---

18. J. A. Spencer: *Sketches of Travels in Egypt and the Holy Land*, 1st ed. London 1850, p. 256.
19. Ibid., p. 262.

place, where a settlement will have to be imposed by an all-powerful God, who once and for all will find the right and just measure:

> "…I verily believe, that God is intending, in His wise Providence, to effect the return of His people to the Holy Land (…) The way – if we may venture to speak thus of the future – is preparing for such a result. The imposture of Mohammed is fast sinking into ruin and disgrace: the Turks are losing their power and influence; and the Christian nations of the West, as they are but agents in the hands of the Supreme Ruler of the Universe, so they are, unconsciously it is true, yet only waiting the time when He shall see fit to sweep away every vestige of Mohammedanism, and plant anew the banner of the cross on every hill-top and tower of the Holy Land."[20]

Spencer reimagines Palestine in contrast to what he sees as a contemporary disgraceful situation. To speak with Cresswell we can say that for Spencer Palestine is becoming a kind of "raw material for the creative production of identity" in a fictitious future, which we will experience when time comes. The land and its small cities are symbols of a Palestine as a place of a higher order, where the tangible realities and the future dream melt into a vision for Palestine. Palestine is furthermore referred to as a place, the meaning of which is changing over time. Palestine represents an intersection, where the claim to locality is crucial for the author. Palestine perceived in this way underlines the historical dimension of Palestine (and Jerusalem) and this presence of history and the resulting changes in perspective are emphasized in many of the travelogues from the nineteenth century.

Place, imagination and history

Several other travellers are describing how Palestine are imagined and reimagined, as for instance the American traveller Bayard Taylor, who, like Spencer, travelled in Palestine in the first half of the 1850s. Taylor

---

20. Ibid., p. 486.

is (pretending to be) surprised by what he sees, when approaching Jerusalem:

> "From the descriptions of travellers, I had expected to see in Jerusalem an ordinary Turkish town; but that before me, with its walls, fortresses, and domes, was it not still the city of David? I saw the Jerusalem of the New Testament, as I had imagined it. Long lines of walls crowned with a notched parapet and strengthened by towers; a few domes and spires above them (...) for one brief moment, I knew that I was in Palestine; that I saw Mount Olivet and Mount Zion; and – I know not how it was – my sight grew weak, and all objects trembled and wavered in a watery film."[21]

For Taylor the image of Palestine is exceeded by the actual reality and the experience of seeing the place creates a mental experience beyond the natural. Maybe it is history itself which produces this extraordinary perception of Palestine and especially Jerusalem. As described by the English historian Arthur Stanley, Palestine is in a class of its own in the sense that it more than other countries is a land of historical remnants:

> "This is the most convenient place for noticing a peculiarity of the present aspect of Palestine, which though not, properly speaking, a physical feature, is so closely connected both with its outward imagery and with its general situation, that it cannot be omitted. Above all other countries in the world, it is a Land of Ruins."[22]

Palestine as place is lived history. As Stanley mentions the ruins are not on a scale equal to those of Greece, and still less to those of Egypt, but "there is no country in which they are so numerous, none in which they bear so large a proportion to the villages and towns still in existence."[23]

---

21. Bayard Taylor: *The Land of the Saracen; Pictures of Palestine, Asia Minor, Sicily and Spain*, 1 ed. New York 1855, p. 58.
22. Arthur Penrhyn Stanley, D. D.: *Sinai and Palestine. In Connection with Their History*, 2 ed. New York 1870, pp. 117-18.
23. Ibid., p. 118.

It is an important point that history has not left the ruins unaffected. The ruins have been made use of for building purposes, "Western Palestine has always been the resort of a population which, however rude and scanty, has been sufficiently numerous and energetic to destroy and to appropriate edifices which in the less frequented parts beyond the Jordan have escaped through neglect and isolation."[24]

Palestine represents a unique reshaping of the relation over time between space and the political and whereas the land behind the Jordan River has been relatively sparsely populated and therefore has left the ruins of for instance Baalbek, Jerash and Palmyra comparatively well-preserved, this is not the case in the area west of the Jordan River. Symbolically the ruins of Palestine can be articulated in Foucauldian terms as representing geographies of resistance, as coined by David Featherstone.[25] The American writer Samuel A. Cox seems to disagree with Stanley regarding the "land of ruins", but reminds us of the Turkish presence in Palestine, while describing the road from the Mediterranean Sea to Ramallah – on the way to Jerusalem:

> "Some ruins, mostly of churches, here and there appear; while square windowless, Turkish guard-houses are seen at intervals, at whose doors are the Turkish soldiers, with guns and cigarettes (...) There is not much to see on the road until you come to Ramleh. Beggars and backsheesh, and some old relics as crusading reminders are here, and one very conspicuous object. The latter is a square tower, with a winding staircase (...) It is over one thousand years old, and has many Moslem associations. Ramleh has been the scene of much contest..."[26]

The contestation of the Palestinian town of Ramleh is obvious for the American traveler and the different historically founded expressions of hegemony are contrasted with the contemporary Ottoman dominance, represented by the Turkish soldiers. History and hegemony are inter-

---

24. Ibid.
25. David Featherstone: "Spatialities of Transnational Resistance to Globalization: The Maps of Grievance of the Inter-Continental Caravan," in *Transactions of the Institute of British Geographers* 28, no. 4 (2003), p. 408.
26. Samuel S. Cox: *Orient Sunbeams or from the Porte to the Pyramids, by Way of Palestine*, 1 ed. New York 1882, pp. 276-277.

mingled in the Palestinian history and constitutes an example of how political conflicts can be thought of in spacial terms. Different spacial practices belonging to different times construct "geographies of power in antagonistic ways"[27] and in Palestine the historical configurations of "power geometry" – to speak with Massey[28] – are obviously present and analytically important. The American Professor of Ancient Languages and Literature Henry M. Harman mentions in his travelogue that:

> "...the smallness of Palestine does not diminish its importance in our eyes. No country in the world has had such an influence upon the human race. Here lived the Patriarchs, Prophets, and Apostles (...) No spot on earth can compare with this in sacredness (...) In the moral world as in the physical, there must be a plan; and the Jewish and Christian revelation, made originally to Abraham and his posterity in the descendants of Jacob, embraces this plan (...) While in Palestine we felt that the Bible, in all its allusions to geography and to local customs, belongs to that land, but that in the theology and devotional strain it soars far above the Holy Land."[29]

Harman ascribes specific characteristics to Palestine because of its religious past. The extraordinary sacredness explains the importance of the country. Obviously the Christian Western travellers very much focus on the religious dimensions of being in the country. The biblical allusions to a specific geographical context endow Palestine as place with a status as a destination you have to visit – almost as a religious duty. Palestine and Jerusalem become places of pilgrimage and a journey to the Holy Land – as it characteristically is called – gives the traveller a possibility to establish a mental template, which produces a better understanding of not only the holy texts but of their geographical context, their place (of origin). For the traveller Palestine is becoming a part of his or her

---

27. Featherstone: "Spatialities of Transnational Resistance to Globalization: The Maps of Grievance of the Inter-Continental Caravan", p. 409.
28. Doreen Massey: "Power-Geometry and a Progressive Sense of Place" in *Mapping the Futures: Local Cultures, Global Change*, ed. J. Bird, et al., London 1993.
29. Henry M. Harman, D. D.: *A Journey to Egypt and the Holy Land, in 1869-1870*, 1 ed. Philadelphia 1873, pp. 216-17.

identity – the sense of self. The identity is rooted in the place and the hardships on the way are to be tolerated in order to reach the physical place and the higher insight.

Topography and being

Topography and being, formulated in this particular syntactic sequence, refers to a world of experience and a logic of being (without entering psychopathological explanations) which is intimately connected to the concept of Palestine and the myths that cling to this particular place. In J.L. Porter's *A handbook for travellers in Syria and Palestine* the ambiance and emotive approach to the geography of Palestine is both permeated and absorbed through this religious symbolic logic. "Palestine is the stage on which the most wondrous events of the world's history were enacted. Every nook and corner of it is "holy ground"."[30]

The origin of the name Palestine is in its very foundation based on a contestation. Behind this controversy historians and geographers would on one side credit the Greek traveller and historian Herodotus (484-424 B.C.) as the originator of the term[31] whilst others would reject this thesis by arguing that later translations of Herodotus' maps was subject to prior knowledge of the translator turning Philistine into Palestine. Others[32] credit the Roman emperor Hadrian (76-138) as creator of the term linking Hadrian's plot to destroy the Jewish people by reinventing the ancient archenemy of Israel – The Philistines – who had been extinct since the sixth century B.C.[33] By erasing or influencing existing geography and renaming the territory, Hadrian re-established the ancient mythological dispute and affected the geometrical imaginary and memory of the place.

---

30. Josias Leslie Porter: *A Handbook for Travellers in Syria and Palestine*, vol. 2. J. Murray 1868, p. 5. The inserted quotation mark on *holy ground* is by Porter.
31. D. Asheri et al.: *A Commentary on Herodotus*, Oxford 2007, p. 154.
32. This discussion is very common amongst religious and politically involved people with interest in the area. The point is not to reflect on the right interpretation, but to emphasize the mythological incongruence.
33. R. Lambert: *Beloved and God: The Story of Hadrian and Antinous*, Phoenix 1997, p. 175.

To sense or rationalize through mythological geometrics beyond the stratified human remains (usually associated with archaeology i.e. place as possessing a specific and physical character) place can be mythologized through imaginative and ambient constructions. The uses of eternal and timeless myths influence the topographical order, justifying the present reality through the linkage between geography and the myths of prehistoric times and eschatology. Thus do the past and future intersect into the present and is constantly underlying in the hierarchy of the topographic valuation. Even though the mythological perception often has a factor of fear, it still has a familiarity to it that frames existential distance and makes it a more confidential companion. The nature and composition of myths often reflect a polar tension or principles of time, space and existential features that mutually define and compliment/exclude each other. In this sense the myth serves as a text or script for the dramatization and staging of events on the world stage. In this context people, time and spaces are not viewed as strictly separated from each other, but as acting in static congruency or incongruency.[34]

The intense imagination of Palestine is not unfamiliarly characterized by the mythological frame of religion and its unaccountable dissidents who all claim a territorial and historic dogmatic pact to Palestinian soil. Herein exists a dynamic activity around a variety of religious, political and cultural communities of remembrance claiming exclusive understandings of reality. All three monotheisms also have undisputed textual affiliation with the land respectively calling it *The Promised Land* and *The Holy Land*.[35] Being a place on the premise of mythology, mind you different proclaimed mythologies, Palestine undergoes a constant topographic metamorphosis through both tangible and imaginary transformations with changing historical and narrative validity. The Handbook, with its advisory approach to geography and account of the manners and cus-

---

34. Gerhard J. Bellinger and Jørgen Hansen: *Mytologisk Leksikon*, 3. udgave, Copenhagen 2002, pp. 5-7.
35. Palestine as the *Promised Land* of the Jews is mentioned several places in the Hebrew Bible (ex. Numbers 34:1-12). For the Christians the reference to *The Holy Land* and its geographical specifications are explicit in the four gospels which all take place in Palestine whereas the Qur'an assigns *The Holy Land* to the Muslims in Sura 5,21

toms[36] of the population, would often reflect this textual ambience of a religious ordering. In *A handbook for travellers in Syria and Palestine*, the religious order is explicitly present as the first introductory line: "The Bible is the best Handbook for Palestine; the present work is only intended to be a companion to it."[37] The handbook also has suggestions for further reading on the geography of Palestine (*Authorities on the Geography and Statistics*)[38] that includes "Robinson's *Biblical Resources* (…) Drew's *Scripture Lands*; Wilson's *Lands of the Bible*",[39] which all have the biblical denominator as the topographical reference.

This distinctive atmosphere or ambiance of metaphysical presence and contestation is central in the guidebooks and travelogues of the 19th century, where the manners and customs of the inhabitants are given materiality in accordance with the historical mythologies. The racial references are in this sense static and always localizable as analogical with the mythological *other*. In this regard the "unnatural behaviour"[40] by the Jews, as noted by Lorenz, or the "The imposture of Mohammed"[41] as noted by Spencer are held and intermixed with the unchangeable mythological *other*. The racial taxonomy and the frequent linkage to prescribed religious values constitute a significant part of the traveller's intense experiences with Palestine's religious history and conflict.

---

36. In the mid-19th century English explorers often applied what was unofficially named the Manners and Customs genre. This nineteenth-century term evolved in response to the British reader's desire for knowledge, and if possible, to sympathize with the ways other people lived differently from themselves. The term *Manners and Customs* was among the most common among travel literature titles in the nineteenth century and could, because of its typological structure easily be adapted to the Handbook (guidebook)
37. Porter: *A Handbook for Travellers in Syria and Palestine*, p. 5
38. Ibid., p. 15
39. Ibid., p. 15
40. D.E. Lorenz, Ph.D.: *The Mediterranean Traveller*, 4 revised ed. London and Edinburgh, New York, Chicago, Toronto 1911, p. 225.
41. Spencer: *Sketches of Travels in Egypt and the Holy Land*, p. 486

Mythological Cartography

The traveller's experiences with the geographical complexities of Palestine is not at least reflected in the cartographic systemization of the area that intersects Asia, Africa and Europe and could almost be said to epitomize cartography in itself.[42] In this sense the topographic mapping of Palestine was from the beginning caught between conflicts of mythological significance. Because of the religious importance of Palestine the mapping progresses as a reversed composition where it is the mythologies that reflect the structure on the topographic coordinates, and not topography that represents the course of events.[43] Based on this topographical conceptualization Palestine would from one angle epitomize The Promised Land showing the Old Kingdoms of Judea and the marking and subdivision of the 12 Tribes, confirming their locations in accordance with the ancient prerequisite as indicated in the holy Jewish scriptures.[44] From another historical or religious angle the topography would correspond with a different political or religious accentuation. In this sense the Holy Land becomes an imaginary or a topological metaphor in the traveller's memory more than an actual representation of a geographical systemization.

Following this logic, space and place are constructed and held together on a totality of mythological coordinates co-distributed and co-activated through contextual imaginary signs (contextual cues) and co-occurrences.[45] As an example of politics of place and its relation to cartographic heterogeneity you have on one hand Al-Istakhri's map of Palestine from 952 that (appears to be) upside down with south at the

---

42. Kenneth Nebenzahl: *Maps of the Bible Lands: Images of Terra Sancta through Two Millennia*, London 1986, p. 8.
43. The first scientific map of Palestine was produced in the late 18th century by Napoleons chief cartographer, Pierre Jacotin. Ibid., p. 8
44. See for instance Emanuel Bowens map of Palestine from 1752 on *American Memory*. http://www.worldmapsonline.com/historicalmaps/kr-1752-palestine.htm (January 2013).
45. Both concepts, "contextual cues" and "co-occurrence" are borrowed from S McDonald and M Ramscar: "Testing the Distributional Hypothesis: The Influence of Context on Judgements of Semantic Similarity" (2001), p. 612.

top.⁴⁶ This orientation could reflect the desire to place Mecca above all else or that Islam expanded into Africa and across the Indian Ocean.⁴⁷ On the other hand you have as contrast the *Situs Hierusalem* map from around 1100 which frames Jerusalem as the cosmographic centre of the Christian World. On *Situs Hierusalem* the churches and the achievements of Crusaders function as the coordinates that served in renewing the European interest in geography. In this perspective the objects or geometrics become meaningful when the interpretation of the visual (or just imaginary) sensory perception is organized in relation to the (imaginary) context. In other words, the "unknown" can be recognized or identified with something (imaginary) known. Michel Maffesoli calls this retrospective formation of meaning dialectic between the everyday and the archetypical.⁴⁸ In other words it is suggested that the causality of meaning which crystallizes into two levels as a frame in a frame, that on one level permits a private experience of perceived time, space and place, but on another level draws on (or conflicts with) what Charles Sanders Peirce calls an outer-world-reference.⁴⁹

Place and politics

The topographical order of Palestine is therefore an important part of the journey and an integral part of the travelogues. The physical character of Palestine is described as for instance in the comprehensive topographical work edited by the British engineer and officer Colonel Wilson, written

---

46. It should be mentioned that cartography before becoming a scientific field would often depict the angle of the sovereign or be in accordance with the political situation in a given area. In this sense the cartographical point of reference could be taken from all kinds of angles.
47. Nebenzahl: *Maps of the Bible Lands: Images of Terra Sancta through Two Millennia.*, p. 8.
48. Michel Maffesoli: "Everyday Tragedy and Creation," *Cultural Studies* Vol. 18, no. No. 2/3 March/May (2004), p. 206.
49. According to Peirce, the outer-world-reference is our ordinary conception of the world tied to practical experience from the outside world and vice versa: our actions in the practical world depend on our operations with mental or imaginary scenarios. For more information see Charles S. Peirce et al., *Collected Papers of Charles Sanders Peirce Vol. 5. Pragmatism and Pragmaticism.* Bristol 1998, p. 487; H.L. Hansen: *Litterær Erfaring og Dialogisme*, Copenhagen; 2005, p. 108.

by a "writer on sacred geography"[50] as they are termed in the foreword of the four-volume "Picturesque Palestine. Sinai and Egypt". The large work is dedicated to a meticulous and extravagantly illustrated description of Palestine. Below is a description of Akka (Acre), a small Palestinian town, which for a period during Ottoman rule was a sanjak. The description is not, however, written without any reference to the political field, as can be seen:

> "The distinctive feature of 'Akka is its complete isolation. There are people still living who remember when (during the peaceful rule of Suleiman, who became pasha of 'Akka a few years after the death of the tyrant Jezzar Pasha, in 1804) the plain north of the city was planted with pines and firs and graves of the rapidly growing Melia Azederach, commonly called the 'Pride of India', a favourite tree for plantations in Syria and Palestine, with tender green foliage and pendent lilac blossoms, which are succeeded by clusters of yellow berries. But all trees within a mile and a quarter of the city were cut down by order of Abdallah Pasha (the successor of Suleiman as governor of 'Akka in 1820), lest they could serve as places of ambush for an enemy."[51]

Acre is one of the Palestinian sanjaks in the 19th century. The fate of the town was bleak as with the trees in the description above. The physical state of Palestine was a result of its history, influenced by the political conditions, in this case the Ottoman ambitions of being able to control their Arab province. The conflicts between the Ottoman rulers and the Arab subjects constituted the most obvious and important source of unrest in Palestine in the 16th, 17th and 18th century. In the 19th century other actors entered the scene and became decisive for the development in the region, first of all the Europeans, who gradually became dominant if not hegemonic as the Ottoman grip on their empire was replaced by disintegration and local attempts at establishing autonomy. Palestine was no exception, but the special status in relation to European interests

---

50. Colonel (Ed.) Wilson: *Picturesque Palestine Sinai and Egypt, I-IV*, 1 ed. London 1880, Vol. I, p. vii.
51. Ibid. (vol. III, p. 74)

resulted in changes where the ethnic composition and power structure saw new configurations.

Related to that there seems to be a development over time in the descriptions of the conditions in Palestine for the local population. Palestine witnessed late in the 19th century and especially in the beginning of the 20th century immigration from Europe, which first of all was Jewish. This is reflected in the portrayals of the country. Early accounts notice specific characteristics related to the conditions for the Jews, who are described in a negative narrative, being exposed to persecution by the non-Jewish population of Palestine, as it can be seen in a British travelogue from 1889, written by the British traveller T. Dargue. As he mentions in the "To the reader" preface, the book is basically his travel diary, which he published "[U]nder the pressure of a pretty wide circle of acquaintances", he is as such an early tourist, travelling for his own pleasure:

> "From here we went to the Jews' market-place, where a great amount of bartering was going on, surrounded by dirt and filth of every description. The poor Jews are really the most miserable of all the people one comes across, and they have the filthiest streets in all Jerusalem. Their squalor and misery may, in some measure, be accounted for by their being down-trodden and persecuted by their neighbours."⁵²

The description of the Jews indicates that Dargue is talking about a group of people whose misery in some measure might be explained by the conditions they have been exposed to in Palestine, but who also themselves are to blame for their difficult situation. The historical background is used to explain the superiority of the Christians compared to the Jews. They never wanted to listen to Christ and – according to Dargue – what was true when Jesus lived might as well be true today (i.e. in 1889): "Would they have treated him any differently now. To judge from their fanaticism and superstition, I am inclined to think that many of them would have treated him just as their forefathers did."⁵³ In some of the travelogues

---

52. T. Dargue: *Through the Holy Land Being a Tour in Egypt, Palestine, Syria, Asia Minor, and Greece; Returning Via Italy, Switzerland, and France*, London 1889, p. 44.
53. Ibid., pp. 45-46.

we can find formulations implying that the Jews living in Palestine recently arrived from many parts of the world. The Jewish immigration is a growing reality as it is explained in the guide book written by Ph.D. D.E. Lorenz in 1911:

> "While the Mohammedans, Jews, Greeks and Armenians have their distinct Quarters (...) there being at least forty languages spoken in this city of 60.000 people.
> The Jews are as a rule the most degraded and despised of all, and have little freedom from insult save in their own Quarter. Fully half of them remain citizens of the various countries from which they come (...) These Jews are of many types and from every nation in the world, and a small proportion of them are thrifty and self-respecting, but the great majority give very little occasion for enthusiasm to the Zionist."[54]

The identity of Palestine is changing and in the 20th century Palestine no longer is an Arab province under the Ottoman Empire – even if this officially is the case until the end of World War I. Palestine is regarding its population becoming a heterogeneous place and the Jews are contributing to the process. The very negative and discriminatory remarks by Lorenz are not untypical; emphasizing that anti-Semitic statements without problems can be put in a guide book if we go back before World War II: "The moral degeneracy of the people as a whole is incredible. Profanity and obscenity are said to be mingled in the speech of the common people to an extent unknown among almost any other people on earth."[55] The "enlightened" Western traveller sees what he wants to see and prefers clearly the Western reality to the Orient.

Oakes is claiming that place is often associated with a progressive political agenda. Travelogues representing globalism and modernity here seem to point into other directions, and, as he shows, "the paradoxical qualities of modernity can just as easily yield a place-based politics which is reactionary, exclusionary, and blatantly supportive of dominant

---

54. Lorenz: *The Mediterranean Traveller*, p. 225.
55. Ibid.

regimes."[56] Modernity in Palestine is coming with European influence, reshaping the place through immigration, Jewish colonizing, and railways (even if these were established by the Ottomans). Indicative for this paradoxicality, as it is coming to the fore in the following quotations from Baedeker of 1912 covering Palestine, is the statement that the railways both promoted the spirit of European culture and the influence of the Porte:

> "The most outstanding feature in the recent history of Palestine has been the marked increase of European influence. The first German colony in Palestine was established in 1868, and there are now seven of them, with about 1700 inhabitants. In 1878 the Jewish colonizing began, and at present 32 such colonies, with about 8000 inhab., exist. (...) The various railways opened since 1895 have also done much to promote the spirit of European culture. On the other hand the influence of the Sublime Porte has also substantially increased. Sultan 'Abdu'l Hamid (...) ordered the building of the Hejaz railway, which is of eminent military importance and assures the Turkish supremacy in the region." [57]

Despite the modernity and the influence from the outside, it is still important to emphasize that travelling in Palestine can be dangerous. We are still in the Orient and there might be some hostility towards strangers: "Weapons are unnecessary on the main routes, but advisable on the others, as firearms, conspicuously carried, add a great deal to the importance with which the 'Frank' is regarded by the natives."[58] In Palestine the cities and the main roads are safe, but outside these social control is lacking.

The transformation of Palestine had to do with the decline of Ottoman dominance. This might explain the lack of social control in the underdeveloped areas. But on a different level the growing European influence contributed to the changes in Palestine and as mentioned an important

---

56. Oakes: "Place and the Paradox of Modernity", p. 526.
57. Karl Baedeker: *Palestine and Syria with Routes Though Mesopotamia and Babylonia and the Island of Cyprus. Handbook for Travellers*, 5 ed. London: 1912, pp. lxxxvi-lxxxvii.
58. Ibid., p. xxv.

factor was immigration. This development contributed to modernization processess, as in the beginning of the 20th century the Jewish immigration was accelerating. In the Western guide books it was recommended to visit the settlements or colonies. These could be found in several places in Palestine, for instance close to Jaffa, the old seaport to the west of Jerusalem, as described in Baedeker of 1912:

> "*Jaffa* or *Yafa*, Greek *Joppa*, the seaport of Jerusalem and the chief town of a Kada of the Liwa of Jerusalem, contains about 50,000 inhab., including 30,000 Moslems, 10,000 Christians, and 10,000 Jews (...) the Jewish Colony Petah Tikweh, the largest of the Jewish colonies in Judæa (pop. 1600), founded in 1878. Return on horseback, along the cost.
>
> Travelers interested in the Zionist movement may visit the following JEWISH COLONIES to the south of Jaffa (...) About 1¼ hr. to the S. of Rishon le-Zion lies the colony of Wadi el-Khanin (150 inhab., founded in 1882), and ¾ hr. to the S.E. that of Rektoboth (600 inhab.), the latter, established in 1990, being the second-largest (in area) of the colonies in Judæa."[59]

As it can be seen the population changes as a result of the developments mentioned above are limited. According to Baedeker "[T]he population of Syria and Palestine amounts (...) to 3.326.160 souls, of whom 700.000 in Palestine." A little more than one tenth of the 700.000, around 78.000, were Jews, "comparatively recent settlers from Europe (...) [T]he causes of this continuous and undiminishing immigration are less of a religious than of a political and social nature, such the oppressions suffered by the Jews in Russia, Roumania, and other lands." A transformation of the conditions for the Jews in Palestine seems to take place, as a result of the immigration.

The fact that the Jewish newcomers are economically in a better situation than the native Jews, contributes to this. But also less tangible factors, such as attempts at creating a specific Jewish culture, add to the change of identities in Palestine: "Of recent years strong efforts have been made to resuscitate Hebrew and to make it the popular speech of

---

59. Ibid., p. 7.

the Jews. As a matter of fact it forms a connecting link between the various factors and is already quite commonly spoken."[60] The description of the transformations indicates that the Jews will become more dominant later in the 20th century, but still "El-Islam is the most extensively disseminated of the great religions and its power is still on the increase",[61] as it is mentioned in the Baedeker section on "Population. Religions. Costumes and Customs."

Conclusion

It has been the ambition of this chapter to analyze travel literature as expressions of Western thought regarding Palestine as contested place. The travelogues and topographical descriptions have been discussed as contemporary narratives demonstrating perceptions of struggles over place. Obviously it has not been the intention of the chapter to rewrite the history of Palestine, but rather to shed light on contradictions and paradoxes in the travel literature related to societal changes in Palestine with a focus on the 19th century. Taking a historical perspective as point of departure the chapter has demonstrated how Palestine as place was represented in a dynamic and conflictual, changing reality in the 19th century.

Palestine was in the 19th century exposed, with a concept from Sassen, to a destabilizing of hierarchies. The Ottoman Empire was challenged by the Egyptian expansion in the Levant and as mentioned only European intervention secured an Ottoman restoration in Palestine. With the gradual weakening of Ottoman hegemony, new identities developed representing nationalities and subnationalities related to spacial delocalizations, as for instance when the sanjak structures changed in connection with the transfer of power from Acre to Jerusalem. Quoting Tim Cresswell the travel literature demonstrates how place provides "the raw material for creative production of identity rather than an a-priori label of identity". As pointed out the travel narratives show how place produces conditions of possibility for social practice, demonstrated in

---

60. Ibid., p. lxiv.
61. Ibid., p. lxvi.

three different perspectives related to place in the period under Ottoman rule.

The first perspective was termed "place, geography and identity". The early guide book by Conder points at the multiple identities attached to the Palestinian space being a loosely defined area under Turkish hegemony, a land defined by local authorities, different nationalities with different physical features. As shown in the narrative by Spencer, Palestine is a contested place in the sense that a contemporary disgraceful situation should be rectified by a higher order in the future. The meaning of Palestine is changing over time, not only in contemporary times, but also in a fictitious future. Spencer is anticipating clashes with the Muslims in Palestine and emphasizes through this historical focus that Palestine (and Jerusalem) can be perceived as an intersection which should find a solution, where the down to earth realities and a dream of the future melt into a vision for Palestine.

Secondly, a perspective was given the headline "place, imagination and history" with the intention of looking at how the historical dimensions of Palestinian identity were imagined and reimagined in travel narratives. As mentioned by Taylor Palestine and Jerusalem have an imagined depiction for all humans – in his case creating a mental experience beyond the natural. Taking Stanley's characterization of Palestine as a land of ruins it was shown how place is lived history when it comes to "the holy land". Two American travellers to Palestine, Cox and Harman, emphasize in their respective narratives the historical dimensions. Cox is pointing at the development in the Palestinan countryside, referring to contestations, which have taken place in Ramallah (Ramleh). Harman is underlining the discrepancy between the physical size of Palestine and the importance of the place, and mentions how the "feeling" of the Bible was present while travelling there. For the traveller Palestine is becoming part of the sense of self.

The two, much interrelated perspectives on the *Topography and being* and *Mythological Cartography* encompass a third perspective which is meant to illustrate how the pre-existing religious and topographic determination of the concept of Palestine makes it a contested and destabilized space. In this sense the topographic being and discourse on Palestine are based on where you place the coordinates of interest and what value the coordinates should have. The topographic layers of history fold in harmonious order alongside the concept of travelling, but heterogeneous within the politics of geography. In this regard the framing of Palestine functions as a metaphor that has an inseparable content of geography, religion and politics that finds its different attachments to the layers of history. The cartographic contestation could on this reflection be said to mirror the topographic conflict between "the everyday and the archetypical".

With "place and politics" the fourth perspective was put forward as analytical frame. The politics of Palestine as place was shown by Wilson, who presented the relation between the local authority in Acre and the regime in Istanbul, the Porte. The travel diary of Dargue introduces social aspects of the ethnic-religious diversity in Palestine, which – in his narrative – are given a religious explanation. As the travel narratives are approaching the 20th century they more explicitly focus on political dimensions of religious contradictions, first of all the growing conflict between the Palestinians and the Jews, whose immigration to Palestine is referred to in the travel narratives.

Several of them suggest that the Jewish colonies are visited by the travellers to Palestine, who – in the beginning of the 20th century – are referred to as tourists. Behind the local conflict in Palestine the travelogues and guide books conjure up an image of a more fundamental conflict between European and Oriental culture. European culture comes to Palestine and a reshaping happens with the place – as a result of the railway, the growing cities and the Jewish immigration. The paradoxical character of the development is for instance pointed at by referring to the fact that the railway, built by the Ottomans, at least potentially assures Turkish supremacy in the region.

Summing up the ambition has been to analyze contradictions and paradoxes in Western travel literature and guidebooks with a focus on societal changes in Palestine in the 19th century. It has been the idea to put emphasis on place as analytical framework in a historical context. The discursively constructed development from a situation characterized by Ottoman hegemony and local relocations, via "culture wars" in the late 19th and the first part of the 20th century and to a seemingly endless conflict has been examined in Palestine as contested place. Taking the Western travelogues, topographical descriptions and guidebooks as empirical point of departure is has been the ambition to contribute to the historiography of place and thereby add new dimensions to the construction of a history of Palestine.

Dominion and Transportation – Constantinople as Contested Place

Christian Høgel

Among contested places, the city of Constantinople looms largely. The city placed on the crossing between Asia and Europe, straddling the water passage from the Mediterranean – through the Sea of Marmara – into the Black Sea, had its long history, only to be conquered and continue its life as first Ottoman, then Turkish Istanbul. Throughout the Middle Ages, Constantinople caused awe and attraction among visitors, merchants, believers, and not least conquerors. And being the centre of a variety of activities for all these groups, it exhibited a very complex city structure, an intricate religious position of its own, and a wealth and splendour to be envied and sought after. The story often told of the Ottoman conquest in 1453 is that of a paradigm change, of a clear-cut shift from Byzantine rule and culture to Ottoman. In terms of direct rule, this is certainly true. A Byzantine, and thereby necessarily Orthodox, emperor ruled the city until 29 May, 1453; after that day the Muslim sultan Mehmed II the Conqueror was in power. Still, much of what is perceived as cultural change pertains precisely to these polities rather than to the life of the city as such. The city was repeatedly an object of contention between warring parties; it was for centuries a contested place, but putting too much stress on winners and losers occludes an understanding of the many strands of continuity that persisted, some of them until the present. In fact, seen in a larger perspective – or in time-space, as D. Massey has coined it[1] – the city acquires a quite stable identity based on its geography, an identity or manner of sustainment where specific historical means of transportation

---

1. Doreen Massey: "Places and Their Past," in *History Workshop Journal* 39 (1995), p. 182-92.

and domination constitute the major factors of change. Thus, the space that Constantinople, and later early modern Istanbul, filled for centuries shifted repeatedly back and forth between being a place of contestation and a centre of dominion, until modern international treaties and nationalistic policies infused more profound changes into the city's life. Disregarding this continuity of constant shift between contestation and dominion leads, among other things, to some common but erroneous notions of how and why the city was conquered in 1453, and these will be taken up more specifically in this chapter. Likewise major periods in the history of the city and its area will be established across the ordinary chronological dividing points. In fact, a three-phased periodization of the city's story, more based on its geographic position and options (and using the concepts offered by Massey) than on the identity of its possessors, offers itself. In this, the advent of Rome (and land roads) and of modern times (and international treaties) will constitute the dividing lines. Transportation and the means for it thus come out as crucial in the city's development. Constantinople – and its predecessors Troy and Byzantion – were founded on spots that for centuries were points of intersection. From here various types of trade and control were possible, all depending on the technical abilities of the specific age. These parameters defined its history to a larger degree than did the ruler of the city. In fact, the lack of a locally based ruler marks a much more important issue than who was in power within the city. And times of dominion would interchange with periods where power would be established elsewhere, thus producing the long-term pulse in the story of the city. Tension on the city would thus accrue and diminish. This holds even today, where tension in the area is low, and where Istanbul – no longer a capital – may in many ways be seen rather to form a bridge not only for sea and land transportation but also for culture, whereas its status as power base has waned.

―

The city of Constantinople – bordering on the waters of the Bosporus – lay on a geographical hotspot, as had other cities before it. Already by the second millennium BCE, the city of Troy had been founded at the other narrow passage between the Mediterranean and the Black Sea, at the Dardanelles. Here it had excellent command of the traffic attempting to conquer the winds and currents that often obstructed an easy entry into the Sea of Marmara. Troy became –when judged from both an archaeological and a Homeric perspective – a very rich and well-guarded place.[2] Its city walls, though mostly pre-dating Homeric times, were renowned and play an important role in Homeric imagination. It is from these walls that the captured Helen can point out the Achaean leaders to the Trojan elders, just as it is these city-walls that the Trojans themselves, as the first, break asunder when joyfully receiving the treacherous gift of the Achaeans, a large wooden horse full of armed men.[3] Thus, according to the Homeric tales, all the well-protected splendour of Troy was taken and ravished by the foreign Achaeans, men from the islands and the mainland to the west that was later to become Hellas. Homer offers an almost romantic explanation for the Achaean expedition, giving as origin of the war Paris' abduction of Helen, leading to the deployment of the former wooers' pledge to bring her back to her husband Menelaus. But tales of robbed women or wives often function as narrative explanation for cultural exchange and ensuing wars,[4] and archaeology will have us believe in quite a different background to the war, namely a dispute over wealth. The remains of Bronze Age Troy are surprisingly impressive, and the sheer size of the city (echoed in Homer's 'city of the wide avenues') can only be explained through its port, river outlets of which have now silted up leaving the ruins of ancient Troy several kilometres from the sea. Trade through this harbour must have been the origin of Troy's wealth. Whether or not the city in some way belonged to the Hittite sphere, it certainly was in control of the nearby sea transportation, from the Mediterranean into the Sea of Marmara and probably on to the

2. On Troy as historical reality, see Trevor Bryce: *The Kingdom of the Hittites*, Oxford 2004, 357-71; Joachim Latacz: *Troy and Homer: towards a solution of an old mystery*, trans. Kevin Windle and Rosh Ireland, Oxford 2004.
3. The story was told in the 'Homeric' *Ilioupersis* from the Epic Cycle, Jonathan Burgess: *The Tradition of the Trojan War in Homer and the Epic Cycle*, Baltimore & London 2001, and in the second book of Vergil's *Aeneid*.
4. See e.g. Herodotus *Hist*. 1.1.1ff. claiming to offer – right from the start of his historical exposition – the Persian version of the origin of the wars with Greece. According to this, Phoenicians coming to Argos abducted the princess Io and other women and took them to Egypt. The examples are legion: the Roman rape of the Sabine women, etc.

Black Sea.[5] In myth this seaway was imagined as that of the *Symplegades*, the 'clashing rocks' that would make the passage hazardous for Jason and the Argonauts in their attempt to reach the Golden Fleece, guarded by a dragon at Colchis in the southeastern corner of the Black Sea. The epithet 'golden' is no coincidence; sailing this way was done in view of riches.

Sea transportation was also, it seems, the reason for the establishment of several Greek colonies all along the Dardanelles (or Hellespont), the Sea of Marmara, and the Bosporus in the eighth and seventh century BCE.[6] The most important colony for our purpose is that of Byzantion, said to have been founded in 667 BCE by Byzas of Megara, who came upon an excellent spot for his city on the triangular peninsula on the west side of southern Bosporus. This emplacement, the future site of Constantinople and Istanbul, together with all the other colonising activity, clearly demonstrates the importance of Black Sea maritime trade even in archaic times. Later, in the Classical period, grain import from the Black Sea would become one of the central means of alimentation supply for mainland Greece, where the soil could not yield enough food for the population. In order to protect this transportation, Greek military interventions were constantly witnessed in the region. Miltiades, the general who led the Athenians to victory at the battle of Marathon in 490 BCE, had before Marathon been the ruler of Thracian Chersonese (modern Gallipoli, i.e. the peninsular forming the northern side of the Dardanelles). But due to the Persian subduing of the Ionian revolt in 494 BCE, he had to relinquish this and flee to Athens. Soon all Greek colonies in the region were under firm Persian rule and remained so until the conquest of Alexander the Great. But their mercantile function stayed the same.[7]

Thus, before Constantinople other cities performed a similar function of controlling sea transportation through the straits. The importance of the Bosporus and the Dardanelles as crossing points for land transportation played a much lesser role at this point, i.e. before real (meaning

---

5. See Latacz: *Troy and Homer*, esp. part I.
6. On the colonisation age and its connections to the Homeric world, see Robin Lane Fox: *Travelling Heroes in the Epic Age of Homer*, London & New York 2008.
7. See Herodotus, *Histories* 4.137ff.

in most cases Roman) roads had been built. Armies and nations on the move certainly passed the straits – as did the Gauls or Galatians in the third century BCE – but these instances were exceptional and difficult. In 482 BCE, when preparing his expedition against Greece, the Persian king Xerxes had a pontoon bridge produced to allow his army to cross the Dardanelles. A storm destroyed it, and Herodotus is quick to paint in vivid colours the angry king, purportedly ordering a literal lashing of the uncooperative waters.[8] But a new bridge was soon built and Xerxes' army succeeded in crossing the Hellespont, which was already in Herodotus' time seen as a watershed between two continents, the lands of the earth being divided into three continents, Europe, Asia, and Libya, (separated by three large waters, the Black Sea, the Red Sea, and the Atlantic).

But despite controlling the watershed between continents, the city of Byzantion, or any other city in the area, hardly played major political roles from the Classical age and into the early Roman period. When Alexander the Great crossed over into Asia, the important cities lay further south, on the west coast of Asia Minor, though he did visit the site of Troy. Also Caesar and Augustus, who claimed to be the descendants of Aeneas, ally of Troy, paid Troy special attention.[9] Thus, the fame of the Homeric heroes was enormous, but the power and to some extent riches of the area was a thing of the past. The sea passage was certainly still indispensable for bringing commodities back and forth between Mediterranean ports and especially the cities of the Crimean, but after the Mithridatic wars in the first century BCE, secure Roman domination guaranteed safe passage. Thus, the cities of the area led a comparably easy life and were, with the possible exception of Cyzicus on the brink of the Sea of Marmara, minor sites. No really important city was placed there before Constantine the Great came upon the idea to establish his New Rome at the site of Byzantion in the early fourth century.

Other emperors before Constantine had thought of placing a capital, i.e. an emperor's administrative and residential palace within an urban setting, somewhere in the eastern part of the empire, not least because the Parthians and, after the third century CE, the Persian Sassanids

---

8. Herodotus: *Histories* 7.35ff.
9. Augustinus: *De Civitate Dei* 3.7.

threatened Rome from the east. In the third century CE, the emperor Diocletian made Nicomedia, situated about one hundred kilometres south of the Bosporus, his new capital. Some decades later, the emperor Galerius seems to have fancied Thessalonica, well placed on the Egnatia road leading from the west coast of mainland Greece to the Bosporus and on to Asia Minor. But Constantine's founding in 324 CE and consecration in May 330 of the city of Constantinople was very soon to overshadow all former attempts to establish an imperial urban centre in the Eastern Empire, and a probable reason was the double control of land and sea that the city commanded together with its role as well-protected seat of domination.

Constantine did not choose an empty spot. His new city encompassed the whole triangular peninsular the tip of which Byzantion had occupied since its foundation in archaic times. But having sided with Pescennius Niger in his attempt for the throne, the old colony of Byzantion had suffered severely from a siege and capture in 196 CE by the emperor Septimius Severus, Niger's more successful opponent. Now on its remnants a new and much larger town was planned by Constantine, who himself walked the perimeter of the new city.[10] Naturally equipped with an excellent harbour – the bay of the Golden Horn – and soon furnished with city walls, the city of Constantinople apparently had what it took to make a city flourish from Late Antiquity and throughout the Middle Ages and into modern times. Constantine's walls, which had encompassed a huge area when seen in comparison to a standard ancient city, were less than a century later even outdone by those of the Theodosians, whose walls were built even further west and with hitherto unseen dimensions of outer and inner walls, with a wide ditch added on the outside.[11] Walls were soon also built to protect the city from the sea, just as a long chain would at least later in the city's story block the harbour of the Golden Horn to unwanted intruders. But if Constantine's reasons for establishing a new city to the east may be explained through comparison with other

---

10. For the foundation of Constantinople, see Gilbert Dagron: *Naissance d'une capitale. Constantinople et ses institutions de 330 à 451*, Bibliotheque Byzantine Etudes, Paris 1974, p. 29-43.
11. A.P. Kazhdan and alii: *The Oxford Dictionary of Byzantium*, 3 vols., New York 1991, 'Constantinople, walls'.

similar projects, his visions for his city were certainly novel. As part of his new attitude towards Christianity, churches were built in the city, but also pagan temples. As in Rome, a Senate with senators was established,[12] as well as an imperial palace and a hippodrome, a compound easily comparable to the Palatine and the Circus Maximus in 'Old' Rome. Already Constantine, as many later emperors did, had statues and relics from all over the empire moved and put on display to glorify this new centre of the empire.[13] The level of ambition is clear, though it is hard to ascertain just how Christian this 'New Rome' of Constantine was meant to be. The city's, and its patriarchate's, claim to a central role within Christendom was for centuries to be contested, but gradually its centrality as the seat of the Orthodox Church became irrefutable. Its role as a Christian capital was sealed with the Theodosian reforms at the end of the fourth century CE.[14] Its unique religious position was further enhanced both through the alienation from (Old) Rome – the controversies in 1054, though unobtrusive at the time, turned out to be of a more permanent nature – and through its position as mother church for churches in the Slavonic world and elsewhere. And since the patriarchal and the imperial systems soon formed an interrelated system, much of the city's splendour belonged to both these worlds. Coronations of new emperors were from the sixth century performed by the patriarch in the Hagia Sophia, Justinian I's architectural masterpiece. And throughout the Middle Ages, Byzantine ceremonial and visual capacities were renowned as surpassing just about anything else, and Byzantine emperors knew the importance of being stingy with imperial titles, robes, and insignia.[15]

As with any large city, old or modern, a certain amount of cultural plurality soon characterized the city. Being a Roman city, Latin dominated from the start all parts of imperial and military life, but as it was placed in the Eastern part of the empire, Greek was the most common civic and cultural language. Thus, when Theodosius II in 425 CE estab-

---

12. Dagron: *Naissance d'une capitale*, p. 119-210.
13. See Sarah Bassett: *The Urban Image of Late Antique Constantinople*, Cambridge 2004.
14. On this process, see Fergus Millar: *A Greek Roman Empire*, Berkeley 2006.
15. See the policy described in the words of a Byzantine emperor Constantine Porphyrogenitus VII, who ruled 945-59 in Gy. Moravcsik and R.J.H. Jenkins, eds.: *Constantine Porphyrogenitus. De administrando imperio*, Budapest 1949, p. 66-67, ch. 13.

lished chairs in various academic fields (thus forming a 'university' in early Constantinople), 15 of these chairs were in Latin, 16 in Greek.[16] But under Justinian I (who ruled 527-65 CE) and his successors Latin was gradually replaced within law and in the military with Greek, and it soon thereafter all but ceased to be used. But that did not make the city monolingual; other languages, and cultures, were present and at times conspicuously. Syriac-speaking monks and clergy featured largely in the city, as did speakers of Armenian, Georgian, and later also Slavonic and Turkish.[17] At times, also Arabic could have been heard.[18] Gradually also Latinate groups – i.e. Italians and other westerners – made their presence felt, especially in trade operations. Greek was, nevertheless, the completely dominant language in the higher spheres of society and at court. This was – until 1453 – a Greek-speaking empire of 'Romans', in Greek *Rhomaioi*, as the citizens of the empire would call themselves throughout the Byzantine era and beyond ('Byzantines' being an eighteenth century, Western appellation).[19]

With all its wealth and glory, Constantinople attracted many who would want a share in these, whether peacefully or forcefully, and attacks feature largely in the history of the city. Although having been besieged before by pretenders to the throne, the city faced its first serious threats from Arab troops. After losing most of their middle-eastern possessions, first to the Persians and then, after its recapture, to the Muslim Arabs, Byzantine emperors had to face Muslim troops much closer to the capital. In 676 came the first Arab siege of the town, which only remained in Byzantine hands due to the introduction of the so-called Greek fire, a napalm-like, almost inextinguishable burning substance that would set attackers' ships, weapons, and men on fire.[20] Thus, though the Persian Empire had within decades given in to the Muslim power, Byzantium

---

16. Whether the term 'university' is at all applicable in Byzantium is discussed. See a good presentation with bibliography in Kazhdan and alii, *ODB*, 'University of Constantinople'.
17. On languages in early Constantinople, see Millar: *A Greek Roman Empire*, p. 84-129.
18. See Albrecht Berger: "Sightseeing in Constantinople: Arab travellers, c.900-1300," in *Travel in the Byzantine World*, ed. Ruth Macrides, Aldershot 2002.
19. On this, see Anthony Kaldellis: *Hellenism in Byzantium. The Transformations of Greek Identity and the Reception of the Classical Tradition*, Cambridge 2007, p. 42-119.
20. See Kazhdan and alii: *ODB* 'Greek fire'.

held out – another eight centuries or so, before losing to another Muslim power, the Ottomans.

Ever since the construction of the Via Egnatia in the second century BCE, the conditions of land transportation from western Greece (and Italy) to the straits of Bosporus had been much ameliorated. Roman roads were built not least to serve a smooth imperial and military infrastructure, but various types of trade would soon follow, even if heavy land transportation was in pre-modern times always kept to a minimum, sea transportation being the first choice. Thus, even if goods now reached the Bosporus and – from the fourth century CE also Constantinople – through Greece, the most important contribution of the Egnatia was the military and administrative transportation it served, and the ensuing cultural contact it facilitated.[21] But any kind of land transportation arriving at Constantinople would need to be sailed across the strait, a fact that especially the city of Chalcedon, on the Asian side across from Constantinople (today's Kadıköy), seems to have gained much from. Romantic stories would soon catch on, reflecting in fiction upon the need to cross the waters even if it had to be done by swimming, as did Leander when keen to reach his beloved Hero.[22] Also the knights of the first and second crusade had to get across, and in order to get this sea transportation, they were obliged to promise to hand back to the Byzantine emperor all future conquered land that had formerly belonged to the Byzantine Empire. Well across, they continued along the Byzantine roads of Asia Minor, forgetting all about their promises.[23] Thus, in a very new and rare manner, the Byzantine Empire, later just Constantinople itself, became a sort of buffer state, being in this process also ruled by Westerners for more than half a century (1204-71). Yet, Constantinople for long still retained its place as seat of an empire.

---

21. See K. Belke: "Roads and travel in Macedonia and Thrace in the middle Byzantine period," in *Travel in the Byzantine World*, ed. Ruth Macrides, Aldershot 2002, p. 73-90.
22. Hubert Cancik and Helmuth Schneider, eds.: *Brill's New Pauly: encyclopedia of the ancient world* 2002-10, 'Hero'.
23. For a brief account, see Michael Angold: *The Byzantine Empire 1025-1204. A political history*, London & New York 1984, p. 137-45. A very readable exposition is still Steven Runciman: *A History of the Crusades*, 3 vols., Cambridge 1955-57.

When presenting the gradual emergence of a Christian urban centre and the ensuing – also – interreligious competition as to its possession, we step from a narration that is mainly based on myth and old time structures into paradigms that are obviously applicable in a modern frame. Though other perspectives may be central to some modern observers – such as for example nationalistic feelings among Greeks today – the central story told of the Ottoman conquest is that of one religion taking over the secular space of another. Orthodox Christianity lived on, but the Byzantine Empire that had ensured the most resplendent display of its glory was no longer, even if successor states for instance in Trebizond lingered on for some decades before also being included in the Ottoman realm.[24] But just as some issues in this transition are not clear to historians today, for example the precise status of the Christians after the conquest, one may reflect upon aspects of how this succession story is often told, and claim that its seemingly paradigmatic nature owes much to simplification and even to mythic overlaying. In fact, one could contemplate the possibility that the mythic tale of Troy's conquest has to some degree influenced the narratives of the fall of Constantinople. Both cities were renowned for their riches, their city walls, and their most resplendent city life. Their riches stemmed from their emplacement at the junction of trade ways; trade was their manner of sustainment. Under siege, both cities were for quite some time reduced to the area enclosed by the city walls; these were apparently cities that could live on for long without a hinterland.[25] And once the cities were taken, fugitives such as the Trojan Aeneas or Byzantine intellectuals would find new homes primarily in Italy. Thus, a correlation between Troy and Constantinople – in terms of place and function – makes sense, even if the parallelism cannot be extended to the actual question of succession, since Homer tells us nothing of what post-war Troy looked like. And as to the religious/cultural supersession

---

24. See Anthony Bryer: "The Roman Orthodox world 1393-1492," in *The Cambridge History of the Byzantine Empire c. 500-1492*, ed. Jonathan Shepard, Cambridge 2008, p. 852-80.
25. See Cyril Mango, Gilbert Dagron, and Geoffrey Greatrex, eds.: *Constantinople and its Hinterland: papers from the Twenty-seventh Spring Symposium of Byzantine Studies, Oxford, April 1993*, Aldershot, Hampshire & Brookfield, Vt. 1995. For the many Homeric tales, especially from the Epic Cycle, on expeditions and captures in the hinterland of Troy, see Burgess: *The Tradition of the Trojan War*.

of Ottoman upon Byzantine, modern notions seem rather to intervene. Here we often witness simple cultural models being adopted in order to make narration fulfil what we take to be obvious procedures.

In fact, as we will now point out, quite a few notions that may be found stated or implied in short historical accounts or in popular presentations today are somewhat misleading. To name just three commonly expressed:

1. The Ottoman conquest was the case of an Eastern power taking over a more Western empire.
2. The power and riches of the city were the key magnets, rather than the city's religious function.
3. The city's name was, subsequent to the conquest, changed from Constantinople into Istanbul.[26]

These common notions are in a simple way just wrong, but in being wrong and nevertheless voiced they conceal more important features that are central for understanding the Ottoman takeover. Central to this are the actual features of continuity that often vanish in accounts of the shift from Byzantine to Ottoman rule. Let us therefore begin by stating what is correct.

1. In 1453, the Ottomans conquered Constantinople from the west. Not only was the crucial blow dealt to the city through land bombardment of the western walls using a very large cannon, designed and built for that specific purpose, and the city walls supervened from the west,[27] but the Ottomans had, since 1365, had their court in Adrianople/Edirne in European Thrace; their headquarters had thus for almost a century been in Europe.[28] This may seem a minor point and a quarrel about details, but

---

26. All three notions are expressed or implied in e.g. Andrew Baruch Wachtel: *The Balkans in World History*, Oxford 2008, p. 51-52 and in many other short – or popular – presentations.
27. See Kritovoulos' description §158-160 of the cannon in *Kritovoulos. History of Mehmed the Conqueror*, trans. Charles T. Riggs, Princeton 1954, p. 254-55.
28. Stanford J. Shaw and Ezel Kural Shaw: *History of the Ottoman Empire and Modern Turkey*, 2 vols., Cambridge 1976-77, 1.17-22; see also Çiğdem Kafescioğlu: *Constantinopolis/Istanbul. Cultural Encounter, Imperial Vision, and the Construction of the Ottoman Capital*, University Park, Penn. 2009, p. 16-18.

in their annexation of the city, the Ottomans – perhaps also because of their already established dominion over large parts of the Balkans – soon entered upon a cultural policy that may in many ways be termed more Westernizing than what the Byzantine had been. Mehmed the Conqueror had his portrait painted by the Italian painter Bellini; an Ottoman hospital was built in the city in a most Italianising style.[29] Through contacts with Westerners, and being now also firmly settled on the borders of the Adriatic, Ottoman rule placed Constantinople at the centre of a realm that reached further west than it had done for centuries, and this soon became visible within the city. Viewing the Ottomans as a more Eastern nation taking over a more Westernized Byzantium is a simplification, at least when considering the first period after the conquest.

2. Constantinople had obviously for a long time been attractive to outsiders, whether humble believers or pilgrims, merchants or official guests, marauders or conquerors. The amount of gold found in the city was legendary, even if these legends were not always true.[30] The markets and trading areas must have offered just about the largest variety of goods to be found anywhere at the western end of the Silk Route. And the sheer amount of urban territory found within the city walls of Constantinople was enough to make people wonder how such an urban centre functioned. Seljuk and Ottoman Turks had been to the city in a variety of roles;[31] now the Ottomans came as conquerors, but this did not mean that power and wealth, or plunder, was all they had in view. Among the attractions, the church of Hagia Sophia featured impressively in visitors' accounts; its architecture and liturgy were repeatedly lauded. "We knew not whether we were in heaven or on earth," as Russian guests in 987 returned saying. The liturgy, with choirs and castrato singers, made

---

29. Kafescioğlu: *Constantinopolis/Istanbul*, p. 72-75, and James Cuno: *Who owns antiquity? Museums and the battle over our ancient heritage*, Princeton & Oxford 2008, p. 68-69, with further examples.
30. On the economy in general, see Mark Whittow: "The middle Byzantine economy," in *The Cambridge History of the Byzantine Empire c. 500-1492*, ed. Jonathan Shepard, Cambridge 2008.
31. Charles M. Brand: "The Turkish Element in Byzantium, Eleventh-Twelfth Centuries," *Dumbarton Oaks Papers* 43 1989, p. 1-25.

similar impressions,[32] and the building and its sanctity was also praised by Muslim authors.[33] In a similar spirit, the contemporary author Tursun Beg describes how Mehmed the Conqueror looked at the Hagia Sophia in awe, citing the Persian poet Sadi when seeing its destitute environs.[34] Mehmed did not come as a non-reverent conqueror; his plans for the city were also religious.

However, Mehmed's piety as regards Constantinople seems not to have made much impression on his men. To them Constantinople obviously still represented a certain amount of wealth to whomever could take possession of it; it was still a trading port, and much of value was still gathered in the city. But it had long lost its hinterlands, whether to the European or the Asiatic side, and to many of Mehmed's men not cities but land was what should be sought after, and that had already been conquered. In fact, they suggested to Mehmed that he pull down the rest of the city and build a defensive wall around the Hagia Sophia.[35] Mehmed answered evadingly, probably pleased at his men's acceptance of the church as a holy site, but to him the church was part of the city and what it could be used for. It held a special possibility of combining political and religious power, as it had done to Byzantine emperors.[36] Thus, Mehmed's wish may be put in connection with the bestowal of the sultan title on one of his predecessors, the Ottoman ruler Murad I, in 1383.[37] When Mehmed entered Constantinople, the Hagia Sophia was turned into a mosque, and he thereby gained an old sanctified spot from which to wield his sanctified power. Some years later Mehmed would, however, launch a building program including spectacular mosques that would eventually demote the Ayasofya mosque to a somewhat secondary position.[38] Still, his plans for Constantinople included a religious aspect.

---

32. On the *Primary/Russian Chronicle*, see Kazhdan and alii: *ODB* 'Povest' vremennych let'; on castrato singing, see Neil Moran: "Byzantine castrati," *Plainsong and Medieval Music* 11 2002, p. 99-112, esp. p. 107-108.
33. Kafescioğlu, *Constantinopolis/Istanbul*, p. 20.
34. Ibid. p. 20.
35. Ibid., p. 18-20.
36. Ibid. p. 18-22.
37. Shaw and Shaw: *History of the Ottoman Empire*, p. 22-27.
38. Kafescioğlu: *Constantinopolis/Istanbul*, p. 66-109.

3. Unlike what is often said, the city retained its name after Mehmed's conquest, or to be precise, in many official Ottoman documents it was referred to as Konstantiniye.[39] This official name was not a new name, but a Turko-Arabic rendering of the Greek name, literally meaning 'Constantinian' (probably in analogy with names as Iskenderiyya/ Alexandria). This official name was, however, not used much outside official registers. Elsewhere the originally Greek 'Istanbul' or rather 'Stambul' (spelled variously, but all reflecting the Greek *stim boli*/στην πόλη, meaning 'in/to the city') gradually became current. However, this was not an outcome of the conquest, but more a result of a vernacular expression becoming dominant. And Constantinople/Istanbul was *the* city in those parts.

Thus, three features that may in short and popular accounts pop up as defining marks for the Ottoman conquest may simply be refuted as untrue. If we think of the city's life in general, much else also continued as before. Trade remained the central means of income, and as before the conquest this was mainly in the hands of Italian communities.[40] Even the composition of the population did not change dramatically. It remained multi-national and, even if much of the original Greek population did not remain alive or in the city after the conquest, Greeks and others soon moved in. And all the way up till the early twentieth century the city retained a very mixed population.[41] The Greek population of Istanbul – numbering some 400,000 – were not exchanged in accordance with the Lausanne treaty of 1923; the most serious exodus from the city actually came after riots and attacks on Greek shops and quarters in 1955, the so-called Septembriana.[42]

These strands of continuity were furthermore actively enhanced by Mehmed's policy of making Constantinople appear as inscribed in a Muslim narration. According to a near-contemporary source, the grave

---

39. Ibid., p. 227 n. 2.
40. On 'Latins' in Constantinople and Byzantium in general, see Whittow: "The middle Byzantine economy," p. 476-78.
41. Cuno: *Who owns antiquity?*, p. 70-71.
42. Ibid., p. 79-80.

of the Arab leader of the first siege of Constantinople, Ayyub al-Ansari, was discovered during Mehmed's siege of the city.[43] Legend had it that this Ayyub had been a near acquaintance of the prophet, and through buildings and processions Mehmed made the presence of his grave an instance of a long-ranging Muslim presence in the city, an 'envelope of time-space' as Massey calls it.[44]

In addition the city and the possibility of dominion it offered remained for long the same. Istanbul became and remained the centre of the Ottoman Empire, much as it had been in the Byzantine Empire. But as Ottoman power waned, former tensions again accrued in the area of the city. As Russia extended its borders firmly onto the Black Sea in the eighteenth and nineteenth centuries, the region became a hotspot of European interest. The Crimean war and later the Russian occupation of north-eastern Anatolia demonstrated Russia's wish to secure a firmer hold on the region, primarily provoked by its need to have an outlet into the Mediterranean. History could have repeated itself with a foreign takeover of the city; instead the outcome of World War I was that the Ottoman Empire collapsed, leading soon to the establishment of the Turkish state.[45] One of the central battlegrounds for this nation birth was Gallipoli, the place where Miltiades had ruled, and in close proximity to ancient Troy. A new order of nations was established, and various treaties, eventually formalized under the Montreux convention of 1936, from that time secured the straits as an international trading sailing route, leaving it to Turkey to control the passage of military ships from non-Black Sea countries.[46] As before in Roman times, such an establishment of free passage led to less tension in the area, but also to a diminishing importance of the city. There were also nationalistic reasons for the move, but it is tempting to see the decision of the new Turkish state of moving its capital to Ankara in this light. Istanbul had lost some of its centrality, not only because it was seen as an old Ottoman centre, but also because its geography was no longer vested with

---

43. Kafescioğlu: *Constantinopolis/Istanbul*, p. 45-52.
44. Massey: "Places and Their Past," p. 188.
45. Feroz Ahmad: *The Making of Modern Turkey*, London & New York 1993, p. 30-51.
46. Ibid., p. 68.

the same interest. This 'de-centralisation' of Istanbul is to a large extent the background for Orhan Pamuk's *hüzün*, the Istanbul melancholy of early-mid twentieth century.[47] Seen, in his *Istanbul* from 2006, as characterizing both his own generation and that before him, Pamuk clearly leaves the impression of a city left in a time gap following upon the collapse of Ottoman rule and culture.

When overlooking the city's long history, we see that even across centuries or millennia the story of Constantinople/Istanbul, and that of its region, displays a surprising amount of continuity, due to its geographical setting. Trade and transportation have been crucial to the interests invested in the area, whereas domination and control of this has at times been placed right at its centre, at other times beyond it. The combination of an excellent harbour and (almost) impregnable city walls secured Constantinople (and Troy) a long and prosperous life. The city's position as the meeting point of continents, as defined since Herodotus, may also have contributed to its importance, though the two other junctures (Gibraltar and Suez) hardly attracted such a long-term interest in the respective areas, or generated the existence of comparable cities. Other geographic parameters – Massey's 'geographical beyond'[48] – need to be taken into account, i.e. the Silk Route (which did not always pass this way), the Black Sea (which is both a real divider like the Atlantic, and a trading area like the Red Sea), the proximity of vast farming areas especially in Asiatic Bithynia, etc.

However, in addition to the continuity, there seems to be a certain rhythm in the city's life. Based on this rhythm, a three-phase model in which to insert its story seems to emerge. In the early phase only sea transportation plays a role, and mythic tales blend with early historical accounts of unusual land crossings. At the end of this period, the second phase, which may be loosely placed at the advent of Rome and the construction of (better) roads, saw new demands – not least the Persian threat in the East – make the foundation of a large city centre at the spot

---

47. Orhan Pamuk: *Istanbul: memories and the city*, trans. Maureen Freely, New York 2006.
48. Massey: "Places and Their Past," p. 183.

of a former minor colony useful. Thus, Constantinople was born into a world of warring empires,[49] which despite clear-cut religious differences still viewed the city's assets in much the same way, whether dressed in Byzantine or Ottoman garb. Only in modern times, our third period, did the tension concentrated on the city loosen somewhat. This may be seen in the choice of modern Turkey to have its capital moved to Ankara. What is more, in 1935 the Hagia Sophia was turned into a museum, having served during the Ottoman period as a mosque. Treaties ensured the safe passage of all trading ships through the straits. But the modern age has also brought the city's ethnic composition to the point where it mirrors that of the country, through the mass influx of people from rural areas in Anatolia, and by way of emigration of other, non-Turkish ethnicities. The modern age has smoothed things according to national or even nationalistic parameters, with some loss of the former Byzantine/Ottoman plurality. Within a Turkish national setting, the spot has been made passable, and millions of inhabitants of present-day Istanbul can cross between Asian and European suburbs of the city not only by ferry, but also by two impressive bridges and soon also through an undersea tunnel.

Modern Istanbul is certainly not an 'unspoilt place' in Massey's sense of a city that looks as we think it did in some not too far away past.[50] Despite its many historical sites and attractions, there is a clear disruption in its modern history, a disruption that is felt both by some inhabitants, as in Orhan Pamuk's *Istanbul,* and by some ex-inhabitants, as in Petros Markaris' *Palia, poli palia,* a modern Greek detective story searching for the remnants of a Rhomaian culture, the culture of the Greek-speaking dwellers of the *poli,* 'the city' as Constantinople/Istanbul may still be called in modern Greek.[51] Much of the disruption seems to lie in the – perhaps apparent – taming of the forces inherent in the city's structure. Should a more uneasy future show up, geography could probably again put pressure on the site. The building of pipelines for gas and oil from

---

49. On warring empires converging towards monotheism, see Garth Fowden: *Empire to Commonwealth: consequences of monotheism in late antiquity,* Princeton 1993.
50. Massey: "Places and Their Past," p. 183-84.
51. Petros Markaris: *Old, Very Old,* Milan 2007.

Russia and Central Asia and towards the west has in recent times shown how much the peace and quiet in the area depends on international diplomacy and cooperation. In the meantime, more than as a contested place, today's Istanbul stands forth, perhaps with some degree of *hüzün*, as the only city in the world bridging two continents.

Detroit's River Rouge as Contested Space

David E. Nye

One of the most common tropes in writing about the United States is that of enormous changes being made in what was once an empty space. Alexis de Tocqueville generalized this trope in a description of the rapidity of American progress. The Anglo-American race, as he called them, "fells the forests and drains the marshes; lakes as large as seas and huge rivers resist its triumphant march in vain. The wilds become villages, and the villages towns. The American, the daily witness of such wonders, does not see anything astonishing in all this. This incredible destruction, this even more surprising growth, seems to him the usual progress of things in this world. He gets accustomed to it as to the unalterable order of nature."[1] Whether describing the creation of Chicago, the construction of Brooklyn Bridge, or the erection of a great factory, one repeatedly finds the contrast between a wild, unutilized space and a magnificent example of progress and civilization. These contrasts oversimplify. They erase previous inhabitants, wars, species extinction, pollution, destruction of habitat, and other damage. The history of each place is far more nuanced than the dramatic trope of progress suggests, and it can be dangerously misleading to adopt the notion that human beings transform abstract space into place. In case after American case, one finds that human beings erased vestiges of the past to create the illusion of an abstract space, in order then to imagine a pristine beginning. Certainly this was the case as regards the River Rouge factory. It is far more accurate to examine it

---

1. Alexis de Tocqueville: "A Fortnight in the Wilds," in *Journey to America*, ed. J. P. Mayer, Yale University Press 1960, p. 329.

as the site of cultural intersections, one that is always being revised and reconstructed.[2]

Arguably the most famous factory site in the United States is Henry Ford's vast River Rouge Plant, usually referred to simply as "The Rouge."[3] In *Middlesex*, Jeffrey Eugenides described Ford's River Rouge plant as "that massive, forbidding, awe-inspiring complex we saw from the highway, that controlled Vesuvius of chutes, tubes, ladders, catwalks, fire, and smoke, known, like a plague or a monarch, only by a color: 'The Rouge.'"[4] For an employee going to work there each day, the factory was first distant clouds of smoke, then a chemical smell, then "a fortress of dark brick," and finally clamoring, tangled, converging assembly lines that stretch beyond the factory to the mines and forests where they suck raw materials out of the earth. In 1930 it was the largest factory complex in the world. Guides enthusiastically cited statistics to the hundreds of thousands of tourists who came each year to see it. The complex employed 100,000 workers, had 16 million square feet of floor space and 92 miles of railway track. It consumed 86 tons of soap every month. Its powerhouse made enough electricity to light all the homes in Chicago. It used more water than the cities of Detroit and Cincinnati combined. Working at top speed, The Rouge could transform iron ore, coal, limestone, sand, and other raw materials into a functioning car in just 28 hours. This icon of productivity still hosts factory tours in 2012.

This chapter will examine the changing uses and conflicted meanings of this site, beginning long before it had industrial uses. It will focus less on production inside the factory than on the changing social production of this place and its continual redefinition. Indeed, this single site provides a microcosm of the history of North America, as it was successively inhabited by Native Americans, the French, the British, American farmers, small-scale industries, and the Rouge Plant, which in recent years has been transformed into a "green factory." The Rouge exemplifies the contestation of place in North America, between Native American tribes,

---

2. Doreen Massey: *For Space*, London 2005, p. 9.
3. I thank The Henry Ford for access to its research center. Other research was completed at the Boston Public Library and at the libraries of MIT.
4. Jeffrey Eugenides: *Middlesex*, New York 2002, p. 93.

between the French and the British, and between different groups in the United States.

The dominant US mythology was for a long time that American space was scarcely touched by Native Americans and came into the hands of Europeans as an unspoiled wilderness. Nineteenth-century Americans had an ideology of space as raw and unfinished nature that it was their duty to develop. From this perspective, the land awaited a second creation that would complete the work that Providence had begun.[5] History was understood to be the movement from wilderness to civilization, from raw to refined, from birch bark canoe to railroad, from simple production using hand tools to modern assembly line factories. Many sites once seemed to embody this progressive vision of American history, perhaps none more completely than the River Rouge factory. This was the perspective that most observers brought to the Rouge Factory for at least half a century, beginning in c. 1920. In contrast, the same physical space can be seen as a contested zone where quite different geographies of power seek domination: Native American vs. European colonizers; agriculture vs. industry; capital vs. labor; industrialism vs. environmentalism.

What any observer "sees" is a combination of his or her own mental representations and the scene that impinges on consciousness at a particular moment. A visitor to the Rouge River scarcely brings an "innocent" eye to the site. The historian who sees it for the first time brings the stranger's unfamiliarity to the experience combined with a wide range of reading and imagery. I saw it first in 1972, again in 1984, and a third time for a more detailed look in 2011. Learning to see the River Rouge takes time, not just the time spent physically walking around and looking, but also the mental triangulations that incorporate two-dimensional representations of the site by painters, photographers, and cartographers, each of whom had different purposes. There is no objective observer but through a range of strategies one begins to understand the site's complexity in time and in space. One discovers soon enough that the progressive narrative, in which raw nature was conquered and improved, is based on erasures and simplifications. American space has continually been reconstructed, beginning with (and not after) the Na-

---

5. David E. Nye: *America as Second Creation*, Cambridge, Mass. 2003, pp. 9-14.

tive Americans, whose interventions were more extensive than early European explorers realized.

Mound Builders and Native Americans

The River Rouge is 125 miles long, and its watershed includes about 400 lakes and ponds. It drains a portion of Southeast Michigan into the Detroit River, and its waters ultimately are discharged into the Great Lakes and the St. Lawrence River. Michigan has considerable rainfall, and the Rouge discharges an average of about 180,000 cubic feet of water per minute, with significant but short-term variations, from as little as 40,000 cfpm in winter to as much as 240,000 cfpm during floods.[6] The river's appearance does not change as much as this variation might suggest, as it falls slowly through a rather flat region. Lower discharge does not mean a sharp change in depth but rather slower flow. Much of the low-lying area where the Ford factory would later be built for a long time remained marshland, which Native Americans utilized as a rich natural habitat for fish and game. The Rouge River is also part of an important crossroads zone, where the Great Lakes contract, allowing easier north-south passage into what is now Canada. Alternately, this area's waterways link Lakes Erie and Ontario to the east with the three largest of the Great Lakes to the west. The Detroit area is one of the major crossroads of North America, and it would have been surprising had a city not emerged there.

A millennium or more ago the River Rouge served as a center for Mound Builders who constructed "elaborate enclosures, embankments and mounds... apparently for religious purposes." They were an agricultural society that built defensive military works with considerable precision, including "large squares, circles and regular polygons" which required some knowledge of surveying. Several were along the River Rouge near Ft. Wayne. "The largest and most interesting of the mounds is located near the mouth of River Rouge, at Delray. This is believed to

---

6. http://nwis.waterdata.usgs.gov/usa/nwis/uv/?cb_00060=on&cb_00055=on&format=gif_stats&period=&begin_date=2012-3-04&end_date=2012-10-25&site_no=04165710 (January 2013).

have been originally 700 to 800 feet long, 400 feet wide and possibly 40 feet in height; not all of which, however, was artificial. The top of the mound gave a commanding view of the river and may have originally carried some form of structure…"[7] Although little is known about the religion of the Mound Builders, it seems certain that these burial sites were the nodal points of ritual. Their prominence and orientation to the sun and moon[8] certainly suggest that they were spaces meant to link heaven and earth, the dead and the living, the sacred and the profane.[9] But if the River Rouge Mound was primarily a burial site, it also provided a lookout point. From it, a sentry could survey a wide area, with nothing to obstruct the view in any direction.

The Mound Builders lived along the Mississippi and Ohio Rivers and their tributaries, with large developments at present-day St. Louis and Marietta, Ohio. In Wisconsin alone they built more than 15,000 earthworks at 3,000 different locations, primarily in the southern part of that state, where they are "clustered along lakes, beside rivers, and on hilltops, often arranged in complex patterns that harmoniously, even artfully, blended with the natural topography."[10] While not an industrial civilization, they mastered technologies of agriculture and fishing, and they were successful enough to amass the surplus labor needed to build the mounds. Their major sites often were the central points of river commerce that Europeans would later develop, in the process destroying much of the archeological evidence. The Mound Builders' culture collapsed in c. 1200, replaced by other Native American peoples. After c. 1610, Europeans began to arrive on the Atlantic coast, driving other tribes westward, causing wars, contestations, and relocations. In this process, the Huron Tribe was forced into the River Rouge area, and soon allied itself with the French against the British and their Native-American allies, the Iroquois.

---

7. W. H. Sherzer, State of Michigan Geological and Biological Survey, Publication 12. Geological Series 9. "Geological Report on Wayne County, Lansing Michigan." State Printers, 1913, p. 8.
8. See, for example, The Midwest Archeological Center's newsletter, http://www.nps.gov/mwac/hopewell/v6n2/one.htm (January 2013)
9. Mircea Eliade: *The Sacred and the Profane: The Nature of Religion*, San Diego, Calif. 1959.
10. Robert A. Birmingham and Leslie E. Eisenberg: *Indian Mounds of Wisconsin*, Madison, Wis. 2000, p. 3.

French and British

The first white settlers in the Detroit area arrived during French explorations through the Great Lakes, which left their trace in many local place names, including the "Rouge" River itself. Étienne Brûlé came as early as 1618, followed by Jean Nicolet in 1634 and Father Jacques Marquette who built the first permanent settlement at Sault St. Marie a full half century after Brûlé passed through the area.[11] Waterways, not roads, remained the main pathways through the region, and the early settlers located in navigable areas.

Detroit itself was first settled by Antoine Cadillac, who arrived with a company of 50 soldiers and 50 artisans and traders in July 1701. From that time the white population grew slowly. The settlement was focused on the fur trade more than on agriculture, and the goal was not to replace the Native Americans but to yoke them to the marketplace and focus their energies on trapping. From the perspective of the trading companies in Montreal and Quebec, the Rouge River was important as a waterway and as a watershed area abundant in beaver, a resource not to be disturbed by too many settlers. "It was not unusual for a merchant to make a profit of one thousand percent on the trade goods to be exchanged for furs" and for the furs to appreciate another thousand percent by the time they were sold in Europe.[12] The fur trade soon reduced the available game, and it set one Native American tribe against another, while making them dependent on traders for rifles, needles, blankets, traps, and metal tools.

The French approach to colonization was quite distinct from that of the British. The British form of imperialism was far more aggressive, and emphasized "expulsion of the native population from the colonized area and the creation of a frontier of separation between the two peoples."[13] This approach also included the transformation of the landscape, from one supporting a Native American way of life to one based on European agriculture. In contrast, the French form of imperialism was a more "be-

---

11. Russel B. Nye: *Michigan*, New York 1966, p. 118.
12. Ibid., p. 66.
13. D. W. Meinig: *Continental America, 1800-1867*. Vol. 2, New Haven 1993, p. 70.

nign articulation of the two peoples at a point of exchange. Each group operating largely within a separate territory, but bound together in an encompassing economic system, as in Canada."[14]

The French therefore had only a minimal presence in the Detroit area, and they did not settle on the River Rouge itself. However, after the defeat of Chief Pontiac in 1763, as part of the more general British victory in the French and Indian War, colonization by expulsion soon followed.[15] To be sure, the English did attempt to limit westward migration after 1763, but this angered the American colonists and was one of the many causes of the rebellion that led to independence. Once the United States emerged as a separate nation, it continued British-style colonization by expulsion. Moreover, the American government adopted a new system of land division that effectively erased the past. All the lands to the west of the original thirteen colonies were surveyed based on an abstract geometrical system of squares, in which every plot of land was oriented to the points of the compass. This new system ignored all former uses of the land, treating North America as a vast checker-board, in which every square was an identical commodity, to be sold at the same price to whomever first staked a claim.[16]

Early Industrial Development

The Detroit region was therefore surveyed according to this abstract system, which is still easily visible in contemporary maps. The geometrical pattern effectively proclaimed that the entire region was open to development, and that every part of it had potential use value, whether wetland or forest, Indian mound or meadow. New roads further articulated the grid pattern, chopping the land into squares. Within this abstract pattern, however, two ideologies battled for supremacy. Thomas Jefferson, the leading proponent of the grid pattern, championed the idea of an agrarian nation with as little industrialization as was consistent with national

---

14. Ibid., p. 72.
15. Michigan Writers Project: *Michigan, A Guide to the Wolverine State*. Oxford 1942, p. 213.
16. Nye: *America as Second Creation*, pp. 21-42.

defense. He saw the independent small farmer as the ideal citizen for the new democratic nation. Jefferson opposed Alexander Hamilton, who wanted the United States to develop into an urban, industrial nation, and thought the propertied class, not farmers, would be its bedrock of stability. Jeffersonian values long prevailed among voters, especially in agricultural regions such as nineteenth-century Michigan. The developments along the Rouge were part of that larger contestation between Jeffersonian and Hamiltonian values.

The common system of land division and the national railway system together opened up "a gridded wilderness" where "industrious settlers could shape the land." Moreover, they embraced the principle of replication, building virtually identical structures in all parts of the nation. "By 1845 a great skein of remarkably similar forms overlay the distinctly regional artifacts dating to colonial times."[17] In the Detroit area, almost all traces of the French or the Native Americans were erased, except for some place names. The emerging city had a layout and appearance that seemed familiar to any American newcomer.

The River Rouge was an artery of transportation, but much of its watershed remained wild or rural until after 1860. The first steamboats arrived in the 1820s, linking Detroit to Buffalo, the new Erie Canal, and New York City. By 1832 additional steamers began service to Chicago,[18] and Detroit grew as immigrants poured in. At times during the antebellum period, small boats on the Rouge also carried escaped slaves toward Canada on the underground railroad.[19] The westward tide of expansion into the treeless Middle West created a demand for lumber, which was abundant in Michigan. All of its rivers became arteries to carry logs out to sawmills, with the Rouge watershed one of the first to be exploited and exhausted. The logs were floated down the river to be cut into timber or hauled away to be processed elsewhere. Part of the demand came from railroads, which needed wood for the ties that held their rails in place. In this and many other ways they began to redefine the landscape. The first railroad charters were already granted in 1830, when the first line was

---

17. John R. Stilgoe: *Common Landscape of America, 1580 to 1845*. New Haven 1982, pp. 132-133.
18. Russel B. Nye: *Michigan*, pp. 51-52.
19. George B. Catlin: *The Story of Detroit*, Detroit 1923, p. 327.

begun in Baltimore. By the 1850s railroads linked Detroit to the emerging national system.

The shores of the Rouge River near the city became an industrial zone so productive and promising that in the 1880s more than $8 million was invested to dredge several miles of its channel, so that factories could receive ocean-going ships. The Rouge Improvement Company created an industrial park primarily devoted to manufacturing iron stoves and other metal products, but also producing salt that, using the Solvay process, was transformed into soda ash and caustic soda. By 1890, Detroit employed 38,000 industrial workers,[20] and its population had reached 206,000.[21] Few traces of these earlier industrial uses of the Rouge remain, and the most recent Ford biography mistakenly assumes the region was remote and rural in 1915, when the automobile company sent anonymous agents into the area to purchase 2,000 acres.[22] When the public began to realize that Henry Ford was behind these purchases, the pretense was that the land was to be used for a tractor factory, but the plans were far more ambitious. The transition marked the shift from small-scale, regional industry to the international corporation.

The Ford Rouge Plant

The world's largest factory stamped a new geometry on the land, excavating, filling, flattening, and imposing an industrial order. When completed in the 1920s, it covered 1,096 acres, not counting access roads and parking lots. Much of the raw material arrived in freighters and barges discharging iron ore, limestone, coal, and other materials at the docks of the canal slip. This was only possible after dredging, deepening, and straightening of the river, a process completed in 1923.[23] Until then, the emerging Rouge factory shipped and received construction materials

---

20. Conot: *American Odyssey*, New York 1974, pp. 94-95.
21. Catlin: *The Story of Detroit*, p. 650.
22. Stephen Watts: *The People's Tycoon: Henry Ford and the American Century*, New York 2005, pp. 280-281.
23. Ford R. Bryan: *The Rouge: Pictured in its Prime*, Detroit 2003, p. 25.

through the Detroit, Ironton and Toledo railroad that Ford also owned. For example, 50 railroad cars of cement arrived every week from Thomas Edison's factory in New Jersey.[24]

When completed, the Rouge factory exemplified vertical integration, as Ford sought to eliminate reliance on outside suppliers and to apply his assembly line method to the manufacture of all the Model T car's parts. Workers didn't merely assemble cars; they also smelted 52 kinds of steel, made tires and safety glass, produced light and power, and made virtually everything that went into each car from the engine to the steering wheel, from the front bumper to the rear window. The River Rouge plant even made its own coke from coal, in the process producing ammonium sulfate (sold as fertilizer), benzol (which was mixed with gasoline and used in cars), and gas and tar (both of which the plant burned as fuel).[25]

Albert Kahn, the architect of the factory buildings, used steel-reinforced concrete to create large interior spaces without many columns or other supports, and worked closely with the company to lay out the floor plan. The complex as a whole had a functionalist design, yet the use of space wasn't rigidly preconceived. (Illustration). The builder for the whole project of which Kahn's buildings were a part, was William Verner. He studied the process of making the Model T and laid out each section of the new factory in consultation with Ford's managers. The flow of the work determined the placement of each building. Since a Model T's main ingredient was steel, Verner began with the railroads and canals that transported the raw materials needed to produce it.[26] Once the location of railroads and canals had been worked out, he built two blast furnaces, completed in 1920 and 1922, and then a foundry for engine blocks, rolling mills and all the facilities needed to make sheet steel, and a stamping plant to make car hoods, doors, roofs, and panels. The transportation of raw materials and parts between buildings was designed into the architecture. Details of every section of the new plant were developed in consultation with the Highland Park factory managers who were going to

---

24. Ibid., p. 25.
25. Tom McCarthy: "Henry Ford, Industrial Ecologist or Industrial Conservationist? Waste Reduction and Recycling at the Rouge," in *Michigan Historical Review* 27:2 (Fall 2001), p. 57.
26. William F. Verner, personal notebook from 1919 to 1920, Henry Ford Archives, Accession 521.

move to River Rouge. For example, Logan Miller helped lay out the new motor department, making use of his experiences at Highland Park. "In the new motor building," he recalled, "we changed the flow of material considerably" as many conveyors were added. By contrast, at Highland Park "parts were kept in stock bins and there were few conveyors."[27] In a 1915 book titled *Ford Methods and the Ford Shops* Horace Arnold and Fay Faurote had praised part bins and their replenishment as a form of efficiency, but at River Rouge managers tried to get rid of such buffer inventories.[28] Instead, "conveyors acted as storage places from one operation to another." This might suggest that because River Rouge was large the work was spread out. But, Miller noted, "the machine shop setup was more compact. We studied the setup of machinery so there was no wasted space. We tried to move the machines as close together as possible to eliminate the movement of stock." Such changes exemplify what David Harvey has called the "compression of space and time" that are hallmarks of advanced forms of capitalism.[29] The assembly-line factory compressed the space of production as part of its process of speeding up time.

Moreover, the new factory was designed for further innovation and greater compression of production. Logan emphasized that there was no permanent layout for the machine shops, because the "production people… had the idea that there were going to be many changes in the makeup of the automobile."[30] The River Rouge plant was built to accommodate changing production flows, without creating a rigid arrangement that might constrain further innovations. This modern factory was no longer merely a container for men and machines; it was a master machine that organized and expressed the whole system of production. This was a master machine that transformed itself into ever more efficient arrangements. By 2013 just 3,000 Ford workers in one factory routinely produced

---

27. Logan Miller: *Reminiscences.* Owen Bombard Oral History Collection. Henry Ford Archives, pp. 14-15.
28. Horace Arnold and Fay L. Faurote: *Ford Methods and the Ford Shops.* Engineering Company 1915.
29. David Harvey: *The condition of postmodernity: An enquiry into the origins of cultural change.* Oxford 1990, p. 232.
30. Miller: *Reminiscences,* p. 15.

300,000 automobiles a year. They were roughly five times as productive as the workers of 1913.[31]

Like the Highland Park plant where the assembly line had been invented, the Rouge became as tourist magnet. To ensure that visitors understood the factory as a comprehensive system, Ford ensured that they had elevated views presenting a vast landscape of harmonious production.[32] One journalist described the overall effect on a visitor: "He sees these units not only in their impressive individual and astounding collective magnitude, but he also sees each unit as a part of a huge machine – he sees each unit as a carefully designed gear which meshes with other gears and operates in synchronism with them, the whole forming one huge, perfectly-timed, smoothly operating industrial machine of almost unbelievable manufacturing efficiency."[33] A German engineer, Otto Moug, toured the River Rouge plant in the late 1920s and found it an uplifting, almost religious experience. "No symphony, no Eroica, compared in depth, content, and power to the music that threatened and hammered away at us as we wandered through Ford's workplaces, wanderers overwhelmed by a daring expression of the human spirit."[34] The workers on the factory floor had a far harsher experience than these words suggest, but this could not be grasped in a short visit during which most of the viewpoints were Olympian rather than close to individual workers.

The painter and photographer Charles Sheeler, under commission by the Ford Motor Company, depicted the factory in a series of landscapes. Sheeler first spent six weeks at River Rouge in late 1927, just as the Model A was going into production. "The subject matter," he wrote to a friend, "is incomparably the most thrilling I have ever had to work with."[35] He submitted 32 photographs to the Ford Motor Company, subsequently used in advertising and publicity, but also exhibited today in museums. These images became the basis for a series of landscape paintings that he worked on until at least 1935. He concentrated on exterior views, show-

---

31. David E. Nye: *America's Assembly Line*, Cambridge, Mass. 2013, pp. 249-250.
32. William Littmann: "The Production of Goodwill: The Origins and Development of the Factory Tour in America," in *Perspectives in Vernacular Architecture*, Vol. 9 (2003), p. 77.
33. Cited in David Lewis: *The Public Image of Henry Ford*, Detroit 1976, p. 161.
34. Cited in Robert Casey: *The Model T: A Centennial History*, Baltimore 2003, p. 33.
35. Karen Lucic: *Charles Sheeler and the Cult of the Machine*, London 1991, p. 92.

ing mountains of coal, iron ore, and other raw materials, heaped symmetrically alongside the company's shipping canal and railroad tracks. In *American Landscape* there is not a single bush or tree or even a blade of grass, nor are any workers visible. The only signs of activity are the smoke from the powerhouse chimney and the railroad cars along the canal. The immediate impression is one of stasis, calm, order, and absolute control over the environment. The 1930s cultural historian Constance Rourke wrote approvingly: "He has accepted industrialism and renders what he sees as its essential forms."[36] Sheeler subtly simplified every object into an almost platonic form. His static Rouge factory was emptied of people and almost etherealized. Eugene Jolas, in the literary journal *transition*, found "a remarkable sense of dynamic magic" in Sheeler's photographs.[37] Many praised these landscapes, and *Fortune* reproduced several of them.

Sheeler focused on rhythmic patterns and formal aspects of the industrial landscape. He is often classed together with several contemporaries as "precisionists." Their paintings not only present somewhat idealized machines and factories but also efface the artist's labor from the canvas. The brushwork becomes invisible, as if the canvas were produced without human intervention. Precisionism was the visual correlative of modern industrial efficiency, naturalizing the transformation of space, so that it appeared unambiguously positive. Sheeler declared that he wanted "to eliminate the evidence of painting as such and present the design with the least evidence of the means of accomplishment." Similarly, a critic said of Stefan Hirsh that "his pictures seem to have been done without any effort."[38] Such canvases presented the transformation of the Rouge River as a benign inevitability. They visualized the narrative of progress.

Even as the Ford factory was being completed, perhaps as a kind of compensation for industry's ruthless assimilation of nature, the city of Detroit purchased 1204 acres further up the river and dedicated them as a park in 1925. Ever since the opening of New York's Central Park in 1873, American cities had set aside large tracks of land ostensibly to preserve

---

36. Cited in Joan Shelley Rubin: "A Convergence of Vision: Constance Rourke, Charles Sheeler, and American Art," in *American Quarterly* 42:2 (Jun.1990), p. 208.
37. Eugene Jolas: "The Industrial Mythos," in *Transition* 12 (Nov.1929), p. 123.
38. Sharon Corwin: "Picturing Efficiency: Precisionism, Scientific Management, and the Effacement of Labor," in *Representations* 84 (2003), autumn, p. 156.

a part of nature and make it freely available to citizens, although in fact these sites were extensively bulldozed and landscaped into new forms. The resulting parks were not natural in the sense of being untouched, but they were public spaces where the individual was expected to recover from the harshness of urban life and find new energy through contact with an idealized Nature.[39] Detroit's park contained not only 11 miles of bridal paths for equestrians but also, appropriately for America's automotive capital, "a series of winding automobile drives." Much of the space was given to team sports that had become popular after industrialization, including a football field, two baseball fields, three children's playgrounds, a track and field athletic field including "jumping and vaulting pits," an 18-hole golf course, 18 tennis courts, an Olympic-sized swimming pool and "picnicking facilities.... scattered throughout the grounds." During winter, the park offered "a 6-acre skating rink and six 700-foot toboggan slides." More ominously, the park also contained "in a natural hollow" a pistol range for the Detroit police and stables for the US National Guard.[40] The proximity of armed forces would be useful to the Ford Company in labor confrontations during the 1930s.

The Workers' Rouge

During the Great Depression, the centralization and vertical integration that in prosperous times had seemed the great advantage of Ford's River Rouge plant became a serious problem. As Alfred Chandler explained: "Ford was the world's most integrated automobile company. To be sure of constant, tightly scheduled flows of materials through his huge plants... and thus to enhance the economies of scale, Ford made massive investment in the production of steel and glass, parts and accessories." When output declined, however, Ford couldn't escape the high fixed costs of such equipment, and "unit costs rose much more rapidly than did those

---

39. John Sears: *Sacred Places: American Tourist Attractions in the Nineteenth Century*, Amherst 1989, pp. 116-121.
40. Michigan Writers Project, p. 282.

of his competitors."[41] One response to the problem was to invest in machines that could eliminate jobs. By 1935, an eight-spindle boring machine required only one operator to drill sixteen valve and pushrod holes in V-8 engine blocks. Because of the huge investments in plants and machinery, to remain competitive Ford had to wring more work out of every man and woman on the line. The speed-up seemed a logical necessity to management in order to keep the cost of cars from increasing.

Workers immediately realized that the speed-up meant fewer people had jobs. Only half as many labored at the Rouge by 1932, when Detroit's auto workers were desperate. Thousands had used up their savings, cashed in their life insurance, and lost their homes. More than 3,000 joined a protest march to the gates of the River Rouge plant, where they met armed resistance. The marchers moved freely through Detroit, but once they reached the city limits of Dearborn police demanded that they turn back. When they refused, the police fired tear gas; the workers responded by pelting them with rocks. As the police retreated, the workers marched forward until they reached the Rouge. There the police and private security forces opened fire, killing four and wounding many more. This "Dearborn Massacre" was a literal contestation of space that angered workers in all parts of the United States. In Detroit more than 20,000 people turned out for a defiant funeral. The River Rouge Plant had become a central site in the battle between capitalism and unionized labor.

During these tense years the work discipline imposed by the movement of the assembly line itself was supplemented at Ford by a strong security presence. One labor organizer believed that "at least 15 out of every 100 employees" were either foremen, security personnel, or spies. The undercover men were instructed to use violent methods to quell disturbances. One Ford worker testified to the National Labor Relations Board that he had been told to swing a lead pipe freely and to hit anyone he had to hit in order to quell disturbances that might erupt on the shop floor. Ford also made an alliance with the American Legion for support in case of labor troubles.[42] In these years, historian Steve Meyer writes, "American automobile workers felt angry, degraded, and

---

41. Alfred D. Chandler: *Scale and Scope*, Cambridge, Mass. 1990, p. 208.
42. Carl Rauchenbush: *Fordism*. League For Industrial Democracy, 1937, pp. 34-35.

emasculated... [until] the swift rise and the gradual consolidation of the United Automobile Workers Union reversed the social and economic decline of automobile workers' lives, permitted a venting of deep-seated anger and hostility, and sanctioned a reassertion of dignified masculine aggressiveness."[43] The unionization of the Rouge Plant proved the most difficult and took longer than elsewhere in the automobile industry.

As the last bastion of anti-unionism, Ford resisted violently. On May 26, 1937, four United Auto Workers (UAW) men, including Walter Reuther, went to an overpass near Gate 4 at River Rouge to hand out leaflets urging workers to join the union. Men from Ford's so-called Service Department (a security force) beat them severely in an incident that became a national news story and subsequently was called "The Battle of the Overpass." The UAW continued to organize and to press for recognition for more than two years. For example, in January 1938 the UAW erected large billboards close to the River Rouge factory that read "STOP speed up, service spies, discrimination. GAIN real seniority, labor rights, collective bargaining."[44] This confrontation between capital and labor was only resolved after a new European war had begun. Ford was forced to the bargaining table at the moment when the struggle with labor was dwarfed by that much larger struggle. The great contestation of war justified resolving the smaller contestation within the factory gates. Labor won the exclusive right to represent the workers, after which they held union elections inside the Ford factories. Thus, the Rouge became a symbol of labor's successful but often bloody struggle for recognition.

The Cold War Rouge

Yet World War II led the American mass media almost immediately to transform the meaning of the Rouge. The Ford Motor Company and mass-production industries in general were reconceived as the guarantor that the United States would never run short of trucks, ships, planes,

---

43. Steve Meyer: "Rough Manhood: The Aggressive and Confrontational Shop Culture of U.S. Auto Workers during World War II," in *Journal of Social History* 36 (2002), no. 1, p. 127.
44. Bryan: *Pictured in its Prime*, p. 218.

weapons, or supplies. In 1940 *Life* magazine devoted eleven pages to a photographic essay on Ford's River Rouge. In addition to a detailed diagram of the whole plant and pages of photographs of the foundry and various machines, the story also included some human-interest material, such as a photo of men lined up at a lunch wagon and one of a man operating a large floor cleaner. There was not a critical word.[45] The same issue of *Life* carried a long story on Hitler's rise to power, with more than 60 photographs documenting his life. Shortly after the United States entered the war, *Time* magazine declared: "Something is happening that Adolf Hitler does not yet understand – a new re-enactment of the old American miracle of wheels and machinery, but on a new scale. This time it is a miracle of war production, and its miracle-worker is the automobile industry." American mass production was expected to overwhelm the Germans and the Japanese. *Time* declared: "Endlessly the lines will send tanks, jeeps, machine guns, cannons, air torpedoes, and armored cars. Ford's River Rouge plant, where Ford steamships dump coal and iron ore and limestone to be magicked into steel and glass and machinery, has turned its two square miles of self-contained industrial empire to the tools of war."[46]

After World War II, the Rouge factory once again emerged as a popular tourist site that produced millions of cars and trucks for American consumers. Henry Ford had built the River Rouge complex as a self-sufficient plant that could make everything needed to build a car, including the steel, the electricity, the body, the engine, and all the automotive parts. Simultaneously, he conceived it as the center of a world automotive empire, with branch factories in Britain, France, Germany, Russia, Japan, and elsewhere. This global reach was highlighted in the Ford Rotunda, where tours of the River Rouge factory began. This structure was first erected at the 1939 New York World's Fair and later moved to Dearborn. Ten stories high, it was "cylindrical in plan and modernistic in outline, resembling four different-sized gears, one above the other." Inside, the enormous circular wall was covered by photographic murals 190 meters long and 6 meters high that showed "the Rouge Plant in all its activities."

---

45. *Life Magazine*, Aug 19, 1940, pp. 37-48.
46. *Time*, March 23, 1942.

At the center of the enormous room stood a six-meter high "revolving globe" with Ford's activities clearly marked.[47] The clear intention was to impress upon visitors both the enormous and intricate complexity of the nearby factory and its role in spreading mass production to the rest of the world.

The River Rouge factory thereby was inscribed at the center of a narrative of triumphant progress. It became an icon of the Cold War, and an exemplary place worthy of replication everywhere. Ford's factory served as an exemplar of "People's Capitalism" that the United States Information Service promoted as the antidote to communism. The People's Capitalism campaign sent brochures, speakers and exhibits around the world, to persuade Europe and emerging nations that American-style mass production assured a better future than any centralized, state-owned productive system. It argued that American society had already achieved what communism only promised.[48] Similar ideas underlay the many exchange programs that brought foreign engineers and managers to the United States, almost invariably to visit an assembly line factory, often the River Rouge Plant itself. For Americans, too, the River Rouge remained an icon of productivity and progress. In 1964, 227,561 people went to see it.[49] Yet during the energy crises of the 1970s production declined, and in the 1980s Ford was challenged by Japanese lean production methods, which it had adopted by 1991. Gradually, the Rouge stopped making many of the parts for vehicles it assembled, and portions of the site fell into disuse. Entire buildings were closed, and the Ford Rouge canal received little traffic. (Illustration 2). Production was decentralized, and outsourced parts arrived in containers. This internationalization undermined well-paid workers in Detroit, not only because Asian and Latin American labor markets were less expensive but also because their factories had weak (or no) unions, demanded long hours, and spent little on safety. Ford's global reach led to de-industrialization inside the United

---

47. Michigan Writers Project, p. 221.
48. Laura Belmonte: "Modernization and US Overseas Propaganda." In *Staging Growth: Modernization, Development, and the Global Cold War*, ed. David C. Engerman et al., Amherst 2003, pp. 119-122.
49. Rotunda & Plant Visitors Attendance Statistics, 1924-1964, accession 1222, Ford Archives.

States and the decline of Detroit as a whole and the River Rouge Plant in particular. The US automotive industry relocated many factories, and it produced more cars with fewer workers. Downtown Detroit slowly collapsed as the city's population fell from 1.5 million in 1970 to just over 700,000 in 2010.

The Green Rouge

During a century of industrial use, the Rouge industrial zone became seriously polluted. In 1989 The International Joint Commission (IJC), a bi-national organization of the United States and Canada, "identified the Rouge River as one of the 43 worst pollution 'hot spots' in the Great Lakes area.[50] The Rouge contained high levels of bacteria, heavy metals, organic chemicals, and polychlorinated biphenyls (PCBs). The Commission called for a $900 million cleanup that would take twenty years. By 1991 $500 million had been appropriated by state and local authorities for improved sewers and wastewater treatment, including a more complete separation between storm and sanitary sewer systems. In addition, more than 300 illegal points of discharge were identified and eliminated.[51] While government spearheaded the cleanup, volunteers also played a major role. Between 1986 and 1992 the Friends of the Rouge organized "an annual clean up of the Rouge River, known as the 'Rouge Rescue'" in which 15,000 volunteers "removed over 19,000 cubic yards of debris, including approximately 500 log jams."[52] Twenty communities participated in this process. However, it was also becoming clear that more than $1 billion would be needed to complete the program. Companies that legally discharged into the Rouge watershed under permit included a steel plant, Shell, Mobile, and Amoco Oil, Ford, General Motors, and a wide range of smaller factories and businesses.[53]

In 2000, William Clay Ford, great-grandson of the founder, decided to

---

50. River Rouge Remedial Action Plan, Annual Report, 1992, p. 3.
51. Ibid., pp. 9-11.
52. Ibid., p. 14.
53. Ibid., pp. 31-32.

Ill. 1: Aerial view of Rouge plant.

Ill. 2: Abandoned Rouge.

Ill. 3: Green Rouge.

spend $2 billion rebuilding the River Rouge factory with the environment and lean manufacturing in mind. It became a flexible-production factory with three assembly lines that could produce nine different models. A new living green roof covered 15 acres and greatly reduced water runoff as well as providing insulation. (Illustration 3) The parking lots were also redesigned to absorb rain rather than shed it as runoff, and the site allows water to percolate slowly through marshy areas before entering the Rouge River. The soil was full of industrial chemicals, but plantings were carefully selected to neutralize or break down toxic substances. Such plantings were cheaper than replacing tons of soil, and they beautified the grounds. Furthermore, a wetland area cost millions of dollars less than building new storm sewers. Inside, the rebuilt factory has abundant natural light and many energy-saving features.[54] Ford also hired Harley

---

54. K. Naughton: "Growing a Green Plant," in *Newsweek*, Nov. 13, 2000, pp. 58-60.

Ellis Devereaux to design a visitor center that in 2009 earned an environmental award, LEED gold certification. Like the Rouge next door, it has a green roof.[55]

The architect in charge of the makeover of the River Rouge plant, William McDonough, became an international spokesperson for integrating product recycling into the system of production. In 2002 he co-authored *From Cradle to Cradle* that made the case for improving productivity by planning for reuse at every step in the manufacturing process. "Building a truly sustainable automobile industry," McDonough asserted, "means developing closed-loop systems for the manufacturing and re-utilization of auto parts. In Europe, the End-of-Life Vehicle Directive [passed by the EU in September 2000] makes manufacturers responsible for automotive materials, pushing companies to design for disassembly and effective resource recovery. Cradle-to-cradle systems, in which materials either go back to industry or safely back to the soil, are built for effective resource recovery."[56]

Older recycling methods reduce waste, but the materials recycled are degraded in quality and purity. For example, a car shredder mixes together high-grade steel, copper, and other metals. When smelted, this yields a lower-grade product that can't be used to make new car bodies. To avoid such "down-cycling," McDonough develops products that can truly be recycled. He advocates thinking about industrial production as part of a "technical metabolism" that "can be designed to mirror natural nutrient cycles; it's a closed-loop system in which valuable, high-tech synthetics and mineral resources circulate in an endless cycle of production, recovery and remanufacture." Society needs disassembly lines that recover materials without degrading them for reuse in new products.[57] In its best form, the "technical metabolism" mirrors biological metabolism and is powered by wind and solar energy. The goal is not to minimize harm but to maximize environmental benefits. "The health of the site is measured not in terms of meeting minimum government-imposed standards but

---

55. *Design News*, Oct 1, 2009, p. 11.
56. William McDonough and Michael Braungart: "Restoring the Industrial Landscape," at http://www.mcdonough.com (January 2013).
57. William McDonough and Michael Braungart: *Cradle to Cradle*, New York 2002, pp. 164-165.

with respect to things like the number of earthworms per cubic foot of soil, the diversity of birds and insects on the land and of aquatic species in a nearby river, and the attractiveness of the site to local residents."[58]

Conclusion

The Rouge factory is evolving into a technical metabolism that mimics natural recycling. This is an appropriate reconception of industry in an ecological age. When integrated into the Native American Mound Builder society, the Rouge was used for transportation, hunting, fishing, and agriculture, as well as serving as a ceremonial site. The French valued the Rouge as part of the fur trade, and only after their defeat did Anglo-Americans settle and farm along its banks. After the arrival of steamboats and railroads, the same area was converted to industrial uses, including iron making, stove production, and chemical refining, before Ford decided to build the world's largest factory there. It became an icon of mass production in the 1920s, a symbol of successful labor struggles by the end of the 1930s, a major center of military production during World War II, and an exemplar of "People's Capitalism" during the Cold War. By 2013, however, the site was less industrial than it had been in 1930. Some of the area had been returned to wetland, and even the roof of the factory was planted with grasses and fed wild birds. The Rouge had become a new kind of factory, and its managers took seriously the search for more environmentally sustainable production. If there is no possibility of rebuilding the ancient Indian burial mounds, neither is there any possibility of returning to the vision of nature as mere raw material to be endlessly transformed. The conception of this (or perhaps any) site as a palimpsest mistakenly suggests that nature is merely an original or bottom layer, with additions and erasures on top. At the Rouge, the river and the land have survived many iterations of culture and industry, each of which has disappeared or declined. The new green factory recognizes nature's persistence and seeks to imitate it by developing a technical metabolism. Rather than treat Nature as abstract space

---

58. Ibid, p. 162.

that exists in order to be exploited, the new industrial ideal is to live in harmony with the landscape.

If the mound builders and the Native Americans remain under erasure (save for their recognition in a few automobile names such as the Pontiac), if the grid system continues to carve the land into a succession of squares, nevertheless many of the places inside Detroit have disappeared. By 2010 more than 80,000 houses and apartments had been abandoned, and more than 40 square miles of the city were vacant. There were vegetable gardens on abandoned lots.[59] What had been neighborhoods were disappearing to become what was long the least American of spaces, the ruin. Many of the automobile plants, and much of the old Rouge was also in ruins. The ruins of Detroit mark the death of the old progressive narrative from wilderness to factory, from empty space to civilization. The wetlands of the River Rouge again have value, and a factory more modest in size and with a smaller carbon footprint expresses an emerging willingness to live within limits.

---

59. Nye: *America's Assembly Line*, p. 215.

London Lived and Intersected: Anti-Israeli Gaza War Demonstrations in London in 2009

Kirstine Sinclair

On 27th December 2008, Israel launched attacks on the Gaza strip following a number of Palestinian rocket attacks across the border to Israel since the end of a ceasefire between the Hamas-led government in Gaza and Israel earlier that month. According to the Israeli government, the attacks on public buildings and infrastructure in Gaza was a necessary means of stopping the Palestinian terror targeting Israeli civilians. According to the Hamas, on the other hand, the Israeli aggression was out of proportion. As evidence of this, they referred to the number of lives lost on the two sides: 13 Israeli soldiers as opposed to between 1100 and 1500 Palestinian civilians.[1] The attacks continued into January 2009 and across the world, anti-Israeli and pro-Gaza demonstrations took place. There were demonstrations throughout Northern and Southern America, across the Middle East, Africa, South and South East Asia, Australia and in the majority of European countries.

The Israeli aggression in the winter of 2008-09 was, of course, part of the long and on-going conflict between Israelis and Palestinians over the territory today known as Israel, West Bank and Gaza, which has been a highly prioritised and contested political issue for the international so-

---

1. There are many reports and news analyses providing estimations of the number of losses. A couple of examples from new sources are found here: http://news.bbc.co.uk/2/hi/middle_east/7855070.stm (June 2012), http://www.aolnews.com/2011/04/03/israeli-officials-cheer-after-goldstone-rethinks-war-crimes-repo/ (June 2012).

ciety as well as the Middle Eastern region since the birth of the State of Israel in 1948. However, the specificities of the conflict are not the point of interest here. Rather, this chapter will focus exclusively on the responses to the Israeli attacks on Gaza as they were performed by different actors in the British capital, London, in January 2009. The aim is to analyse how a selection of actors used London to communicate their criticism of the Israeli aggression. The questions are: How did different British actors respond to the Gaza conflict in anti-Israeli demonstrations in London in January 2009? Where did they march and what symbols did they use to express their opposition to the Israeli aggression? What does this say about the understanding of the conflict, the actors and their use of the London city space? And what does it say about London?

In order to limit the object of the analysis, three demonstrations protesting against the Israeli aggression in Gaza have been singled out: those of 3rd, 4th and 10th of January. On 3rd and 10th of January 2009, the Stop the War Coalition organised two demonstrations which will be compared to a demonstration organised by Hizb ut-Tahrir taking place on the 4th of January 2009. As British organisations affiliated with the Muslim Brotherhood were part of the Stop the War Coalition demonstrations, the comparison is not between Islamists on the one side and non-Islamist organisations on the other, but rather between different kinds of Islamist organisations or organisations affiliated with Islamists. The point being that this is not about Muslims or political Islam but about how a political message can be delivered differently by comparable actors within the same frame of time and space and still appeal to very different audiences through the use of place.

The demonstrations will be analysed using concepts from cultural geography, namely "Lived Space" and "Intersections", in combination with perspectives from Goffman's sociological studies of performance and identity making. In the following, I aim to analyse these organisations' choice of routes through London and their use of symbols and in some instances violence in order to make the argument that the use of London, the way different actors single out different routes, monuments and destinations for their demonstrations, reveals who their audiences are as well as their political agendas and their ideas of what kind of a place London is.

The differentiated usage of London as city space becomes very obvious when one focuses on how the city is used and what activities are taking place. It is, to paraphrase Cresswell, when one looks at London in terms of verbs rather than nouns and asks not "who does what?", but rather "what do they do?" that new narratives about London appear.[2] In the following, I hope to demonstrate how looking at London as made up of intersecting activities and people performing political ideas rather than a place defined by its geographical boundaries, contributes new stories about what London is.[3]

London as a World City

Apart from being the British capital, London is also (one of) the biggest cities in the European Union with more than 8 million inhabitants (2011). It is the world's leading financial centre alongside New York City, has had a central role in developments in arts, design and fashion, just as it has been one of the world's most visited cities, a magnet for people seeking work, for tourists, students and business people of all sorts, for centuries. Today, London hosts 43 universities and around 300 spoken languages have been registered in the greater London area. Facts like these are what makes London a "global city" or "world city".[4]

To political activists, whether international or based locally, London has a special role, too. A former member of Hizb ut-Tahrir has explained how London had a special status according to Hizb ut-Tahrir's strategy for creating awareness about its cause and political goal. They would have publications for broad distribution throughout the British Isles, and publications that were only distributed in the capital. And the same

---

2. Tim Cresswell: *Place: a Short Introduction*, Malden, MA 2004, pp. 43-51, Tim Cresswell: "Introduction" in T*hamyris/Intersections* no. 9, 2004, p. 2012.
3. As accounted for in the introduction of this volume, space and place have been viewed differently at different times, and still today, there are many ways of analysing and understanding place and space. In the following analysis of demonstrations in London, I use the concepts of "lived space" and "intersections" borrowed from Tim Cresswell and Doreen Massey respectively: Tim Cresswell: *Place*, Doreen Massey: *for space*, London 2005.
4. See for instance Doreen Massey: *World City*, Cambridge, UK 2007.

was the case with demonstrations. Some would be repeated widely in cities like Birmingham, Manchester and Sheffield, some only took place in London. The anti-Gaza war demonstration in 2009 only took place in London. This was because London was regarded the "Okaz Fair" of current times. Okaz Fair was an event that went before the pilgrimage at the time of the Prophet Mohammed. All leaders of tribes would meet before performing the pilgrimage, and the Prophet would summon them to God. In other words, at this fair, he would have access to all relevant political representatives.[5] Comparing London to the Okaz Fair means seeing London as a place where one can reach the attention of all relevant political leaders; a platform from where Hizb ut-Tahrir can address Muslims worldwide.

The activists involved in the Stop the War Coalition's demonstrations represented both Muslim and non-Muslim organisations. The Muslim activists involved were affiliated with either the Muslim Council of Britain and the Muslim Brotherhood or Jamaat-i-Islami, and together with activists from the Respect Party and the Public Service Trade Union "Unison" among others, they used their participation to show identification with the Palestinians and frustration with events in Gaza, to address British politicians, to draw the public's attention to the situation in Gaza, and to some extent to let off steam in the shape of street violence near the Israeli Embassy. But from an organisational perspective, The Muslim Council of Britain and Jamaat-i-Islami used the demonstrations to unite with left-wing activists and a wide range of British opinion makers and public figures and thus emphasised the council's affiliation with British political culture and recognised valves for political frustration.

---

5. Conversation with former member of the Hizb ut-Tahrir leadership in Britain, June 2012. More details about the fair can be found here: "The History of al-Tabari", Vol. VI, *Muhammed at Mecca*, Albany 1988, pp. 120-22.

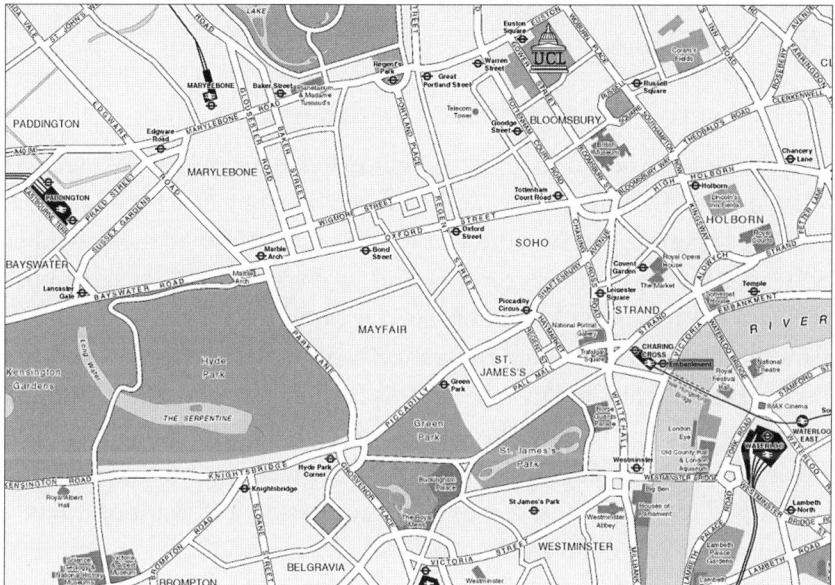

As we shall see in the following, the solidarity with the Palestinian cause is expressed in a variety of ways covering both cultural, religious and political issues and aims, but the solidarity is also situational and opportunistic.[6] Some groups, such as the British Stop the War coalition, can use the cause because it fits in with their wider political agenda while others use the cause to promote a different political goal, such as the establishment of the Islamic state, the Caliphate, as is the case of Hizb ut-Tahrir. In this way, political demonstrations are expressions of strategic public relations considerations on many simultaneous levels, and while that is perhaps a banal point, it becomes less banal when analysing such factors with a point of departure in place. The world city London is an ideal open-air stage without backcloth or fixed audiences. From this stage, actors can address the whole world, just as they can alter the scenography as they go along.

---

6. Arjun Appadurai: *Fear of Small Numbers: An Essay on the Geography of Anger*, Durham 2006, pp. 25-26.

The Three Demonstrations

THE TWO STOP THE WAR COALITION DEMONSTRATIONS

On January 3rd 2009, over 12.000 people marched from Embankment via Westminster, Downing Street and Trafalgar Square to the Israeli Embassy.[7] The organiser, the Stop the War Coalition, was formed in September 2001 after the terror attacks on New York and Washington on September 11th and the following launch of the War on terror by the Bush administration. Its aims are to stop the war on terror and to "oppose any racist backlash generated by this war" and, as further stated on the coalition's homepage: "(...) to stop the erosion of civil rights."[8] Today, in 2012, however, the homepage gives witness to the fact that the coalition has developed its field of interest to cover aggression and war not directly linked to the War on Terror.

The coalition's President is Tony Benn, a retired Member of Parliament for Labour who used to belong to the left wing of the party. Vice-Presidents are: George Galloway, Tariq Ali, Anas Al-Tikriti, Louise Christian, Tam Dalyell, Caroline Lucas (Member of the European Parliament), Alice Mahon, Kamal Majid and Keith Sonnet (Head of the Public Service Trade Union "Unison"). All of the above are very prominent members of the British left and engaged in politics, journalism, law, human rights activism and/or trade unions. To give just a few more details, Galloway used to be a member of parliament for Labour until he was expelled for his vocal opposition to the Iraq war. In 2004, he formed the new political party called Respect and is today a member of parliament representing this party's constituency in Bradford. Tariq Ali is a British Pakistani military historian and journalist with Marxist leanings who has published a number of books on Pakistan and military history and who writes for the daily left-wing newspaper The Guardian. Ali has had a long history as a

---

7. See for instance *The Guardian*: http://www.guardian.co.uk/world/2009/jan/04/gaza-israel-demonstration-trafalgar-square for an estimated number (June 2012).
8. See the Coalition's homepage for a full description of aims: http://stopwar.org.uk/index.php/about/what-we-stand-for (June 2012).

public political activist dating back to opposition to the Vietnam War in the late 1960s.[9]

The idea behind the coalition is to attract individuals and organisations sympathetic to the stated aims and let local committees branch out and organise their own events. This has resulted in cooperation with organisations representing a great variety of political opinions, religions and ethical standpoints. And this also explains the Coalition's involvement in the Anti Gaza-war demonstrations in January 2009.

On 10th January 2009, the number of participating demonstrators had grown from 12,000 to a much larger number: One estimation said between 50,000 and 200,000 individuals, making it the largest demonstration expressing sympathy for the Palestinians in the history of the United Kingdom.[10] This time, the demonstration had Speaker's Corner in Hyde Park as its starting point and from there it went via Bayswater and Kensington Gardens before terminating in front of the Israeli Embassy, like the demonstration on 3rd January 2009. In the demonstration on 10th January, leaders of the Muslim Council of Britain which is associated with the Muslim Brotherhood and the Pakistani Islamist organisation Jamaat-i-Islami, walked side by side with representatives of Jews for Justice, Amnesty International and a whole range of other socially engaged activist enterprises.

Despite the fact that the involved organisations differ regarding views on Hamas's rocket attack on Israeli civilians for instance, and how the conflict between Israel and Palestine should be approached more generally speaking, they nevertheless were united in protesting against Israel's attacks across the border into Gaza. Under the banner of the Stop the War Coalition, the protesters agreed on the following: the perception that Israel's occupation of the Gaza strip since 1967 is as an "apartheid-like"-regime which is provoking resistance from Hamas and that the current

---

9. For a full list of Presidents and Vice Presidents in the Stop the War organisation see this link: http://stopwar.org.uk/index.php/about/steering-committee-and-officers (June 2012). For a list of Ali's publications, please follow this link: http://literature.britishcouncil.org/tariq-ali (June 2012).
10. The organiser, Stop the War, claimed the number of participants was six times higher according to *The Guardian*: http://www.guardian.co.uk/world/2009/jan/04/gaza-israel-demonstration-trafalgar-square (June 2012).

Israeli occupation and the blockade of Gaza by Israel and Egypt must be terminated in order for "Gaza's infrastructure and democracy to recover", and finally, that Israeli generals should be tried for war crimes. The latter claim was based on observations reported by UN and Red Cross officials.[11]

The two Stop the War Coalition demonstrations on January 3rd and 10th both finished in front of the Israeli Embassy, but they went along different routes before reaching what would appear an obvious point of termination: the official Israeli representation to the United Kingdom. The first of the two demonstrations went from the banks of the Thames via Westminster, Downing Street and Trafalgar Square to the Israeli Embassy. It had Embankment as its point of departure, which, apart from being centrally located and thus near the points of interest for the demonstration, is also the location of a tube station and just across the river from the Waterloo rail station. From this practical starting point, the demonstration went to Westminster, the British Parliament, continued to Downing Street, the official residence of the Prime Minister and up past Trafalgar Square marked by Nelson's column. Trafalgar Square is often considered the closest equivalent London has to a "town Square", it is home to the National Gallery and several consular buildings, such as for instance Canada House, and it is also used to mark holidays or cultural events. For instance the square is used for official New Year celebrations and similarly the Muslim holiday marking the end of the Ramadan, Eid ul-fitr, is marked by a major event on the square. However, Trafalgar Square is perhaps best known for Nelson's column in the centre of the square. As most readers will be aware, Admiral and Lord Horatio Nelson is considered a national hero in the United Kingdom after he successfully led the British fleet in battle against the French and Spanish fleets attempting to invade the British Isles in 1805. The demonstration stopped at Trafalgar Square where speakers in turn addressed the audience, before the crowd continued to the Israeli Embassy in Kensington.

---

11. Please find the UN report here: http://www2.ohchr.org/english/bodies/hrcouncil/special-session/9/factfindingmission.htm (June 2012). The so-called Goldstone Report was later criticised as described here: http://www.washingtonpost.com/opinions/reconsidering-the-goldstone-report-on-israel-and-war-crimes/2011/04/01/AFg111JC_story.html (June 2012).

As shown in the above, the demonstration on 3rd January connected sights of political and historical interest as well as symbolic value through having people walk the distance of approximately 2 kilometres from Embankment to the Israeli Embassy in Kensington, south-west of Hyde Park via the mentioned places. Furthermore, by walking past the British parliament and the home of the Prime Minister before reaching the Israeli embassy, the demonstration connected the representational British democracy and institutionalised power with the official Israel.

The strategy of addressing official representatives and institutions is typical for western civil rights movements and has been seen on many occasions throughout history. For instance the popular opposition to the Vietnam War took the shape of demonstrations at the Mall in Washington and has since been repeated in connection with recent anti-war-on-terror demonstrations too. 300,000 people gathered in Washington in 2007 and listened to Joan Baez sing: "Where have all the flowers gone?" to the Bush administration in the White House. [12]

The second demonstration organised by the Stop the War Coalition had Speaker's Corner in Hyde Park as its point of departure. By this time and based on previous experiences the week before, the organisers must have felt certain that they would be able to gather enough people to make Speaker's Corner a good assembly point. Choosing the right settings for a demonstration is crucial to getting your message through to the public: If you have a big square or venue as your starting point and only a few people show up, your event looks like a failure and your message will not be heard. If, on the other hand, you fill a major square, your event is a success. The underlying logic being that the number of participants is important for the reception of the message: 500 people marching and no one will listen. 50,000 people marching and the message will be heard by those in power just as it is likely to be covered by the media and thus reach the wider public.

Speaker's Corner in the north-east corner of Hyde Park is the epitome of free speech and open debate and is regarded with pride by Londoners and the whole of Britain. It is in all its simplicity a place where people

---

12. Personal account to the author from Maj Vingum Jensen who participated in the demonstration in Washington in 2007.

with any kind of messages can make their voices heard. Passers-by will be more or less interested and there is of course no guarantee of an audience, but with no set time frame or programme, it is a magnet for people seeking out an audience for their messages, be they political, religious or something altogether different. Thus, Speaker's Corner has special connotations of civil rights and democracy in general and freedom of speech more specifically. From Speaker's Corner in Hyde Park, the demonstration went via Kensington Gardens to the Israeli Embassy. Kensington Gardens is the westernmost part of Hyde Park and hosts the home of the late Princess of Wales, Lady Diana. It is, however, also directly on the way from Speaker's Corner to the target of the protest, the Israeli Embassy.

The march began largely peacefully and included many young British Muslims as well as members of political parties. The crowd listened to speakers including trade unionists, representatives of Palestinian exiles, and celebrity campaigners such as Brian Eno and Annie Lennox. But in both instances, the demonstrations ended in violence. On 3rd January 2009, the London Metropolitan Police had to protect the Israeli Embassy from a crowd of 5,000 individuals. The crowd attacking the embassy had broken away from the demonstration at Trafalgar Square and was dominated by young British Muslims armed with fireworks. As described by The Guardian:

> *"Officers with riot shields sealed off local roads as a small group of angry protesters tried to storm the building. Older protesters were seen trying to calm sections of the crowd. As darkness fell the atmosphere became more heated, vocal and aggressive."*[13]

The demonstration on January 10th 2009 also ended in violence in front of the Israeli Embassy. Here another report from The Guardian:

> *"The march began in Hyde Park, where Speakers' Corner was turned into a sea of Palestinian flags and banners condemning Israel, before making its*

---

13. http://www.guardian.co.uk/world/2009/jan/04/gaza-israel-demonstration-trafalgar-square (June 2012).

way to Kensington Gardens. There were scuffles outside the Israeli embassy as the march passed by the gates leading to its entrance. Missiles were thrown at police guarding the way and a number of loud bangs – believed to be firecrackers – were heard as riot police drew batons and attempted to push the crowd back from the gates. A number of younger masked demonstrators attempted to climb on to the gates, near Kensington High Street, and hurled pieces of placards and other items at police lines. Panic rippled through the crowd, which included young children, and a number of people fell to the ground amid the scuffles."[14]

The organisers behind the demonstrations did not apologise for the violent behaviour by some of the participants. And as the participating Stop the War Vice President, historian and journalist Tariq Ali, said after the second demonstration on January 10th:

"You always have on any demonstration a group of people who get very angry and sometimes that comes out in violence, but for me the most appalling violence is happening in Gaza. A few punch-ups outside the Israeli embassy is neither here nor there."[15]

In other words, the violence by some of the participants in the Stop the War Coalition demonstrations was regarded minor incidents compared to the bigger picture – the Gaza war – or just an unfortunate side-effect, rather than activities compromising the organisers' agenda.

Summing up, based on the routes of the two Stop the War coalition demonstrations as well as the symbols and slogans used, the aim of the demonstrations was to highlight the consequences of the Gaza war for the Palestinians in Gaza and to get official Britain, politicians and diplomats, to put pressure on official Israel, politicians and diplomats, to stop the aggression.

---

14. http://www.guardian.co.uk/world/2009/jan/04/gaza-israel-demonstration-trafalgar-square (June 2012).
15. http://www.guardian.co.uk/world/2009/jan/10/gaza-london-protest-march (June 2012).

THE HIZB UT-TAHRIR DEMONSTRATION

As opposed to the two demonstrations connecting places of political importance and cultural interest with the embassy of Israel, Hizb ut-Tahrir's demonstration took a slightly different route through London. At a demonstration on Sunday 4th January 2009 organised by Hizb ut-Tahrir Britain, around 3,000 demonstrators called on the armies of Muslim majority countries to defend Gaza from what the organisation perceived as brutal Israeli onslaught – or simply state terrorism. The demonstration began at Paddington Green, made a halt at Marble Arch where speakers from Hizb ut-Tahrir urged the Muslim armies to defend Gaza. Then the crowd marched on to the embassies of Saudi Arabia, Syria and Egypt thus leaving out the Israeli embassy.

Paddington Green is close to Paddington Station in a part of London with a substantial Arab population. Here, in the summer, you find rich Arabs cruising in their expensive Gulf Emirates registered cars and Arab book shops and water pipe cafés close by. From this corner of London, the demonstration moved to Marble Arch – a white marble arch originally designed in 1925 to be an entrance gate to Buckingham Palace. The construction, however, was delayed due to rising costs and ultimately the design was changed. Later, in 1960, in connection with re-construction of Buckingham Palace, the arch was dismantled and moved to its current location directly opposite Speaker's Corner at the junction of Edgware Road, Oxford Street and Park Lane.

Hizb ut-Tahrir's demonstration passed Marble Arch on the way to three Middle Eastern embassies: the Syrian, the Saudi Arabian and the Egyptian. All three embassies lie within a short distance from each other in the Mayfair area between Marble Arch and Green Park to the east of Hyde Park. As the Saudi Arabian and the Egyptian embassies lie just one block away from each other, it is understandable that the Hizb ut-Tahrir organisers have wished to include all embassies in their march, but why would they march on the embassies of these three Arab countries rather than the Israeli Embassy?

The short answer is that Hizb ut-Tahrir was accusing the regimes of Saudi Arabia, Egypt and Syria for directly or indirectly supporting what was perceived as Israeli aggression and a failure to help Palestinians. The logic behind this criticism would be that Egypt and Saudi Arabia are both seen as allies of the United States of America and thus as supporters of Israel – Egypt because of the peace treaty with Israel signed at Camp David in 1978 ending 30 years of conflict, Saudi Arabia because of extended collaboration with the US in connection with military operations, bases on Saudi soil and an overall Saudi support of the US War on Terror since 2001. The criticism towards Syria would be based on different reasoning, in that Syria has never signed a peace treaty with Israel and has in no formal way recognised Israel's right to exist. Quite the contrary, Israel and Syria are still in an open albeit cool and somewhat controlled conflict over the territory known as the Golan Heights in the south-west corner of present-day Syria. Regarding the Syrian regime, Hizb ut-Tahrir's criticism is based on what is perceived as a failure to fight for the Palestinians' right to return to Palestine. What exactly is meant by Palestine is not clearly defined but it would be likely to involve the seizure of the existence of the state of Israel according to Hizb ut-Tahrir's general stance on the matter.[16]

In this manner, Hizb ut-Tahrir was accusing the leaders of Saudi Arabia, Egypt and Syria of if not direct responsibility for the atrocities in Gaza then indirect responsibility. And the accusations were followed up bluntly by the use of symbols in the shape of coffins carried by the demonstrators. There were three coffins which carried the writing: "Killed in Gaza" on one side and "Killed by Mubarak", "Killed by King Abdullah" and "Killed by Assad" respectively on the other. Behind the three coffins was a large orange banner carrying the message: "Only Khalifah will Liberate Palestine". As explained in a blog about the demonstration, *"The protestors called for all the current corrupt Muslim rulers to be replaced by a Khalifah (Caliph) who would send the armies from Muslim countries to defend Gaza and liberate Palestine".*[17] After the last stop at the Syrian Embassy, the demonstrators performed a collective prayer.

Seen in this perspective, Hizb ut-Tahrir's demonstration in the Brit-

---

16. An analysis of Hizb ut-Tahrir's stance on the Palestinian issue can be found here: Kirstine Sinclair: *The Caliphate as homeland? Hizb ut-Tahrir in Denmark and Britain*, Unpublished PhD Thesis, University of Southern Denmark, Odense 2010 (chapter 3).
17. The blog was written by Peter Marshall in 2009 and is found here: http://mylondondiary.co.uk/2009/01/jan.htm#hizb (October 2012)

ish capital in January 2009 was using the Gaza conflict to highlight what the organisation understands as a general, unbearable and unjust situation for the Palestinians through targeting Arab parties in the conflict – Israel's neighbours Syria and Egypt and the most influential US ally in the region, Saudi Arabia. Based on the slogans and symbols used and the chosen route of the demonstration, ending the Gaza war was not the primary message for Hizb ut-Tahrir. It was rather the need to remove the rulers who are helping the enemy (read: the West and Israel) and insert a Caliph in their place. For Hizb ut-Tahrir, the need to re-establish the Caliphate is always the message. [18]

Same Place and Same Cause, but...

If we look at the similarities between the three demonstrations, it is clear that all three involved a crowd moving between two points, stopping along the way to listen to speeches and carrying banners with slogans. The Stop the War demonstrations also involved singing. However, while the two Stop the War coalition demonstrations were open and eventually got out of control for the organisers and the authorities, Hizb ut-Tahrir's demonstration was closed and controlled. Albeit different in terms of organisation and participants – open and closed respectively – the organisers understood a large number of participants as a success criteria, the logic being that the larger the number of participants, the larger the political influence. This observation is based on reports made by the organisers and communicated to internet homepage audiences. And furthermore, the number of participants seems to be success parameter for the journalistic coverage of the political events as well.

All three demonstrations were successful in terms of numbers. The number of followers in the Stop the War demonstrations rose from 12,000 in the first to somewhere between 50,000 and 200,000 in the second. While authorities and journalists gave figures at the low end of the scale, the organisers themselves gave the highest figure on the scale, indicating

---

18. Please find an analysis of this phenomenon here: Kirstine Sinclair: *The Caliphate as homeland?* (chapters 4 and 5).

that a high number of participants was a success criterion in and of itself. As mentioned, 3,000 people took part in Hizb ut-Tahrir's event. Hizb ut-Tahrir used to be able to gather up to 10,000 people at conferences (for instance at Wembley in 2003), but compared to standards for attendance after 2005, 3,000 must be recognised as a high number.

The three demonstrations were also successful in terms of making headlines and creating or achieving public attention as well as influencing politicians. As an example of this, The British Foreign Secretary David Miliband condemned the "disproportionate use of violence" by the Israelis in Gaza.[19] However, the coverage brought to the Stop the War demonstrations by the violent development was of course not all positive.

Violence was represented in the demonstrations in different ways and on different levels. All three demonstrations had as their point of departure the Israeli aggression in Gaza. In none of the speeches that were part of the demonstrations was the stance towards the aggression nuanced with details about the Palestinian rocket attacks into Israeli territory, rather, the conflict was seen only from the point of view of Hamas i.e. pointing to the Palestinians as victims. Finally, violence became a very real albeit not planned part of the two Stop the War demonstrations, with participating individuals breaking off from the actual demonstrations and engaging in aggressive attacks on the Israeli Embassy and members of the London Metropolitan Police force.

The surprising factor here is not so much the fact that a number of the demonstrators – the group was dominated by young males with Arab background – were agitated and frustrated enough to react physically, but more that the coalition behind the event did not take a critical stance to the aggression. Instead Tariq Ali, one of the Vice Presidents of Stop the War decided to compare the aggression and violence outside the Israeli embassy to the Israeli attacks on Gaza and came to the conclusion that the violence in London in January 2009 was "neither here nor there". In other words, he was able to justify the violent actions in London and interpret them as a natural reaction to more serious or damaging violence

---

19. See Miliband's comments here: http://tvnewswatch.blogspot.dk/2009/01/army-of-journalists-build-on-gaza.html (June 2012).

elsewhere rather than taking a non-violent position and disstance his organisation from the individuals throwing things at the police guarding the Israeli Embassy in London.

Perhaps to some members of the public it also came as a surprise that it was not the Hizb ut-Tahrir demonstration that got out of control and led to violence since Hizb ut-Tahrir is known for their very harsh rhetorical expressions concerning both the Palestinian issue and Western influence in Muslim countries in general. But the demonstrating Hizb ut-Tahrir members would not be preoccupied with the Gaza conflict despite the fact that the ongoing war was the pretext that brought them to the streets. Rather, the logic behind the accusations of Egypt, Saudi Arabia and Syria would be that Hizb ut-Tahrir claims to have the solution to the Palestinian situation as well as all problems ever relevant to the world's Muslims; namely the re-establishment of the Islamic Caliphate. And because this crowd consisted primarily of Hizb ut-Tahrir members and supporters, they would automatically be a more controlled crowd focusing on getting their long-term political goals through. The argument made in their demonstration was one supporting the Caliphate, not the Palestinian cause. The Israeli aggression in Gaza was just a useful example of how the Muslim populations of the Middle East need a Caliphate. Thus, Israel or the official Britain was never the targeted audience for Hizb ut-Tahrir's demonstration. The real target was Arab Muslims in London, Europe and the Middle East and their "despotic leaders".[20] And the argument made in the demonstration was not one concerning the Palestinians per se but one concerning the political goal of Hizb ut-Tahrir: the re-establishment of the Islamic Caliphate.

While the similarities are many, as seen above, we also see a couple of significant differences between the demonstrations. One is their political messages: The Stop the War demonstrations made the argument that the Israeli aggressions in Gaza should be stopped and made it clear by choice of routes and destination point that the official Britain should pressure the official Israel to come to a solution. Hizb ut-Tahrir on the other hand,

---

20. See Hizb ut-Tahrir's homepage for their version of the events: http://www.hizb-ut-tahrir.info/info/english.php/contents_en/entry_2058 (June 2012).

chose to address Israel's Arab neighbours and allies of the West which demonstrated a different political goal with their demonstration.

Performance in Place

When movements and individuals respond to world politics through activism such as demonstrations and thus demanding public attention it can be viewed as a performance with a carefully chosen stage and audience. In the current analysis, the chosen stage is London, but the chosen audiences vary. However, the choice of stage and audience and the act of performance is, according to Goffman, not something that has relevance only on special occasions like political demonstrations. Performance is also a part of people's everyday social interactions in so far as social interactions can be seen as negotiations and "impression management".[21] Performance making use of staging and audiences is thus something very central to human activities and interactions.

Goffman's performance theory does not focus on place and space as such but rather on how individuals negotiate their sense of self through interactions with others. To bring in the perspective of place and space in the analysis of the demonstrations dealt with here, perspectives from current human and cultural geography are brought forward. As shown, the two perspectives share a focus on negotiations. Where Goffman argues that individuals negotiate a sense of self through interaction with surroundings and other people, Cresswell and Massey argue that individuals negotiate a sense of place through interactions with other people. As we have seen, the three demonstrations involve a lot of activities: people moving through the city, walking, people speaking, cheering, shouting and singing and also people showing aggressive behaviour – throwing objects and threatening the authorities. In other words, with Cresswell's

---

21. Erving Goffmann: *The Presentation of Self in Everyday Life*, Harmondsworth, England 1990 (1959). See also *The Johns Hopkins Guide to Literary Theory and Criticism*, eds. Groden, Kreiswirth and Szeman, Baltimore and London 2005, pp. 726-731, for a discussion of the developments within recent performance studies.

concept of lived space, we have a tool for analysing the demonstrations in terms of verbs and movement.[22]

Massey's concept of "intersections" provides a tool for looking at places as open-ended. If we study demonstrations as intersecting places, this allows for alternative understandings of how individuals in a demonstration connect different parts of the city and how they tell different stories depending on what parts of the city they connect. Another way of explaining "intersection" is to say that places are made up of people and ideas cutting through territory. The three demonstrations analysed here connect different places in London and thus show us different versions of London. Using the concept of intersections, one can argue that London as a scene for these demonstrations consists of more than one narrative about London. In this sense, places are not natural and have no well-defined unequivocal beginning or end like demonstrations do. And demonstrations using London to bring forward a political message, add to the manifold narratives about what London is.

When addressing the Leaders of Saudi Arabia, Egypt and Syria in London, Hizb ut-Tahrir in their understanding re-enact or perform the Okaz Fair from the time of the Prophet, the same week the Stop the War movement addressed contemporary British and Israeli politicians. The imagined gathering of Arab tribal leaders at Okaz Fair is as real to Hizb ut-Tahrir activists as the politicians in Downing Street are to the Stop the War movement.

As we have seen, London was used differently by actors protesting against the same war. The Stop the War coalition and Hizb ut-Tahrir drew different lines through London when they performed their demonstrations. They connected different dots or sights of interest in the city as they marched through it and were thus able to tell different stories about themselves and about London. In their choice of routes, the Stop the War coalition represented classical narratives about who the public is and who holds the power in the British state, whereas Hizb ut-Tahrir represented an alternative narrative about what London is, namely a meeting point for influential Arabian leaders and peoples. In their differentiated use of

---

22. See Cresswell's discussion of the three dimensions here: Tim Cresswell *Place*, pp. 43-51, Tim Cresswell: "Introduction," pp. 2012.

London as a stage for political performance, the actors negotiate who they are and what they want and thus the city contributes to the formation of their identity, and the demonstrators contribute with narratives about what London is.[23]

London as Lived and Open-Ended

Political activist organisations attempt to influence opinions and events through demonstrations entailing not merely the display of messages and slogans but also in a broader sense through embodiment, actual activities and the use of urban spaces. We have seen examples of how two organisations used the same opportunity, the Gaza war in 2008-09, to tell two different narratives about London and to agitate for different political messages and solutions.

Where Cresswell's concept of Lived Space has provided a helpful tool for looking at what people do in places, where they go and how they do what they do, Massey's concept of intersection has been equally useful in understanding the importance of looking at a city as open-ended in order to see the many narratives being told and performed simultaneously. In the case of the three demonstrations studied in this chapter, the idea of looking for activities, performance and intersections has made it clear that a demonstration in London can mean more than what is obvious from the banners and slogans shown: political agendas are revealed by the specific routes and destinations of demonstrations just as routes and destinations show who the targeted audience is. Furthermore, the actual activities, the nature of the speeches and whether events develop into violence or not gives evidence of the self-understanding of the actors involved. While the participants and organisers of the Stop the War demonstrations were at some kind of war with the Israeli authorities, the

---

23. What is important to mention, of course, is that there are groups of secular, intellectual and well-educated Muslims who are not part of either demonstration because Hizb ut-Tahrir and the Muslim Brotherhood are involved, so although the big Stop the War demonstrations were including in their outset, and indeed did include a wide range of organisations and individuals, they were also excluding due to the cooperation with the Muslim Council of Britain i.e. the Muslim Brotherhood.

marching Hizb ut-Tahrir supporters were mentally identifying with the Prophet addressing the leaders of the Arab tribes at the Okaz Fair.

Such findings mean that one has to alter the definition of what London is. London stretches beyond the city limits and it is no longer meaningful to consider London as first and foremost the British capital. Rather, it is a place made up of 8.2 million individuals' ideas of the world and ideas of what London is. It is the imagined Okaz Fair as much as it is Trafalgar Square and Downing Street. In this way, London becomes the sum of (sometimes contradictory) thoughts and persuasions of the people living there, travelling through, engaging in political activities there – thoughts and ideas intersecting the city, continually finding new uses for old monuments and thus telling new stories about London.

BORDERS AS PLACE

Delineating Slovenia: Establishing and Bordering a National Sphere

Peter Thaler

This chapter analyzes the conflicting standards of establishing a Slovenian national sphere in the historic provinces of Carniola, Styria, and Carinthia. Unlike many of its predecessors in northern and western Europe, the Slovenian national movement had no recognized territorial base to proceed from. Not only was there no Slovenian state, but the speakers of Slovenian were distributed among diverse political entities. All the more important for Slovenian activists was the favorable delineation of their projected national space, which could form the basis for a future nation-state.

In this effort, Slovenian nationalists could invoke the legacy of earlier political entities. Most significant was the medieval principality of Carantania, which had encompassed a large segment of the southeastern Alps. As one of the oldest known Slavic polities, it endowed the Slovenian historical tradition with a prestigious legacy, even if most of its territory lay outside the borders of modern-day Slovenia. To compensate for this geographical discrepancy, the considerably smaller tribal polity of Carniola figured prominently among Slovenian historical symbols as well, since it corresponded more closely to the ethnolinguistic realities of the nineteenth century.[1]

---

1. For the early history of the Slovenian-speaking regions, see Bogo Grafenauer: *Karantanija: Izbrane razprave in članki*, Ljubljana 2000; Rajko Bratož, ed.: *Slovenija in sosednje dežele med antiko in karolinško dobo: Začetki slovenske etnogeneze*, 2 vols., Ljubljana 1990; and Günther Hödl and Johannes Grabmeyer, eds.: *Karantanien und der Alpen-Adria-Raum im Frühmittelalter*, Vienna 1993.

Politics did not constitute the only point of contention in the debate about historical legitimacy and national entitlement, however. Historical presence and cultural traditions were issues closer to the heart of many national activists. In their discourse, language merged with culture and genealogy, and the past merged with or superseded the present to become a guidepost for a better and more authentic future. As a consequence, history became of preeminent importance in the discourse of national renewal and liberation.

At the same time, competing national movements employed different standards and principles to establish their superior claims to a territory and its inhabitants. Current linguistic conditions provided the most commonplace set of arguments, but they had to compete with a wide selection of alternative criteria. National activists readily availed themselves of current or past political conditions to counter claims that were based on language and ethnicity. If contemporary language use proved disadvantageous, it was dismissed in favor of more authentic historical antecedents. And finally, depending on their respective implications, one could cite or dismiss the apparent preferences of the local populace. The invocation of conflicting principles along the contested northern fringes of emergent Slovenia forms the centerpiece of the current investigation.

The Volatile Census Results of Šoštanj in Styria

The process of national mobilization among speakers of Slovenian occurred at a time when they were citizens of the Habsburg empire. The final decades of this dynastic conglomerate state have become the classic image of national strife, and a number of important theorists of nationalism and national identity have taken the Habsburg experience as a starting point for their analysis and model-building.[2] Next to the lands

---

2. Notable examples would be Otto Bauer's *Die Nationalitätenfrage und die Sozialdemokratie*, Vienna 1907, and Karl Renner's *Das Selbstbestimmungsrecht der Nationen*, Vienna 1918. But a number of theorists of nationalism that do not focus primarily on Austria are also deeply influenced by this country's experience; one might mention Hans Kohn and Eric Hobsbawm in this context.

of the Bohemian crown with their protracted competition between Germans and Czechs, the Alpine provinces of Styria, Carinthia, and Carniola formed the second focal point of German-Slavic conflict in the Habsburg Monarchy.

The national movements of the era premised the existence of the nation, but it was they themselves who increased the political significance of cultural conditions. This politization of culture formed a prerequisite for turning speakers of a language into members of a nation. To accomplish this objective, nation builders regularly looked to history. Yet as we can see in the case of Slovenia, history does not always render its findings easily.

How should one define Slovenian history? As the history of a sovereign state, it only commenced in the 1990s. Even if one includes the Yugoslav period, its lifespan amounts to less than a century. There are few who would restrict Slovenian history to this brief period. Yet what are the characteristics of Slovenian history before World War I, and how is it demarcated from others? Is it the history of select political entities, including all of its inhabitants? Or is it a personal history of Slovenian speakers detached from the polities in which they lived?

Since the early Middle Ages, the historical experience of Slovenian speakers occurred within an empire, which was sometimes called Frankish and sometimes Roman, sometimes holy and sometimes German. For many centuries, they inhabited several Habsburg crown lands as subjects of the imperial dynasty; the incorporation of Hungary added further Slovenes. They were not the only ones to inhabit those territories, however. In Gorizia, Slovenian-speakers lived together with speakers of Italian and Friulian. In Istria, with speakers of Italian and Croatian. In the county of Vas, with speakers of Hungarian. In Carinthia, Styria, and Carniola, with speakers of German. Whereas Carinthia and Styria were dominated by Germans, Slovenians constituted the largest linguistic group in Carniola. Even in the latter province, aristocrats and burghers predominantly spoke German, however, and for centuries, educational and cultural life was formed in their image.

This was the general cultural and political framework in which a Slovenian national movement took shape.³ From the very beginning, it faced serious challenges. One of its foremost objectives was the preeminence of Slovenian language and culture in the public life of "Slovenia". In order to accomplish this goal, the exact location of that entity needed to be demarcated. At the same time, the national movement struggled to convince all speakers of Slovenian that they belonged to the Slovenian nation, whereas many of them had primarily identified themselves as subjects of the Habsburg emperor, as Styrians, as Catholics, or as members of a number of other identificational alternatives.

The desired change in consciousness was achieved most easily in Carniola, where Slovenian speakers formed a clear majority. In an era of nascent democratization and mass culture, the duchy's German-speaking elites came under increasing pressure. Modernization and industrialization swelled towns and cities with immigrants from their Slavophone surroundings. In contrast to earlier periods, those new arrivals no longer felt the need to assimilate. Improved educational possibilities created a Slovenian-speaking middle class. Carniola and southern Styria increasingly resembled the image of Slovenian nationhood, even if the urban sectors of Styria remained more hesitant.

The cultural environment in the southeastern Alps was characterized by a gradual movement toward homogenization. Thus, the share of Slovenian speakers fell from 32.74 percent in 1880 to 29.38 percent in 1910 in predominantly German-speaking Styria and, even more noticeably, from 29.72 to 21.24 percent in neighboring Carinthia. In Carniola, by contrast, the share of Slovenian speakers rose from 93.67 to 94.36 percent, with a corresponding reduction of the German presence from 6.15 to 5.36 percent.⁴

---

3. For an introduction to the formation of national identities in Slovenia, see Fran Zwitter: *O slovenskem narodnem vprašanju*, Ljubljana 1990; John K. Cox: *Slovenia: Evolving Loyalties*, London 2005; and Joachim Hösler: *Von Krain zu Slowenien: Die Anfänge der nationalen Differenzierungsprozesse in Krain und der Untersteiermark von der Aufklärung bis 1848*, Munich 2006.

4. For all the census numbers in this section, see the *Österreichische Statistik* for the years of 1882, 1892, 1902, and 1912, published by the Statistische Zentralkommission in Vienna, and the overviews in Emil Brix: *Die Umgangssprachen in Altösterreich zwischen Agitation und Assimilation*, Vienna 1982, pp. 436-489, Gerhard Werner: *Sprache und Volkstum in der Untersteiermark*, Stuttgart 1935, p. 204f., and Richard Pfaundler: "Die nationalen Verhältnisse in Steiermark am Ausgange des 19. Jahrhunderts," *Statistische Monatschrift* 9 (1906): pp. 401-430.

In the capital city of Ljubljana, the German share dropped from approximately 23 percent in 1880 to less than 15 percent in 1910.[5]

Below the level of this larger trend, however, there were local idiosyncrasies that underscore the potential instability of national sentiment in border regions. What makes this instability particularly interesting is the nature of the measurement in which it expressed itself. The Austrian censuses of the late Habsburg period did not ask people to identify with a cultural or political entity. Instead, they contained a question about an individual's *Umgangssprache*, a term best translated as that person's language of (predominant) daily use, or primary language. Although this question appears to be directed at an objectively defined characteristic, it soon took on distinctly political overtones. Activists on all sides attempted to turn the answer to the linguistic question into a national plebiscite. The consequences of this politicization can be seen in Styrian census results of the late Habsburg period.

The territory of the modern province of Styria had a long history of German-Slavic coexistence. The Alpine Slavs, who had moved into the area soon after the withdrawal of the Romans, had been subjugated by the Bavarians in the early Middle Ages. The territory was integrated into the Frankish kingdom and the Holy Roman Empire that succeeded it. The Babenberg dukes of Austria and their Habsburg successors tied the region ever closer to the Austrian sphere. In the census of 1880, 794,841 Styrians listed their primary language as German and 388,419 as Slovenian, which made the province two-thirds German- and one-third Slovenian-speaking. This linguistic ratio resulted from an overall compilation and did not reflect local conditions, which tended to be more homogenous, with an almost exclusively German-speaking north and a predominantly Slovenian-speaking south.

Many towns and cities in southern Styria had German majorities, however. Much of the region's ethnic strife revolved around these German-speaking urban centers surrounded by rural Slovenes. The specific

---

5. Brix: *Die Umgangssprachen in Altösterreich*, p. 181. Although much of the reduction of the German proportion derived from the influx of Slovenian speakers into the capital, the absolute numbers of Germans in Ljubljana (Laibach) stagnated at a time of general population growth and even declined periodically.

demographics of southern Styria introduced an element of volatility, which constituted the most noteworthy aspect of the local nationality conflict. In the language statistics of the small town of Šoštanj/Schönstein, this volatility demarcates itself particularly well. In the last four censuses held under Habsburg auspices, the local distribution of German and Slovenian speakers was as follows:

Table 1: Primary Language in Šoštanj/Schönstein according to the Austrian Censuses, 1880-1910

	Total	German	Slovenian
1880	734	118	615
1890	835	410	421
1900	1096	179	908
1910	1257	874	368

Even if one considers the substantial in-migration expressed in the overall population growth, the inconsistency of the results is striking. The citizens of Šoštanj/Schönstein clearly associated primary language with national identification. Their language use could not have vacillated as forcefully as suggested by the census data. They were sufficiently well-versed in both German and Slovenian to see either one as a potential primary language and turned their census replies into conscious political statements. Moreover, many local citizens felt close enough to both national communities to alternate between them. Thus, at a time of protracted conflict between Germans and Slovenes in Austria's Alpine provinces, the inhabitants of Šoštanj/Schönstein would at times be found on the German side, at times on the Slovenian.

Assigning Nationality in Southern Carinthia

National ambivalence or indifference could also express itself in a more fundamental manner. Not all speakers of Slovenian adopted the new ethnonational way of thinking. The resulting ideological split was most visible in Carinthia, which displayed strong geographical coherence, centered on the Klagenfurt Basin and demarcated by mountain ranges. As a consequence, its social and economic exchanges were regionally based. The everyday lives of Slovenian-speaking Carinthians were integrated more strongly with the German core of the province than with Slovenian Carniola beyond the mountains.

In the decades leading up to World War I, the Austrian censuses recorded a drop in the share of Slovenian speakers in Carinthia from approximately 30 to around 20 percent. Although the details of these census results have faced legitimate criticism, the basic trends that emanated from them have largely stood the test of time.[6] Social and educational changes and especially urbanization furthered cultural assimilation in an area where higher education and urban culture were overwhelmingly German. Bilingual schools provided the previously monolingual Slavophones of southern Carinthia with a new element of identificational choice. Although the Slovenian national movement decried this development, it did not consider it its most vexing problem. Much more inexplicable to Slovenian nationalists was the fact that only one segment of the remaining Slavophones supported them.

Confronted with the challenge of national mobilization, the Slovenian-speaking population of southern Carinthia splintered into two significant factions. One of them resembled its equivalents in Carniola and southern Styria. Its members supported the organizations and electoral candidates of Slovenian nationalism and promoted a closer political integration of the Slovenian language area. Although this mobilization largely occurred under the banner of Catholic conservativism, it would be overly generalizing to treat this segment of the population as a coherent ideological entity. It could not but impact Carinthian conditions that the larger Slovenian language area remained divided between liberals and conservatives, seculars and Catholics, as well as pro-Habsburg Slovenian autonomists, trialists in support of a distinct South Slavic polity within the Habsburg Empire, and increasingly separatist Yugoslavists. Yet at the same time, these factions were united in their fundamental conviction

---

6. For the Austrian censuses, see especially Brix: *Die Umgangssprachen in Altösterreich*.

that all speakers of Slovenian formed a natural unity, which ought to be affiliated politically as well.

This subgroup of Slovenian speakers reflected the prevalent path of contemporary European nation-building, which rested on the politicization of culture. In Carinthia, however, another collective identity challenged this sense-of-self.[7] Its adherents valued their local Slovenian dialect and South Carinthian way of life. Yet at the same time, they defined themselves as a part of a larger Carinthian context, even if this crown land was predominantly German. In the nationally divided party system of the late Habsburg Monarchy, this segment of Slavophones tended to support German parties, and it emphatically rejected Slovenian nationalism, not to mention Yugoslavism. It was represented most widely in social and regional environments that were strongly interwoven with German speakers.

Whereas the existence of this group was undeniable, its classification remained controversial. Both the Slovenian and the Carinthian German national movement largely adhered to an essentialist concept of nationhood, which could not meaningfully be applied on these individuals. Slovenian nationalists deprecated them as a *nemškutarji* or *nemčurji*, that is, as beholden to the Germans. They were genuinely puzzled by people who were Slovenian in name and language, but refused to identify with the Slovene nation. In their eyes, they had to be traitors and renegades.

NATIONALITY AS HISTORICAL LEGACY

In 1917, the Carniolian lawyer and politician Gregor Žerjav published the concise study *Die nationale Abgrenzung im Süden*.[8] As a member of the Austrian parliament in Vienna, Žerjav had become one of the foremost representatives of liberal Slovenian nationalism and Yugoslavism. He was subsequently among the signatories establishing the new Kingdom of Serbs, Croats, and Slovenes, in whose government he served in the

---

7. Similar developments, if on a smaller scale in relative terms, occurred in parts of southern Styria.
8. [Gregor Žerjav]: *Die nationale Abgrenzung im Süden: Ein Beitrag zur Realisierung der Selbstbestimmung der Völker Österreich-Ungarns*, Zagreb 1917. In view of his demand to dissolve the existing monarchy and his previous incarceration during the war, Žerjav published the booklet under the pseudonym "by a Southern Slav."

1920s. In his programmatic essay, the Slovene politician criticized Karl Renner's Social Democratic concept of individual nationality and personal autonomy and argued in favor of clear territorial separation.[9] He based this rejection of national self-identification on the pressure emanating from societal elites and public authorities, as well as on a fundamental ideological premise. While accepting Renner's notion that the nation is an aggregation of people, he insisted it is no voluntary association that one can join and leave at will. National affiliation is predetermined, and people can even belong to a nation without being aware of it.[10]

Having established the philosophical and practical necessity for clearly separating different national communities, Žerjav developed his program for an implementation of this principle in the German-Slovenian zone of contact. Before he arrives at national affiliation as the foremost criterion of future bordering, Žerjav emotively invokes the history of Alpine Slavs and refers to place-names throughout Austria as living evidence of past Slovenian losses.[11] When it comes to national affiliation, the author concedes that its objective assessment may be difficult in areas of cultural and political interpenetration such as Styria, Carinthia, or Trieste. It soon becomes clear, however, that Žerjav does not presage modern concepts of ambivalence and hybridity. Instead, he proposes that the inhabitants of outwardly German or Italian cities such as Klagenfurt and Trieste to a large extent are Slavs, even if they may not openly acknowledge this fact. To Žerjav, even assimilated Germanophiles who scorn Slovenian nationalism and Yugoslavism should be counted as Slovenes, as long as they revert to their ancestral tongue in the confessional and on their deathbed.[12]

After listing valid arguments against the accuracy of Austrian censuses organized by nationally predisposed public officials, the Slovenian politician presented his solution. Inaccuracies should not be remedied through improved new censuses, but through a reverting to past condi-

---

9. See, for example, Synopticus [Karl Renner]: *Staat und Nation*, Vienna, 1899.
10. [Žerjav]: *Die nationale Abgrenzung im Süden*, p. 18.
11. Ibid., p. 28.
12. Ibid.

tions as expressed in earlier statistical calculations. National renegades could not form the moral basis for assigning territory; it would offend common decency to create a German language area out of Germanophile Slovenes. Therefore, conscious or unconscious renegades should be counted according to their true ethnicity. Their superficial German veneer would disappear as soon as public pressure had ceased, and they would recognize to which people they truly belonged.[13]

Having thus established Slovenian majorities in many currently German-speaking rural districts, Žerjav directed his attention to the central cities. Due to their size, they could be employed as effective arguments against the inclusion of their less populated surroundings in a future Yugoslavia. Yet Žerjav submitted a solution for this problem as well. In expanding municipalities such as Villach, Klagenfurt, and Maribor, one should pay no heed to current linguistic conditions, but establish the proportion of the population with roots in Slavophone districts. In addition, one should judge a city's national character by its productive classes, such as workers and peasants, and disregard public officials, merchants, and professionals.[14] In a future Yugoslavia, German officials would be replaced and leave, and many merchants and professionals would follow them. Only a minority of the current inhabitants would remain and replenish itself from its Slavic surroundings.

Thus, Žerjav had delineated his approach to the creation of future national entities. An imagined historical point in time constituted the pivot of national decision-making, serving both as the basis for the current political assignment of an area and as the appropriate standard to be recreated. Those who deviated from this representation by having turned their backs on the natural progression of the nation faced a dualistic response. Their present cultural and political preferences were to be disregarded, but their authenticized past legitimized the nation's claim to the area. As individuals, they were destined for reassimilation or emigration.

The German side originally referred to nationally indifferent Slavo-

---

13. Ibid., p. 34.
14. Ibid., pp. 34-37.

phones as Germanophile, or pro-German, Slovenes.[15] Whereas this designation was sober and non-judgmental, its analytical accuracy may be open to debate, since the decisive factor for the rejection of Slovenian nationhood, at least at this early stage, was not identification with German culture, not to mention a German nation-state, but a strong sense of provincial identity and of social and economic integration with German-speaking Carinthians.[16] In time, it was replaced by the term "Windische", which echoed the general designation of neighboring Slavs as Wends among premodern speakers of German and had traditionally been applied to all speakers of Slovenian. As a consequence, one also encounters it in numerous Austrian place names. With the conceptual essentialization of nationhood, however, the term became ideologically charged. German-oriented scholars and activists emphasized the differences between standard Slovene and the dialects spoken by nationally indifferent Slavophones, arguing that formal Slovene was incomprehensible to the latter, whereas they could acquire standard German more easily. They diagnosed a natural assimilatory process and the emergence of a mixed language.[17]

The political instrumentalization of dialectal idiosyncrasies figured prominently in many national conflicts. Politically engaged researchers emphasized the variations within the other language community. They suggested that segments of the national Other spoke a mixed language and therefore should not be associated with the opposing cultural sphere. In his examination of linguistic conditions in the duchy of Schleswig, Danish activist scholar C. F. Allen referred to a "so-called Low German," which was spoken in southern Anglia and so far removed from standard German that the students could more easily acquire

---

15. The German term was "deutschfreundliche Slowenen".
16. The postwar Slovenian historian Janko Pleterski also objected to the term because it seemed to imply that Slovenian nationalism was intrinsically Germanophobe, which Pleterski considered inaccurate. See Janko Pleterski: *Narodna in politična zavest na Koroškem: Narodna zavest in politična orientacija prebivalstva slovenske Koroške v letih 1848-1918*, Ljubljana 1965, p. 205.
17. For an important expression of the theory, see Martin Wutte: *Deutsch-Windisch-Slowenisch*, Klagenfurt, 1927. See also Tom Priestly: "On the Development of the *Windischentheorie*," *International Journal of the Sociology of Language* 124 (1997): pp. 81-83.

standard Danish.[18] His German colleague August Sach, for his part, deplored that the true nature of South Jutish as a distinct language was not universally understood.[19] In Carinthia, by the same token, German nationalists argued that local Wends spoke a Slavo-Germanic creole and constituted an ethnoculturally intermediate population, located halfway between Germans and Slovenes. In addition, they stressed the differences between Carinthia, which in their eyes had formed a cultural, ethnic, and economic unit for centuries, and a culturally and geographically remote Carniola.[20]

In reality, the differentiation between national and non-national Slovenian speakers was based on subjective rather than objective criteria. While it was true that the Slovenian dialects in Carinthia contained many German elements and differed appreciably from the Slovenian written standard, which was based on Carniolian usage and consciously purified of Germanisms, these dialects were used by almost all speakers of Slovenian in Carinthia, regardless of national orientation. By the same token, the mutual assimilation of and extensive intermarriage between German and Slovenian Carinthians was not restricted to select subgroups

---

18. "Children should not only not be educated in High German out of concern for the Danish language in this district. This should also be done out of concern for the Low German language as it is spoken in southern Anglia...
Children who are used to speaking this language have great difficulties in learning High German, whereas they easily learn Danish."
See C. F. Allen: *Det danske sprogs historie i hertugdømmet Slesvig eller Sønderjylland*, Copenhagen 1857, 2:598 and 599. The translations of this and subsequent non-English sources are my own.
And Peder Lauridsen stated in a similar vein: "One way or the other, the Anglian children who spoke Low German had to learn a new language in school – either High German or standard Danish. Yet in vocabulary and sentence structure the latter lay much closer to Anglian Low German than the difficult and elaborate High German."
See Peder Lauridsen: "Vort folks sydgrænse," in *Danmark: Land og Folk*, ed. Daniel Bruun (Copenhagen, 1919), 2:4:108f.

19. "At that time, one cannot expect that civil servants would have fully understood that the Jutish dialect represents a separate language in its relationship to standard Danish." See August Sach: *Das Herzogtum Schleswig in seiner ethnographischen und nationalen Entwicklung* (Halle, 1907), 3:277.

20. Arnold Suppan: *Jugoslawien und Österreich 1918-1938: Bilaterale Außenpolitik im europäischen Umfeld*, Vienna 1996, p. 524.

of the population, notwithstanding modest social and regional variations. Yet on both sides of the national divide, many observers could not truly imagine that individuals could be just as Slovenian in language and heritage as others, but reject the political conclusions of the Slovenian national movement.

NATIONALITY AS INDIVIDUAL RESOLUTION

In the long run, time ran out for noncommittal positions. At the end of the First World War, the Habsburg Monarchy fell apart. The Slovenian national movement fulfilled its fundamental aspirations in their Yugoslav expression. Carniola and southern Styria, including the still German-dominated urban centers, joined the Kingdom of Serbs, Croats, and Slovenes, which was subsequently renamed Yugoslavia.[21]

The new South Slav polity was meant to include large portions of Carinthia as well. In the turbulent months following the disintegration of the empire, numerous border conceptions circulated in public and behind closed doors. In a statute passed on 22 November 1918, the provisional national assembly of German-Austria defined the territory of its nascent state rather open-endedly as including Styria and Carinthia with the exception of the contiguous Yugoslav settlement area.[22] By that time, the newly formed Slovenian national council of Carinthia had already agreed on a program of three political alternatives, according to which at the very least a yet to be defined Slovenian linguistic zone was to join the Kingdom of Serbs, Croats and Slovenes, but preferably also economically important adjacent territories, and ideally the province of Carinthia in its entirety.[23] By all standards, the northern alternative would include numerous German-speakers in the South Slavic state. Its proponents defended it, however, by arguing that it would preserve the integrated economy of Carinthia and compensate the Slovenians for the cultural and territorial losses they had suffered throughout the centuries.[24]

---

21. In this chapter Yugoslavia will also be used as a synonym for the Kingdom of Serbs, Croats, and Slovenes during the period when it did not constitute the country's official designation.
22. *Gesetz vom 22. November 1918 über Umfang, Grenzen und Beziehungen des Staatsgebietes von Deutschösterreich, Staatsgesetzblatt für den Staat Deutschösterreich 1918*, Stück 9, Nummer 40.
23. Suppan: *Jugoslawien und Österreich 1918-1938*, p. 489.
24. Ibid., p. 490.

The implementation of this program proved difficult. Both the German and segments of the Slovenian-speaking population actively resisted the regular and irregular military units that attempted to secure the region for an emergent Yugoslavia. After drawn-out fighting and a fact-finding mission by an international expert commission, the Allies decided to settle the conflict through a plebiscite. The voting was to take place in an area amounting to 2,070 square kilometers and inhabited by approximately 125,000 people; this contained approximately one fifth of the province's land mass and one third of its population. Even though one also has to consider that two smaller districts in the south were immediately placed under Yugoslav sovereignty, the area fell noticeably short of even the most modest Slovenian demands of 1918. Districts in the west were not included; nor was the city of Villach. Within the plebiscite area, the capital of Klagenfurt and its surroundings formed a separate zone II, to vote only if the larger zone I fell to Yugoslavia. Thus, in visible similarity with the arrangements made for the Flensburg region in central Schleswig, the geographically small but populous Klagenfurt area, with its substantial majority of German speakers, was to receive the option of remaining connected to its economic hinterland.[25] Zone I, where the initial vote was to be held, comprised 1,705 square kilometers and 71,800 inhabitants, of which almost 40,000 were eligible to cast their ballot. Until the final resolution of the conflict, the two zones were administratively divided between the two parties involved, so that zone I was administered by Yugoslav and zone II by Austrian authorities.

On 10 October 1920, 37,304 Carinthians in zone I submitted valid ballots, which amounted to 95 percent of all eligible voters. Of these, 22,025, or 59 percent, voted for Austria, whereas 15,278, or 41 percent, preferred Yugoslavia. In the preceding census of 1910, 68.6 percent of the local population had listed Slovenian as their primary language. Even if one premises that almost all German-speakers had chosen Austria, this leaves a substantial minority of around 40 percent of Slovenian speakers on the Austrian side. Divided up by political districts, the distribution was as follows:

---

25. For an examination of national conditions in Schleswig, see Peter Thaler: *Of Mind and Matter: The Duality of National Identity in the German-Danish Borderlands*, West Lafayette, Ind., 2009.

Table 2: Austrian Census 1910 and Carinthian Plebiscite 1920

District	German-speaking	Slovenian-speaking	Austrian percentage of vote	Yugoslav percentage of vote
Rosegg (Rožek)	17.6	82.4	46.3	53.7
Ferlach (Borovlje)	40.4	59.6	56.4	43.6
Bleiburg (Pliberk)	15.5	84.5	49.0	51.0
Völkermarkt (Velikovec)	43.6	56.4	77.2	22.8
Total Zone 1	31.4	68.6	59.04	40.96

Source: Sarah Wambaugh, *Plebiscites since the World War* (Washington, D.C., 1933), 1:198.

A comparison between the census of 1910 and the outcome of the plebiscite indicates that while the census numbers may have undercounted those who practically availed themselves of the Slovenian vernacular, they still exceeded those who identified with a Slovenian nation by a sizable margin. It was this disconnection between language and national identification that proved ominous for the Slovenian national movement in Carinthia. The years between 1918 and 1920 marked its zenith. Its proponents laid claim to all speakers of Slovenian, regardless of their personal sense of identity. In neighboring Styria, this policy succeeded, and within a few years, the German municipalities to the south of the new border, including the city of Maribor, had developed in the manner predicted by Gregor Žerjav. Due primarily to (re)assimilation, national reorientation, and emigration, the number of German-speakers on the territory of interwar Slovenia dropped from 106,255 in the Austrian census of 1910 to 41,514 in the Yugoslav census of 1921 and 28,998 in 1931.[26] In

---

26. Suppan: *Jugoslawien und Österreich 1918-1938*, p. 663. The Yugoslav census used native tongue as its category of classification.

Carinthia, however, the Allies had left the decision to the local population, split fairly evenly between Germans, Slovenes, and the much debated segment of nationally indifferent Slavophones. Žerjav's renegades were permitted to make their own choice after all.

The setback for Slovenian nationalism was even larger than it seemed. During the subsequent decades, Slovenian gradually lost its majority status in many communities of southern Carinthia. On one level, this reflected the continuing socioeconomic and at times also political pressures to assimilate, which had already weakened Slovenian during the late nineteenth century and only gained in significance in the increasingly more urban and industrial society of the twentieth. These societal ramifications can only partially account for the accelerating decline of Slovenian language and culture in Carinthia, however, as many nationally conscious Slovenes initially proved able to retain their identity. In many ways, it was the essentialism of Slovenian nationalism that provided the final catalyst for the integration of nationally indifferent Slovenian speakers into the German sphere. The experience that their Slovenian vernacular had served as justification for Yugoslavia's territorial claims shook many of them to the core and provided effective arguments for assimilation.[27] If you do not want to be part of a Slovenian or Yugoslav state, you must stop speaking Slovenian, Austro-German nationalists explained to their increasingly bilingual compatriots. And as was the case in other comparable regions such as Masuria or Upper Silesia, many heeded these admonitions.[28]

The difference between Slovenian-speaking populations with diver-

---

27. See Andreas Moritsch, ed.: *Vom Ethnos zur Nationalität*, Vienna 1991, p. 69.
28. For an introduction to the postwar history of the Masurians, see Andrzej Sakson: *Mazurzy: Społeczność pogranicza*, Poznań 1990; Leszek Belzyt: "Problem weryfikacji polskiej ludności rodzimej na Warmii, Mazurach i Powiślu," Ph.D. diss., University of Toruń 1987; and idem, "Zur Frage des nationalen Bewußtseins der Masuren im 19. und 20. Jahrhundert," *Zeitschrift für Ostmitteleuropaforschung* 45:1 (1996): 35-71. For a comparative look at contemporary Upper Silesian and Masurian conditions, see Wojciech Łukowski and Tomasz Nawrocki: "Upper Silesia and Masuria in Search of Identity," in *Ethnic Minorities and Ethnic Majority: Sociological Studies of Ethnic Relations in Poland*, ed. Marek S. Szczepański, Katowice 1997, pp. 107-117. For a longer horizon, see also Grzegorcz Jasiński: *Mazurzy w drugiej połowie XIX wieku*, Olsztyn 1994, and Richard Blanke: *Polish-Speaking Germans? Language and National Identity among the Masurians since 1871*, Cologne 2001.

gent national self-identifications surfaces in a comparison between the southern Carinthian communities of Ludmannsdorf-Oberhäusl (Bilčovs-Zgornja vesca) and Tainach (Tinje).[29] Prior to World War I, both communities were overwhelmingly Slovenian-speaking. Their national orientation differed noticeably, however. Whereas only 20.6 percent of the voters in Ludmannsdorf and 31.2 in Oberdörfl voted for Austria, a substantial majority of 85.9 percent of the electorate in Tainach made that choice.[30] Thereafter, this political disagreement visibly impacted linguistic self-assessment as well.

Table 3: Proportion of Self-Identified German speakers in two Carinthian Communities in Select Austrian Censuses

Year	Ludmannsdorf-Oberdörfl (Bilčovs-Zgornja vesca)		Tainach (Tinje)	
	Total speakers	Percentage	Total speakers	Percentage
1880	4	0.3	23	4.1
1910	65	5.7	147	24.6
1923	126	10.5	452	83.4
1934	423	30.7	506	88.5
1951	196	15.0	571	88.8

Source: Andreas Moritsch, ed.: *Vom Ethnos zur Nationalität*, Vienna 1991, p. 83.[31]

The Slovenian speakers of Ludmannsdorf, who to a large extent identified with the Slovenian national movement and supported Yugoslavia in the 1920 plebiscite, continued to express this linguistic identity in Austrian censuses until the early postwar era. In fact, the census of 1951, follow-

---

29. Ludmannsdorf and Oberdörfl were municipally merged in 1957 and are therefore treated as one community in the current investigation.
30. Moritsch: *Vom Ethnos zur Nationalität*, p. 89.
31. It should be noted that individual censuses defined the language in question in different terms and that the numbers listed refer to people who listed only German while excluding those who listed German in combination with other languages.

ing the repression of Slovenian national identity during World War II, even witnessed a drop in the share of self-declared German-speakers. In Tainach, by contrast, the experiences of 1918-1920 irreparably alienated nationally indifferent Slavophones from the Slovenian national tradition. They did not truly cease speaking their Slovenian dialect as quickly as indicated in the censuses, but they gradually adapted their language use to their political identification with German-speaking Austria.

Today, linguistic conditions largely mirror the political frontier between the meanwhile sovereign Republic of Slovenia and its Austrian neighbor. The German-speaking minority in Slovenia only survived World War II in rudimentary traces. The Slovene population in Austria is politically active and highly visible, but there are only few communities left in which it still constitutes the local majority. From the 1960s, at the latest, the linguistic balance shifted so strongly that it also transformed communities with a history of Slovenian nationalism. As a consequence, the Slovenian language is increasingly turning into a symbol of identity rather than an essential practical necessity, as many members of the younger generations grow up more familiar with German as their language of everyday use.

Conclusion

National movements proved highly flexible and pragmatic in their approach to political theory. Even though they are widely associated with essentialist concepts of nationhood, they were more than willing to employ political and voluntarist alternatives, if those provided useful arguments for national aggrandizement. In fact, national activists saw no need to burden their argumentation with excessive consistency. In the aftermath of World War I, Polish nationalists claimed both historically German provinces with Polish-speaking populations and historically Polish provinces with Ukrainian-speaking populations for their reemerging state, alternatively availing themselves of ethnocultural and political criteria. By the same token, the newly founded Czechoslovakia was to comprise the historical crown lands of Bohemia, Moravia and Austrian Silesia in their entirety, regardless of their local ethnic composition, as well as the territories of the linguistically related Slovaks, which for many centuries had formed a part of the Hungarian kingdom.

Thus, places could be contested in numerous ways. National movements struggled over the political affiliation of towns and regions. They tried to change their linguistic composition. They worked toward changing the sense of self of the people who inhabited these regions. They disagreed about the national affiliation of the local inhabitants and categorized them according to their representativeness for local genealogy. And most of all, they forwarded conflicting criteria for assessing the true national character of both the land and its people.

History provided essential arguments for this activism. Yet it was a highly selective use of history. Historical nation-builders searched the past for points in time they considered useful for the contemporary political debate and as an inspiration for the future they desired. As a consequence, Slovenian nationalists put the early Middle Ages as the apex of Slavic linguistic expansion at the center of their historical conception, whereas pre-Slavic Illyrian, Celtic, Roman, and Germanic periods were passed over quickly and subsequent transformations of the area rued as a painful calvary of decay and denationalization. Austro-Germans, by contrast, attempted to project current, more favorable conditions into the past and enhance the Germanic genealogy of Slavophones as yet untouched by Slovenian nationalism. History was omnipresent, but not as an abstract scholarly endeavor, but as an instrument to support the national agenda.

Belonging on the Border. Mexican American Strategies at *El Primer Congreso Nacionalista*, Texas 1911

Anne Magnussen

In September 1911, the editor of *La Crónica*, a Spanish-language newspaper based in Texas, teamed up with the Masonic Order of the *Caballeros de Honor* (*the Honorable Gentlemen*) and organized a conference with the explicit objective to unite the Mexican Americans in Texas. The conference was the culmination of many years of built-up anger against European American prejudice and discrimination against Mexican Americans. The idea was that as one, unified community, they would be able to protect themselves much more efficiently.[1] The Mexican Americans constituted a transnational community that lived on the border between the United States and Mexico, and in their efforts to carve out a place for themselves, they tried to redefine both the Mexican American community and the border as a place.[2]

It was apparent at the time that several factors divided the Mexican American population living in Texas, including socio-economic features, legal status, ideology, and sense of history. Within this complex network

---

1. *La Cronica*, Sept 28, 1911 3; *Primer Congreso Nacionalista verificado en Laredo, Texas, EE.UU. DE A. Los Días 14 al 22 de Septiembre de 1911. Discursos y Conferencias. Por la Raza y Para la Raza.* Tipografía de N. Idar, Laredo, Texas 1912, p. 38-39, 43; Emilio Zamora: "Mutualist and Mexicanist Expressions of a Political Culture in Texas", in Emilio Zamora, Cynthia Orozco & Rodolfo Rocha (eds.): *Mexican Americans in Texas History*. Austin 2000, pp. 83-101 & p. 88.
2. A transnational community should here be understood as one that maintains concrete and/or symbolic connections with several countries at the same time. Alejandra Castañeda: *The Politics of Citizenship of Mexican Migrants*, New York 2006, p. 12.

of factors emerged a contested sense of place and belonging among the Mexican Americans. At the conference, the differences were apparent in the formulation of two strategies concerning how to unite the Mexican American population that were at least partially contradictory and that included sense of place as one of the points of difference. In the broader context of Texas society, the result was a community that was continuously being questioned by both those around them and the Mexican Americans themselves.[3] Below I analyze the contested sense of place and belonging among the Mexican American population in Texas as it was expressed at the conference and the debates connected to it.

There is a rich scholarship about the US-Mexican border as a place of interaction and exchange. A series of studies from the 1930s can be said to mark the beginning of this field of study.[4] From the 1970s the field grew considerably, not least as part of a first generation of studies of identities, minorities and power relations on the US-Mexican border and generally in the United States.[5] Since then, the scientific literature concerning Mexican Americans on the US-Mexican border has only increased. When considering specific questions of Mexican American organizing efforts, the principal focus has been on two periods of time; the 1930s and the 1970s and onwards. In the 1930s and 1940s the first lasting civil rights organizations were established, with LULAC from 1929 and GI Forum in 1948, and the 1970s saw a radicalization of the civil rights movement and identity politics, which involved the emergence of new organizations and the reframing of the existing ones.[6]

---

3. For a discussion of terminology re "Mexican American" and similar terms, see Zamora: "Mutualist and Mexicanist Expressions," pp. 2-3.
4. Most prominently Paul Taylor in *Mexican Labor in the United States. Dimmit County, Winter Garden District, South Texas*, Berkeley 1934, and in *An American-Mexican frontier, Nueces County, Texas*, Chapel Hill 1930.
5. E.g. Jorge C. Rangel & Carlos M. Alcalá: "Project Report: De Jure Segregation of Chicanos in Texas Schools", in: *Harvard Civil Rights-Civil Liberties Law Review*, 7 (1972), pp. 307-391; Pauline R. Kibbe: *Latin Americans in Texas*. New York 1974; Arnoldo de León: *The Tejano Community, 1836-1900*, Albuquerque 1982.
6. George Kiser & David Silverman: "Mexican Repatriation during the Great Depression," in *Journal of Mexican American History* 3 (1973), pp. 139-164; Mario T. García: *Mexican Americans. Leadership, Ideology, & Identity, 1930-1960*. New Haven & London 1989; R. Reynolds McKay: *Texas Mexican repatriation during the Great Depression*, Oklahoma 1982; Mario T. García: "The

Even though there have been studies of identity construction and conflicts focused on the beginning of the 20th century in the border area, they have been fewer and have only to a limited extent focused on organization among Mexican Americans.[7] This is not surprising, as organizing efforts were limited and seldom successful among Mexican Americans at the turn of the century. What makes *el Congreso Nacionalista* from 1911 interesting to study is that it proves that at least some efforts were under way early on. At the same time the participants clearly formulated the major strategies behind the idea of constructing a common Mexican American movement and identity that came to dominate later on. In this sense *el Congreso* can be said to represent an early formulation of – and debate about – questions of Mexican American identity on the border. The strategies analyzed below specify these questions of identity and constitute the point of departure for later organization efforts, both in the 1930s and 40s, and from the 1970s. At the end of the chapter I will therefore include a short perspective concerning the ways in which the strategies and their interrelationship can be used to describe the Mexican American community and its sense of place over the 20th century.

Doreen Massey's definition of place as an intersection of groupings, processes and factors is particularly useful as a heuristic framework for

---

Border as Symbol and Reality in Mexican-American Thought," in *Mexican Studies / Estudios Mexicanos*, 1 (1985), pp. 195-225; Gloria Anzaldúa: *Borderlands / La Frontera*, San Francisco 1987; Cynthia E. Orozco: *The origins of the League of United Latin American Citizens (LULAC) and the Mexican American civil rights movement in Texas with an analysis of women's political participation in a gendered context, 1910-1929*, Los Angeles 1992; Benjamín Márquez: *LULAC. The Evolution of a Mexican American Political Organization*, Austin 1993.

7. Examples are Juan Gómez-Quiñones: "Piedras contra la Luna, México en Aztlán y Aztlán en México: Chicano-Mexican Relations and the Mexican Consulates, 1900-1920," in J.W. Wilkie; M.C. Meyer & E. Monzón de Wilkie (eds.): *Contemporary Mexico. Papers of the IV Congress of Mexican History*, Berkeley 1976, pp. 494-522; Américo Paredes: *With His Pistol In His Hand*, Austin 1958. This period has also been treated as part of general historical overviews such as Sarah Deutsch: *No Separate Refuge. Culture, Class, and Gender on an Anglo-Hispanic Frontier in the American Southwest, 1880-1940*, New York & Oxford 1987; David Montejano: *Anglos and Mexicans in the Making of Texas, 1836-1986*, Austin 1987; Mario T. García: "Americanization and the Mexican Immigrant, 1880-1930," in *Journal of Ethnic Studies*, 6 (1978), pp. 19-34.

the description of a border region such as the one discussed here.[8] According to Massey, "we recognize space as the product of interrelations; as constituted through interactions, from the immensity of the global to the intimately tiny."[9] Place furthermore constitutes a "sphere of the possibility of the existence of multiplicity in the sense of contemporaneous plurality; as the sphere in which distinct trajectories coexist; as the sphere therefore of coexisting heterogeneity."[10] As a third characteristic, place is always under construction.[11] Massey's definition offers the possibility of including a multiplicity of factors in the analysis including socio-economic factors, sense of history, etc., while at the same time including a national dichotomy as one of the central factors that define life in a border region in terms of power relations, identities and conflicts. When place is defined as always under construction it makes it possible to analyze the particular sense of place represented at *el Congreso* as the result of practices, negotiations and power struggles over time. At the same time, it makes it possible for a particular sense of place to be changed by particular activities, for example by the events and speeches of *el Congreso* with consequences for a future sense of place.

While the study of place as intersections opens up a more complete picture of a border region, it also complicates the actual analysis. The high number and complexity of factors and groupings involved are difficult to include satisfactorily in a coherent analysis. In the analysis below I therefore concentrate on a small part of the Texas border region, namely the contested sense of place within the Mexican American community. Afterwards, I discuss how this contested sense can be understood as part of the border as a complex intersection, and offer, as mentioned above, a short perspective on the developments within this area over the 20th century.

---

8. It should be noted that Massey uses the term space differently than the definition in the introduction to this anthology. What Massey refers to as "space" is what the introduction and this chapter would refer to as "place."
9. Doreen Massey: *For Space*, London 2005, p. 9.
10. Ibid.
11. Ibid.

Ethnic communities and Texas society 1911

Despite the shared ethnicity, important factors divided the Mexican Americans living in Texas in 1911. One factor was nationality, as some members of the group were Mexican nationals and others US citizens, either through birth or naturalization.[12] Other differences related to historical background, socio-economic status and demography. Some families could trace their roots back to the times when Texas was Mexican (and, before that, Spanish) territory before 1836. Others had only just arrived from Mexico with the increased immigration starting in the 1890s.[13] Before that, the most popular areas for settlement had been close to the present Mexican border in South Texas and around San Antonio in Central Texas. In these areas, the Mexican American population was more numerous than in other parts of Texas and included a small Mexican American middle class.[14] In comparison, Central Texas (outside of San Antonio) had only recently started to attract Mexican American migrants with the region's new opportunities in agriculture. With some exceptions, the new migrants were laborers.[15]

To be able to unite the Mexican American community, it was necessary to bridge these socio-economic, legal and historical divisions, and at least at the outset European American discrimination helped this process along. In the words of the scholar Elliott Young: "Ironically, in forcing together this heterogeneous group, European racism helped to create an inclusive Nationalist identity."[16] At the beginning of the 20th

---

12. Based on census records, Emilio Zamora calculates that between 40 and 50 percent of people of Mexican descent living in Texas in 1890, 1900 and 1910 were Mexico-born. Emilio Zamora: *The World of the Mexican Worker in Texas*, College Station 1993, p. 211.
13. Manuel G. Gonzales: *Mexicanos. A History of Mexicans in the United States*, Bloomington & Indianapolis 2000.
14. Cynthia E. Orozco: *No Mexicans, Women or Dogs Allowed*, Austin 2010, pp. 17-29.
15. David Montejano: *Anglos and Mexicans*, pp. 109-110. See also Zamora: *The World of the Mexican Worker*, pp. 12-17 & p. 34.
16. Elliott Young: "Deconstructing *La Raza*: Identifying the *Gente Decente* of Laredo, 1904-1911", in *Southwestern Historical Quarterly*, XCVIII (1994), pp. 227-259. See also José Limón: "El Primer Congreso Mexicanista de 1911: A Precursor to Contemporary Chicanismo," in *Aztlan*, 5 (1974).

century, most European Americans living in Texas considered themselves distinct from, and superior to, both Mexican Americans and African Americans. The relationship between European Americans and African Americans was defined according to a racial hierarchy formalized with the so-called Jim Crow segregation, designating institutions and specific areas in public space for blacks and whites, respectively.[17] In legal terms, Mexican Americans were white, but in everyday life they were discriminated against along the same lines as the African American population.[18] In segregated institutions such as restaurants, barber shops, cinemas and hospitals, Mexican Americans were usually sent to the Black section, and in most towns and cities there was a strict ethnic division of neighborhoods.[19]

The discrimination against Mexican Americans was based in part on physical features and race, with Mexican Americans being referred to as colored or "greasers" and as "a degenerated race."[20] However, ethnicity played a role as well, since most European Americans at the time would argue that people of Mexican descent – disregarding actual citizenship – simply did not belong in the US, but in Mexico. At least part of the explanation for this was that the European American majority considered Mexico and Mexicans to be the historical enemy that had been thrown out in 1836.[21]

At the conference and in the Spanish-language newspaper debate

---

17. Douglas A. Blackmon: *Slavery by Another Name. The Re-Enslavement of Black Americans from the Civil War to World War II*, New York 2008, pp. 110-111; Jane Dailey: *The Age of Jim Crow*, New York & London 2009.
18. Arnoldo de León: *They Called Them Greasers. Anglo Attitudes Toward Mexicans in Texas, 1821-1900*, Austin 1983; Neil Foley: *The White Scourge. Mexicans, Blacks, and Poor Whites in Texas Cotton Culture*, Berkeley 1997, pp. 2-4 & pp. 40-42.
19. E.g. *El Regidor*, Feb 10, 1910, 3; *La Crónica*, Dec 17, 1910, 6; Jan 12, 1911,1 & 6; June 29,1911, 1; Aug 10, 1911 1. See also Montejano: *Anglos and Mexicans*, pp. 160-16; Foley: *The White Scourge*, pp. 40-42.
20. *Primer congreso* 1912, p. 14; *La Crónica*, Feb 9, 1911, 1; June 29,1911, 1. See also de León 1983.
21. Stewart and de León: *Not Room Enough. Mexicans, Anglos, and Socio-economic Change in Texas, 1850-1900*, Albuquerque 1993, p. 91; Holly Beacheley Brear: *Inherit the Alamo. Myth and Ritual at an American Shrine*, Austin 1995, p. 2; Anne Magnussen: "New People, New Historical Narratives. When the Mexican-Americans Came to Gonzales, Texas, at the Turn of the Twentieth Century, " in *Diálogos Latinoamericanos* 16 (2009), pp. 16-34.

preceding it, focus was mostly on discrimination within two areas: in the legal system and in education. The practice of lynching Mexican Americans and African Americans was widespread at the time, showing that the legal authorities could not protect individuals against lynch mobs. In most cases the perpetrators of the lynching were not prosecuted, and if they were, they received very light sentences.[22]

The access to and treatment of Mexican American children in the Texas public school system was another subject that generated complaints from the Spanish-language newspapers and the conference speakers. As legally white, Mexican American children should in principle have attended the public white schools, but except for the cities and towns close to the Mexican border with Mexican American majorities, this was rarely the case. In some towns, there was a third category of schools, so-called Mexican schools that Mexican American children were supposed to attend. In some towns and school districts, Mexican American children were not offered any education at all.[23]

For the organizers of the 1911 conference, the discrimination within both the legal system and the schools could only be fought efficiently if they managed to bridge the divisions within the Mexican American community itself. Therefore they continuously emphasized that the invitation was open to all *Mexicanos* who were worried about the community's welfare and progress, "disregarding citizenship."[24] They

---

22. Randolph B. Cambell: *Gone to Texas. A History of the Lone Star State*, New York & Oxford 2003, pp. 325-326; William D. Carrigan: *The Making of a Lynching Culture. Violence and Vigilantism in Central Texas, 1836-1916*, Urbana and Chicago 2004; e.g. "Quejas. Asalto a la familia García 1909" and "Choque entre Americanos y Mexicanos en Falfurrias 1910, *Archivo de la Embajada de México en los Estados Unidos de América*. Secretaría de Relaciones Exteriores, Ciudad de México.

23. Mexican schools in Gonzales (*La Crónica*, Dec 17, 1910, 1; *Sanborn Fire Insurance Maps, Texas* (1877-1922), Perry-Castañeda Library Map Collection, University of Texas Libraries, University of Texas, Gonzales 1912, sheet 1), Seguín (*La Crónica*, Dec 17, 1910, 1; Dec 31, 1910, 1; Sanborn, Seguín 1912, sheet 1), San Angelo (*La Crónica*, June 25, 1910, 1; Sanborn, San Angelo 1913, sheet 1), Kingsville (*La Crónica*, Dec 17, 1910, 4; Sanborn, Kingsville 1915, sheet 1), Del Río (*La Crónica*, Dec 17, 1910, 4; Sanborn, Del Río 1917, sheet 1), Pearsall (*La Crónica*, Dec 17, 1910, 4; Dec 31, 1910, 1; *El Regidor*, Dec 2, 1909, 1; Dec 23, 1909, 1; *La Crónica*, June 25, 1910, 4; Dec 31, 1910, 1; Jan 12, 1911, 1; Feb 9, 1911, 1).

24. Spanish quotes have been translated by the author. *La Crónica*, Feb 2, 1911, 3. See also *Primer congreso* 1912, p. 15 & 1.

invited journalists, representatives of the Masonic Orders and mutual aid societies from around Texas, as well as of the workers' organizations and women's societies. More than 24 towns and cities in Texas sent delegates to the conference.[25] The specific goal was to create an umbrella organization, the *Nationalist League of Benevolence and Protection* with local chapters and in close connection to the already existing societies and organizations.[26]

The voices and opinions that were heard in the papers and at the conference were those of newspaper editors, heads of the local mutual aid and workers' societies, school teachers, professors, and generally respected Mexican Americans who wrote letters to the papers or attended the conference as delegates. They all spoke against discrimination and in favor of unity, but two different strategies materialized when it came to how this unity should be obtained and on which values it should be based. The strategies interacted with each other, both in the actual speeches and texts and with regards to the values and ideas they represented. However, as will be apparent, they also seemed to oppose each other on important points. One of the points on which the two strategies fundamentally differed was on the subject of place and where the Mexican American community belonged.

A nationalist strategy

One strategy was to unite around a nationalist sentiment that defined the Mexican Americans in opposition to the European Americans. In the face of the often violent discrimination, such a strategy of opposition was hardly surprising.[27] The continuous references to Mexican history were at the core of this strategy. In terms of place, Mexico was considered the true and only homeland, while life in the United States was a life in exile.[28]

---

25. *La Crónica*, Aug 10, 1911, 6; *Primer Congreso* 1912, p. 1
26. *Primer Congreso* 1912, p. 39 and 43. My translation from *Liga Nacionalista de Benevolencia y Protección*. All the translations from the Spanish language press and conference material are the author's.
27. *La Crónica*, June 29,1911, 1; Oct 5, 1911, 4.
28. *Primer congreso* 1912, p. 8, 12-13, 15, 24, 28, 30, 32-33.

In this sense, the strategy actively involved and reproduced the idea of the border as a division between two countries, cultures and people. According to this sentiment, the Mexican Americans were physically located on one side, but belonged on the other.

The nationalist strategy was present both in the newspaper coverage and at the conference that represented a "pervasive nationalistic style" according to the scholar José Limón.[29] The speeches were held in Spanish and the dates chosen for the conference coincided with the celebration of Mexican independence (September 15-16). A nationalist focus was underscored by means of continuous references to "la Patria," to the Mexican flag,[30] and through statements according to which Mexicans living in the US could be called on at any time to return and "free [Mexico] from the infamous acts and insults committed by foreigners and traitors."[31] The war rhetoric was strong, and the fact that Mexican society was in serious upheaval with the first phases of the Mexican revolution surely influenced this.[32]

Closely related to the nationalist discourse was the use of historical references. They involved events and historical persons from Mexican independence at the beginning of the 19th century in combination with prominent Aztecs and the Spanish conqueror Hernán Cortéz symbolizing the Spanish conquest. They were all depicted as heroes and together they represented a unique Mexican race, *La Raza*, characterized precisely by its combination of races and its particular ethnic and cultural history.[33]

Only few historical references involved Texas. Taking into account the state's recent past as one of Mexico's Northern provinces, this was somewhat surprising, and there were no explicit demands, for example that the Mexican Americans ought to have special privileges because of this past.[34] A clear-cut distinction between the two nationalities, peoples

---

29. Limón: "El primer congreso," p. 94.
30. *Primer congreso* 1912, p. 8-10, 13, 15, 32-33.
31. *Primer congreso* 1912, p. 32.
32. *Primer congreso* 1912, e.g. p. 23-25 and 33. See also Javier Garciadiego: *La revolución mexicana. Crónicas, documentos, planes y testimonios*, México, D.F. 2005.
33. The conference' motto was "Por la raza y para la raza," (*By the [Mexican] Race and For the [Mexican] Race*). *Primer Congreso*, p. 1 and also p. 7, 9, 15, 25; *La Crónica*, Oct 1, 1910, 1.
34. *La Crónica*, July 13, 1911, 6.

and places was in this sense also upheld in the choice of historical events and periods.

The many references to Mexican Americans living in exile in Texas, the war rhetoric and the idea of a unique Mexican race were all factors that reinforced the idea of the Mexican (Americans) in opposition to the dominant (European) American community. A similar opposition was present in terms of territory, pitting the United States against Mexico.

Within the logic of the nationalist strategy, the Mexican consulates in Texas played a central role in the protection of the Mexicans living in exile. As a case in point, *El Regidor* recommended that everybody should hold on to their Mexican citizenship. In this way they would maintain their national pride, but they would also be able to draw on the consulates in a situation of crisis.[35] Mexican citizenship was in this sense understood both as a strong symbol connecting the individual to Mexico and as an important component in his or her personal protection.

The nationalist strategy was clear and strong in its description of the values and objectives that should unite the Mexican American community living in Texas. However, it also drew attention to the division in terms of nationality between Mexican nationals and US citizens of Mexican descent. More importantly, it counteracted the idea of Texas as a place where Mexican Americans actually belonged – or were even supposed to live at all – with its many references to exile and its insistence on the border as an absolute division between two distinct places and peoples. Other than to recur to the consulates, this strategy seemed to offer very few pointers as to how to act in Texas in the face of discrimination and violence.

An Integrationist strategy

As opposed to the notion of the border as an absolute division, the integrationist strategy represented it as a place in which different ethnic communities could – and should – interact on equal terms. Taking into account the dominant racial dynamics in the US at the time, this meant

---

35. *El Regidor*, Nov 25, 1909, 1.

that according to the integrationist voices the Mexican Americans ought to be treated as whites.[36]

The insistence on equality with the European American community was central to the integrationist strategy, although without leaving behind a Mexican (American) identity. National pride and Mexican values should function as a means to gain respect as dignified white members of Texan society, not as a way of distancing the group from the European Americans. To obtain equality according to this strategy, the Mexican Americans should hold high their Mexican ancestry, while at the same time trying to reshape the image and characteristics of the community within Texas society.

According to the integrationist strategy, Mexican Americans ought to be represented as equally progressive, productive and invaluable for Texas economy and business as were the European Americans – according at least to the dominant European American self-image.[37] Not all Mexican Americans could be educated or rich, but everybody "ought to aspire to improve their class."[38] Thus it was every Mexican American's responsibility to improve himself and his possibilities in Texas, "with [his] head held high and with the satisfaction of a man who fights loyally and honorably for his existence."[39]

These efforts should be understood in relation to the European American stereotype of Mexican Americans. The dominant European American Texas narrative evolved around values such as modernity, progress, democracy and individual entrepreneurship. However, European Americans regarded "Mexicans" in Texas as the Other, representing the exact opposite values, as they were stereotyped as docile, uncivilized and with no sense of progress or democratic values.[40] To oppose this stereotype,

---

36. E.g. *La Crónica*, Dec 10, 1910, 4.
37. *Primer congreso* 1912, p. 32-33; Richard R. Flores: *Remembering the Alamo. Memory, Modernity, & the Master Symbol*, Austin 2002, pp. 1-12.
38. *La Crónica*, April 30, 1910 5.
39. *La Crónica*, April 30, 1910 5. The gender was explicit. Women had another role, as educators of the children.
40. Flores: *Remembering the Alamo*, pp. 1-12; Magnussen: "New People, New Historical Narratives."

all Mexican Americans should therefore work on changing the dominant image of a "Mexican."

According to some of the voices at the conference and in the papers, the Mexican stereotype was only partially false, and speakers criticized the Mexican Americans for being too passive and accepting to work for others for too little money. Mexican Americans were "asleep, [...] dreaming about sublime greatness" while the European Americans acted, fought for their rights and improved their situation in life.[41] According to one conference speaker, the reason behind the lack of business enterprise was that the Mexican was a warrior and a poet (not docile and uncivilized), as opposed to the practical Americans who built railroads and drilled for oil.[42]

The key issue, whether represented as docile, warriors or poets, was that the Mexican Americans should learn from the European Americans and be more practical and more ambitious in work, savings and education.[43] The contrast to the nationalist strategy's war rhetoric and its call to go back to Mexico and fight is apparent here.

Education was a central component in the integrationist strategy, making the school exclusion an important issue. The complaint was not only that the education offered to the Mexican American children was of bad quality if existent at all, but also more specifically that the children were excluded from public schools for European American children. Within the integrationist strategy, the creation of separate Mexican schools was not a solution to the problem but part of it. To be treated on equal terms with the European Americans meant that their children should attend the same schools. According to an early (1907) article in *El Regidor*, the idea of separate schools, "similar to those that exist for colored people [was] a humiliation of the national [i.e. Mexican] dignity."[44] The quote is an example both of the insistence on being considered white and of how the nationalist sentiment was included in the integrationist strategy as an expression of national pride.

---

41. *La Crónica*, March 16, 1911, 5.
42. *La Crónica*, Nov 19, 1910 1; March 16, 1911 5.
43. *La Crónica*, May 7, 1910, 2; Oct 1, 1910 1; Oct 1, 1910, 1; Nov 19, 1910, 1.
44. *El Regidor*, March 7, 1907, 1. See also *La Crónica*, Jan 12, 1911 1, 1 & 6; April 13, 1911, 2.

Closely related to the subject of education, many participants in the debates argued that it was necessary to educate and "culture" the many Mexican American laborers living in Texas.[45] In this context, the issue of social class was introduced. The difference between the majority of laborers and the small, but well-educated and settled Mexican American population in the border cities and towns was decisive here. The conference speakers and editors represented the latter and saw the Mexican American middle class as the ideal, pointing to education and political influence as the means that should improve the Mexican American laborers' socio-economic status as well as their dignity. In this way, it was argued, the respect from the European Americans for the Mexican American community as a whole could be secured.[46]

In terms of race, both strategies included a strong relationship with Mexico and its particular racially and ethnically diverse history as part of the definition of the Mexican American community. Here, the key concept was *la Raza [mexicana]* indicating the Mexican (American) uniqueness.[47] The two strategies differed, however, when it came to the significance of place. Within the nationalist strategy, race primarily strengthened the relationship with Mexico as a place and the role of exiles in Texas. Within the integrationist strategy, focus was rather on the opportunities that being defined as white gave the Mexican Americans in Texas as a place.[48] According to the scholar Neil Foley, middle-class Mexican Americans made Faustian pacts as they took on a "white racial identity and its core value of White supremacy."[49]

The integrationist strategy included, as mentioned, some of the central

---

45. *La Crónica*, Dec 17, 1910 (no p.); Sept 14, 1911, 2); *Primer Congreso* 1912, p. 17.
46. *Primer Congreso* 1912, 19.
47. See also *La Crónica*, Nov 26, 1910, 1.
48. Other racial denominations were used, e.g. the "Latin" and "Anglo Saxon races" (E.g. *La Crónica*, Jan 19, 1911). The point was the same: that they were equal – white – races. Race was sometimes used as a synonym with nationality, but the overriding division was in black and white. *La Crónica*, Aug 6 1910, 3. See also Mora, Anthony. *Border Dilemmas. Racial and National Uncertainties in New Mexico, 1848-1912*, Durham and London, Duke University Press 2011, p. 5
49. Neil Foley: "Becoming Hispanic: Mexican Americans and the Faustian Pact with Whiteness", in Neil Foley (ed.): *Reflexiones 1997. New Directions in Mexican American Studies*. Austin 1997, p. 63.

features of the nationalist strategy, primarily that of national pride, but it differed from it on two interrelated features: the relationship with the European American community and the significance of place. According to the integrationist strategy, the border was (or should be) a place in which the Mexican American community could maintain its ethnic identity while at the same time integrating into the existing European American dominated dynamics, i.e. defined by the narrative of progress and modernity and a specific racial hierarchy.

The integrationist strategy seemed to solve the nationalist strategy's problem of belonging somewhere else (i.e. in Mexico), but it created new problems. The strategy thoroughly depended on the willingness of the European American community to actually accept the Mexican Americans as white and as belonging in Texas. If at all, this acceptance was possible only for a limited section of the Mexican American community, namely the middle classes, who already saw themselves as part of the narrative of progress and who lived in towns and cities with high percentages of Mexican Americans. In this way, the integrationist strategy made social class visible as an important division within the Mexican American community. As a strategy, integration was therefore questioned both by the European Americans and by socio-economic divisions within the Mexican American community itself.

Nationalist and integrationist sentiments, combined: Belonging on the border

Several scholars within the field argue that, in 1911, Mexican Americans in Texas were firmly convinced that a strategy of integration was impossible due to the generalized discrimination against them. From this perspective, the key components of the integrationist strategy looked like wishful thinking, something that was fully recognized at the *Primer Congreso Nacionalista* in 1911.[50]

---

50. Young: "Deconstructing *La Raza*," p. 254; Limón: "El primer congreso," p. 99; Montejano: *Anglos and Mexicans*, pp. 116-117.

The nationalist strategy was quite possibly the stronger of the two at the conference, but as argued above, the integrationist strategy was also evident. The protest against school exclusion, for example, was an important case in point, and so were the foci on US-defined race and socio-economic status. As will be apparent below, it actually made good sense that both partially contradictory strategies were represented at the conference and in the newspaper debate. At the time, the Mexican Americans were to a large extent left alone by both US and Mexican institutions, and in this situation none of the strategies was useful on its own. In combination, however, they offered a potential framework for belonging on the border.

The conference organizers recognized that neither the US nor the Mexican governments were capable of or willing to help them against discrimination.[51] Due to the US authorities' acceptance of the widespread discrimination, Mexican Americans had very little faith in them, be it on state or local level. Even though Mexican nationals living in Texas could in principle draw on the assistance of Mexican authorities, i.e. the regional consulates, the political situation and many concrete cases had shown that this help was often half-hearted and furthermore only accessible for certain members of the Mexican American community, i.e. the Mexican nationals.[52] Most of the Mexican Americans living on the border had "only one possibility, and that [was] to take care of [themselves] for the good of [their] fellow countrymen."[53]

A key feature of dealing with life on the border was taking care of each other as a community by organizing locally in chapters of Masonic orders and of mutual aid societies and in Catholic as well as Protestant churches.[54] Local patriotic celebrations furthermore functioned as important practices of local unity. What makes these celebrations especially interesting in this context is that they very clearly reproduced values from both the nationalist and integrationist strategies. Below the celebrations

---

51. *La Crónica*, Feb 2, 1911 3; Limón: "El primer congreso," p. 92.
52. *La Crónica*, Aug 10, 1911, 1.
53. *La Crónica*, Aug 10, 1911, 1. See also *La Crónica*, Nov 12, 1910, 1.
54. Zamora: "Mutualist and Mexicanist Expressions," pp. 83-101.

will function as a case in point, showing how Mexican Americans drew on both strategies in the construction and reproduction of local Texas based communities.

Local celebrations united the Mexican American community by reproducing the main points of the nationalist strategy, of history and *la patria*. But when it came to place, the celebrations differed fundamentally from the celebrations held in Mexico as they were obviously held outside the national territory. In Texas, part of the celebration was often held in downtown areas otherwise dominated by the European American community.[55] With the visibility that the parades and festivities offered, the Mexican American community was insisting that it also belonged in the particular place, both physically and symbolically.[56] In this sense the local patriotic celebrations strengthened both strategies. On the one hand, they united the local Mexican Americans around nationalist values and a celebration of Mexican national history. On the other hand, the celebrations strengthened the Mexican American community's belonging in a particular place in Texas. The patriotic celebrations were furthermore used as a way of attracting Mexican American visitors to town from the surrounding area, creating contacts and business.

In the areas where discrimination was strongest, not least in Central Texas, the access to downtown was limited, but the increase in discrimination over the first part of the 20th century did not stop the local patriotic celebrations, and there were at least some examples showing that these celebrations continued to take place in downtown areas.[57]

The use of the patriotic celebrations to attract business was most pronounced in the big cities, such as Laredo. In 1910-1911, the Laredo organizers were very explicit about the double objective of the celebrations. They were honoring Mexican history and independence and improving

---

55. Local Texas celebrations around 1910-11: *El Regidor*, Sept 16, 1909, 1; Sept 29, 1910, 8; Oct 13, 1910, 4; *La Crónica*, April 30, 1910, 4; May 17, 1910, 2; June 25, 1910, 1 July 30, 1910, 3.
56. Yi-Fu Tuan: *Space and Place*, Minneapolis 2007, p. 169; Susan G. Davis: *Parades and Power*, Philadelphia 1986, pp. 1-7.
57. In Gonzales 1911 (The Gonzales Inquirer, Sept 21, 1911, 4) and in Karnes City (*La Crónica*, June 11, 1910, p. 1; July 30, 1910, p. 3).

local business at the same time.⁵⁸ Supporting local, Mexican American business, insisting on school inclusion, and celebrating Mexico locally were all efforts that represented network building and strengthened the Mexican Americans' possibilities of education and socio-economic progress locally in Texas. However, these efforts were combined with the core values of the Nationalist strategy and the recognition that equality with the European American community was next to impossible.

Taking into account the complex intersections of race, ethnicity, demography, socio-economic status and nationality, it may not be surprising that the *Primer Congreso Mexicanista*'s objective of uniting the Mexican American population in Texas to fight discrimination did not have much success. The *Nationalist League* did not materialize and discrimination against Mexican Americans in Texas only became more pronounced in the years following the conference.⁵⁹ However, the Mexican Americans continued to live on the border, continuously reproducing and/or questioning both the border as a division and the Mexican Americans as a community. As a grand project, the formulation of a common Mexican American community did not have much success, but when zooming in on the Mexican American neighborhoods in villages around Texas it became apparent how the Mexican Americans used both strategies in their construction of a specific sense of place and belonging.

The two strategies were actively used in the construction of neighborhoods as intersections of local, regional and transnational relations. Through work, commerce, patriotic celebrations and subjects of discriminatory practices, the Mexican American neighborhoods interacted with the town as a whole. The surrounding region was important in that Mexican Americans living on farms came in for business, patriotic celebrations, and to participate in church, society and school activities. The

---

58. *La Crónica*, March 5, 1910, 1; March 12, 1910, 1; July 2, 1910 1; Aug 6, 1910 1. See also e.g. San Marcos (*La Crónica*, July 24, 1910, 4), and Karnes City (*La Crónica*, May 28, 1910, 3; July 20, 1911, 4).
59. William D. Carrigan & Clive Webb: "Muerto por Unos Desconocidos (Killed by Persons Unknown): Mob Violence against Blacks and Mexicans," in Stephanie Cole & Nancy A. Parker (eds.): *Beyond Black & White. Race, Ethnicity, and Gender in the U.S. South and Southwest*, College Station 2004, pp. 35-74; Montejano: *Anglos and Mexicans*.

transnational interaction with Mexico was central in the definition of the Mexican American neighborhoods for various reasons. For one, the patriotic celebrations and the reproduction of cultural practices including language and religion defined the Mexican American neighborhood as a place.[60] Secondly, the migrants who came to work in the harvest and then went back to Mexico or to another part of Texas further reinforced the local neighborhood as a transnational place, maintaining a strong connection with Mexico.

A contested sense of place, over time

As mentioned in the introduction, interaction between the nationalist and integrationist strategies continued to characterize the organizing efforts and identity projects among the Mexican Americans living on the border. In specific periods of time, some features of the strategies dominated over others. This is the case, for example, when the first Mexican American civil rights organization, LULAC, was founded in Texas in 1929. Most of its members represented the growing Mexican American middle class and prioritized an integrationist strategy, insisting on equal rights and integration into the European American middle classes.[61] The integrationist strategy continued to coexist with a pronounced reticence against integration from the many Mexican American labourers, who for the most part were subject to a much harsher discrimination than the Mexican American middle class.

Another example of interaction between the strategies occurred in the 1970s. By then, the Mexican American civil rights organizations were well established. A new generation of Mexican Americans that called themselves *Chicanos* criticized the older generations for their willingness to integrate and insisted on *special* rights rather than equal rights, along

---

60. The transnational dimension of a place should here be understood as one where connections, identities or activities are maintained with several countries. See Alejandra Castañeda: *The Politics of Citizenship of Mexican Migrants*, New York 2006, p. 12.
61. Richard A. García: *Rise of the Mexican American Middle Class. San Antonio, 1929-1941*, College Station 1991.

similar lines as the radical section of the African American civil rights movement. Chicanos defined themselves in opposition to the European Americans and argued that the region's past as Mexican and Indigenous, with reference to the mythical *Aztlán,* gave people of Mexican descent a particular historical right to large parts of US territory. This points to an important and significant change when it comes to a sense of place in between the nationalist strategy of 1911 and the Chicano movement. In the 1900s and 1910s, a nationalist focus considered life in Texas a life in exile because of a dislocation in place – Mexico was the true homeland. By the 1970s, Mexican American nationalists considered themselves to be in the right place as they claimed a historical right of the US southwest region, including Texas. The problem was that somebody else had taken over. Academic titles such as "Foreigners in their Native Land" and "Occupied America" from the 1970s represent this sense of place.[62]

Today, the Mexican American community is even more complex and diversified than at the beginning of the 20th century or in the 1970s, and it continues to evolve and change and so does place. Massey's definition of place as both heterogeneous, consisting of "contemporaneous plurality" and as always under construction is very helpful as a heuristic framework for the analysis of changes in the understanding of the border as place over time. The Mexican Americans constitute a highly diversified group regarding their relationship with Mexico, their socio-economic status, and their relationship to other ethnic groups in the US. Especially from the 1990s, more and more Mexican Americans have moved beyond the immediate border states, and there are now big Mexican American communities in the South, the Mid-West and in the North-Eastern States. This leads to new dynamics, not only within the Mexican American community, but also relating to other communities of Latin American descent. The Mexican American community is continuously being contested or reshaped, and so is the community's sense of place.

---

62. Rodolfo Acuña: *Occupied America. A History of Chicanos,* New York 2004. First edition came in 1972; David J. Weber: *Foreigners in Their Native Land. Historical Roots of the Mexican Americans,* Albuquerque 2003. First edition appeared in 1973.

Schleswig as a Contested Place

Michael Bregnsbo and Kurt Villads Jensen

The territory of Schleswig is today divided between Denmark and Germany so that the northern part belongs to Denmark whereas the southern part belongs to Germany together with Holstein constitutes the German *Land* of Schleswig-Holstein.[1] For centuries Schleswig has constituted the borderland between Denmark and the German Empire and later German state buildings and has as such been contested through the ages. In fact, Schleswig has often had a direct and most important impact on the kingdom of Denmark in general, its international position, self-understanding, identity, fate and occasionally even its very existence.

Because of the fact that Schleswig has thus long been a place of contest, much research in the history of Schleswig has been carried out and much historiography exists. This goes especially for the 19th century, when Schleswig became an all-important issue not only for Denmark and Germany, but in a European context as well. Certainly, national antagonisms have been projected back on former ages in the historiography and used for arguments during the national conflict on

---

1. The spelling "Schleswig" is German, in Danish it is called "Slesvig" or nowadays oftener the Danish part of Schleswig is called "Sønderjylland" (Southern Jutland) to emphasise both that Schleswig is part of the Danish peninsula of Jutland and that it is not the whole territory of Schleswig that now belongs to Denmark. Furthermore, a city in the current-day German part of Schleswig is also called Schleswig. In this chapter, the territory of Schleswig and not the city of the same name is meant. Schleswig means: the creek at the river Schlei (in Danish: Slien). We use the designation to cover the area from the first centuries AD, although it could be argued that Schleswig as a political entity was created only in the high middle ages, around 1100.

both sides.² However, Schleswig was a contested place long before the Dano-German national antagonisms emerged.³ How was Schleswig a contested place even before the age of nationalism, what was the apple(s) of discord through different ages, and how are things with those antagonisms today?

Geography

Schleswig has been of significant importance throughout history, both economically and politically and thus as an ideological marker of identity. This is to a great degree explainable from the geographical and geopolitical location of Schleswig and Denmark.

The Baltic Sea is the outlet of the great rivers of Scandinavia and much of northern and eastern Europe, and until the building of railroads in the late nineteenth century, the Baltic Sea provided the main access to the enormous markets in the east. Denmark consists of a peninsula and

---

2. Until the second part of the 20th century, both Danish and German historiography about Schleswig was strongly influenced by Dano-German national antagonisms and often had the hidden agenda of proving the respective side right. Furthermore, due to the different political, legal, economic and social structures of Schleswig in comparison with the rest of Denmark historically seen, Danish historiography has tended to leave Schleswig out of the general historiography of Denmark and instead let the history of Schleswig be written separately by specialists.

3. Among the most important general reference works are Henrik Becker-Christensen (ed.): *Geschichte Schleswigs. Vom frühen Mittelalter bis 1920*, Haderslev 1999; Karl-Ernst Behre: *Landschaftsgeschichte Norddeutschlands. Umwelt und Siedlung von der Steinzeit bis zur Gegenwart*, Neumünster 2008; Robert Bohn: *Geschichte Schleswig-Holsteins*, Munich 2006; Michael Bregnsbo & Kurt Villads Jensen: *Det danske imperium. Storhed og fald*, Copenhagen 2004; Vilhelm la Cour et al. (eds.): *Sønderjyllands Historie fremstillet for det danske Folk*, vol. I-V, Copenhagen 1930-1943; H. V. Gregersen: *Slesvig og Holsten indtil 1830*, Copenhagen 1981; Hans Schultz Hansen, Lars N. Henningsen and Carsten Porskrog (eds.): *Sønderjyllands Historie*, I-II, Aarhus 2008-2009; O. Klose et al. (eds.): *Geschichte Schleswig-Holsteins 1-8* (vol. 7 and 8 have not yet been completed) 1955-; Ulrich Lange (ed.): *Geschichte Schleswig-Holsteins. Von den Anfängen bis zur Gegenwart*, Neumünster 1996; Klaus-J. Lorenzen-Schmidt & Ortwin Pelc (eds.): *Schleswig-Holstein Lexikon*, Neumünster 2000. Martin Rheinheimer (hrsg.): *Grenzen in der Geschichte Schleswig-Holsteins und Dänemarks*, Neumünster 2006; Lorenz Rerup: *Slesvig og Holsten efter 1830*, Copenhagen 1982; and Peter Thaler: *Of Mind and Matter: The Duality of National Identity in the German-Danish Borderland*, West Lafayette 2009.

a number of minor islands and functions as the delta of the Baltic Sea, and almost all communication between the Baltic Sea and the North Sea and the Mediterranean had to pass through Danish waters.

Schleswig comprises the narrowest part of the peninsula of Jutland, where the distance from east to west, from the Baltic to the North Sea, is only about 15 kilometres.[4] By crossing over Schleswig instead of circumnavigating Jutland, many days' transport would have been saved. At the same time, land-based traffic to Denmark and south-western Scandinavia would have had to pass through Schleswig in a north-south direction, be it traders following the so-called ox-way or be it armies following the same road system, also known as Hærvejen – the army road.

Schleswig is a flat region without any high points that could provide natural fortifications, but the western parts are marshy lands, which until modern times had been difficult to penetrate. Some areas of the low-lying southern parts are fertile land and suited, for example, for cattle breeding, and the natural ports of Schleswig and Flensburg have been important centres for traffic and trade since they were founded in the Middle Ages.[5]

Historians in the twentieth century often assumed that communication was slow in ancient times and northern countries isolated from the main part of Europe, but modern archaeological research has shown that Schleswig and Scandinavia were closely connected to the rest of the European world, both eastern and western. New technology and new ideas were introduced with very little delay. If they came much later, for example as Christianity did only in the tenth century, it is best explained as being the result of a deliberate choice rather than of an isolated geographical situation.

---

4. From coast to coast between Eckernförde and Husum, the distance is about 55 km, but there is only about 15 km between the part of Slien Fjord and river Treene that was navigable in the Middle Ages and earlier.
5. Bjørn Poulsen: "Middelalderens landbrug," in Per Ethelberg et al. (eds): *Det Sønderjyske Landbrugs Historie. Jernalder, Vikingetid og Middelalder*, Haderslev 2003, 458-715; Behre: *Landschaftsgeschichte Norddeutschlands*.

Fortifications since antiquity

That Schleswig was a contested area for at least two thousand years is clearly attested by the impressive and significant works of fortification that had been erected since the first century AD and were maintained and had functioned for hundreds of years.

The oldest fortification in historical times is the Olgerdiget, which stretched south-east from Aabenraa for almost 12 kilometres. It was an impressive construction with several parallel ditches and mounds, and three to five rows of palisades consisting of a total of about 90,000 oak trees. The Olgerdiget was established in the middle of the second century AD and constantly in use for three hundred years. A similar fortification is Æ Vold north of Aabenraa, built in the middle of the third century and running east-west. Æ Vold is clearly a defensive structure directed against Olgerdiget, and the two fortifications are separated by a zone of about 15 kilometres. Both are laid out with great precision and clearly inspired by contemporary Roman fortifications of the northern border of the Roman Empire, of the limes. The area in between, a zone of about 15 kilometres, was probably a kind of no-man's land or populated with heavily militarised peasants of some kind.[6]

The implication must be that the Northern area of Schleswig in the first half millennium AD was contested between two or more rulers who had been inspired by Roman military organisation and architecture. Perhaps they also entered into shifting alliances with the Roman forces to strengthen their local position. This is difficult to prove, but can be substantiated by the great number of sacrifices of military equipment found in bogs and moors in Southern Jutland. Ejrsbøl Moor near Haderslev was used continuously throughout five hundred years and contains equipment from at least four major battles. It is possible to follow over time the changes in fashion and technology and show that the latest and most

---

6. Lars Jørgensen, Birger Storgaard & Lone Gebauer Thomsen (eds.): *Sejrens Triumf. Norden i skyggen af det Romerske Imperium*, Copenhagen 2003; Jørgen Jensen: *Danmarks oldtid 1-4*, Copenhagen 2003, vol. 3, pp. 585-590, p.3.

effective weapons in the Roman arsenals were immediately imported to Schleswig and Scandinavia or imitated.

The huge sacrificial deposits of weapons have often been interpreted as evidence of recurrent major battles in the area, as proof that Schleswig was contested and attractive for neighbouring powers both from the south in Germany and from the north in other Scandinavian countries. It is, however, remarkable that no humans can be found among the offerings, and that no mass graves have been found nearby. It may indicate a more advanced sort of contest among local powers in Schleswig, in the sense that they may have competed against each other by leading expansive and aggressive wars elsewhere from where they brought back booty to be offered to the gods, while the dead soldiers were buried on the fields where they fell.

Changing populations – or changing forms of government?

From the sixth to the eighth centuries, a major movement of populations seems to have taken place in northern Europe. These have traditionally been considered centuries of large-scale immigration of Slavic-speaking peoples from Central Europe and the north and along the Baltic coast to Holstein and Schleswig in the west. In the same period, there may have been emigration from the eastern part of Schleswig, from Angel. Linguistic differences are impossible to trace in archaeological material and all migration theories are uncertain, but from this time it seems – also from the few earliest written pieces of evidence – that Schleswig and Holstein became inhabited by a mixed Slavic- and Germanic/Danish-speaking population. There are no indications that this was considered a problem for any of the groups at this time.

During the eighth century, the Frankish/Carolingian kingdom expanded and came in direct contact with Danish rulers after the conquest and forced through the baptism of the Saxons in 772. The expansion culminated in the restoration of the Roman Empire with the coronation of Charlemagne in the year 800. Schleswig now became and was to remain for centuries the border area and battle area between the Danes and Carolingians or their later successors. It was marked physically in the landscape with the erection of the fortification of Danevirke, which was begun in the mid-seventh century but expanded significantly in the 720s and continued to be elaborated and strengthened for the next five hundred years. Danevirke is a mound or rampart, about 10 kilometres long, with ditches and palisades. It was placed at the narrowest point of the peninsula of Jutland, some 15-20 kilometres north of the Eider River.[7]

Wars to gain political control over Schleswig must have been frequent, although we know little about them. In 811, a peace treaty was concluded between Charlemagne and a Danish King Hemming which specified that the border between the two powers should be the Eider River.[8] It became the southern border of Schleswig, separating this region from Holstein, and it is the first mention we have of a border between Danish and German powers. Shortly before, in 808, the Danish king had supported regional development by destroying the trading centre of Reric in the Slavic area near Wismar and moving the merchants to the recently founded city of Hedeby, at the eastern end of the Dannevirke and at Slien fjord. Hedeby, and its later successor Slesvig, became political and in particular economic centres and subjects of contest in the future.

Conversion and crusades

The inhabitants of Schleswig must have had a fair knowledge of Christianity from an early time, both through military and trading contacts, and the first reports of a mission to the area stem from the early eighth century. A general conversion of the area did not happen, however, until around the year 1000 and was heavily enforced from above. This created a new frame within which to understand conflicts. They could now also be expressed as religious differences.

As early as the eleventh century, Schleswig became the starting point for religious wars against those Slavs in Holstein or further east who were pagans. Christian Slavs worked together with Danes, and the local rulers'

---

7. Jensen: *Danmarks oldtid*, 4, pp. 244-250.
8. Reimer Hansen: "Deutschlands Nordgrenze," in *Deutschlands Grenzen in der Geschichte*, ed. Alexander Demant, München 1990, pp. 89-133.

choice of religion was often influenced by the prospects of strong alliances. Wars were fought with great cruelty, if we are to believe the Christian reports about them, and the borderland became a martyr-producing area.[9] With the general European crusading movement after 1100, the religious wars became better organised and more sharply defined ideologically, and the religious warriors became part of a common European network.[10]

In the early twelfth century, the city of Schleswig was transformed into a holy city whose main church imitated the Holy Sepulchre in Jerusalem and whose inhabitants formed a religious confraternity, heavily armed and obliged to participate in regular raids against the heathens.[11] Duke Knud Lavard of Schleswig expanded his political power far into Slavic pagan areas and became apparently too powerful for the Danish king and was murdered in 1131.[12] Schleswig continued, however, to be the starting point for yearly crusades, which set out in the spring and raided the neighbouring pagan areas. In the 1180s, the pagan areas near to Schleswig and all along the coast to Mecklenburg were brought under the control of the Danish king, and the religious wars were fought further away from Schleswig. The area was no longer contested for religious reasons.

Royal appanage and royal contest

Schleswig became the appanage of the royal family from the beginning of the twelfth century and was held as a duchy by the eldest son while

---

9. Described vividly by Adam of Bremen (1070s) and Helmold of Bosau (1170s); Adami *Gesta Hammaburgensis ecclesiae pontificum*, ed. J. M. Lappenberg, Monumenta Germaniae historica Scriptores 8, Hannover 1876; Helmoldi presbyteri *Chronica Slavorum*, ed. G.H. Pertz, Hannover 1868.
10. Cf. Kurt Villads Jensen: *Korstog ved verdens yderste rand. Danmark og Portugal ca. 1000 til ca. 1250*, Odense 2011.
11. Christian Radtke: "Die Entwicklung der Stadt Schleswig: Funktionen, Strukturen und die Anfänge der Gemeindebildung," in *Die Stadt im westlichen Ostseeraum: Vorträge zur Stadtgründung und Stadterweiterung im hohen Mittelalter*, ed. Erich Hoffmann and Frank Lubowitz, Frankfurt a.M. 1995, pp. 47-91.
12. *The Offices and Masses of St. Knud Lavard*, reproduced in facsimile, transscribed and edited by John Bergsagel with an essay on the historical background by Thomas Riis, vol 1-2, Copenhagen 2010.

he waited to take over the throne. It was militarily important for the Danish kingdom as one of the two main routes towards the popular battle fields in Northern Germany (the other being by ship from the southern islands over the Baltic), but it was also located unpleasantly near German princes and strong independent cities with whom the rulers of Schleswig could ally themselves in possible struggles against their Danish king and overlord. It became dominant during the hundred years from c. 1250 till 1340.[13]

In 1250 King Erik Plovpenning was murdered in Schleswig, to all evidence at the instigation of his brother Duke Abel, who had already some years earlier declared himself king. Abel took over the throne in spite of general suspicion against him, but when he fell in battle in 1252, the third brother Christopher was elected king instead of Abel's son. This resulted in a prolonged struggle for power between the Abel-line and the Christopher-line of the dynasty in which the control over Schleswig became central.[14] The kings attempted to bind local, high-ranking barons to themselves through a personal oath of fidelity, the duke did the same but also allied with other princes such as the dukes of Rügen, the counts of Holstein, and the princes of Brandenburg. In a decisive battle at Lohede outside Slesvig in 1261, the young King Erik Glipping lost and was kept prisoner in Holstein for some time. When he was assassinated in 1286, the Duke of Schleswig succeeded in taking over control of most of the king's men in Schleswig and a substantial part of all royal income. In 1326, Count Gerhard of Holstein could muster enough support in Schleswig and among the Danish nobility to have the young Duke Valdemar of Schleswig elected King of Denmark instead of (another) Christopher, and a civil war followed. It was specified as a condition for the coronation of young Valdemar that Schleswig and the kingdom of Denmark should never be united under one ruler.[15] This became a point of dissent for centuries to come, but as a direct result of this clause, Valdemar abdicated

---

13. Bregnsbo and Jensen: *Det danske imperium*, pp. 39-46.
14. Kaj Hørby: *Status regni Dacie. Studier i Christofferlinjens ægteskabs- og alliancepolitik 1252-1319*, Copenhagen 1977.
15. Esben Albrectsen: "Var Sønderjylland i middelalderen en del af Danmarks Rige?", in *Historisk Tidsskrift* 15. Rk., 3, 1988, pp. 1-17.

as Duke of Schleswig and was succeeded by Gerhard, who now united Holstein and Schleswig under the authority of one single ruler.

In 1340 Gerhard was assassinated by an otherwise unknown Danish petty nobleman, and a marriage alliance reconciled the two lines of the royal family. In the future, counts of Holstein also held Schleswig as an inherited fief. Although the time of mighty and independent dukes of Schleswig was over, the situation was still complicated seen from the perspective of the Danish king, and other agents in the contest for control over the place were ready to intervene.

Schleswig in the Kalmar Union

In 1397, Denmark, Norway, and Sweden were united so that one person ruled over them all. The three kingdoms comprised Schleswig, Finland, substantial areas along the Baltic coast, and the North Atlantic isles including Greenland and Iceland. The king of these lands was also duke of Holstein and of Pomerania. The Kalmar Union became one of the mightiest political entities in Northern Europe, but the political status of Schleswig complicated the smooth governance of the union.

In some lands of the union, the regent inherited power, in others he was elected by the council of the kingdom. In Schleswig and Holstein, he had to be accepted by the local nobility, the *Ritterschaft*, which in the fifteenth century became more and more independent – of the king and of the duke. In 1409, Queen Margaret installed herself as regent on behalf of the young duke, and open war followed in which the king of Denmark's claim to be suzerain of Schleswig was openly disputed by the local nobility. A central element in these controversies was the legal systems. Should disputes about sovereignty be solved according to local, Danish or some kind of German law? In 1421, the Danish King Erik of Pomerania had a Danish provincial court decide that both the northern and the southern part of Schleswig and even some areas further south belonged under Danish law. One specific argument was that the local language and the juridical language was Danish, so for the first time language was used as a decisive political argument.

In the following decades, King Erik elevated the dispute over Schleswig to a higher level by appealing to the German-Roman emperor and claiming that the Holsteinian nobility had forfeited all rights to Schleswig by their rebellion against Queen Margaret. Another argument was that Denmark did not have fiefs at all, only provinces under the crown, so therefore counts of Holstein could not hold Schleswig as a fief. Although the emperor decided in favour of Erik, wars with the Holsteinians continued.

Political strength changed hastily in the middle of the fifteenth century, which internationally saw a prolonged struggle between two principles for government: from above or from below, *regimen regale* or *regimen politicum*.[16] Some argued that authority belonged to kings and dukes and counts, in this order, while others argued that it grew up from below and was expressed by the councils of nobles. In practice, much depended upon the relative strength of the kings versus the nobility. In 1448, the nobility pressed the new Danish king to confirm the agreement from 1326 that Schleswig should never become part of Denmark so that the same person would not rule over both areas – a clear example of regimen politicum. But in 1460, the same nobles elected the same king as count and duke and agreed that Schleswig and Holstein should be kept together forever and undivided.[17] In 1474, the emperor elevated Holstein from county to duchy and significantly enhanced the prestige of the Danish king – a clear example of regimen regale. It also led, however, to a complicated legal situation in which in the future the king of Denmark was to be elected by the nobility of Schleswig as duke, but confirmed by himself and therefore was his own vassal. In Holstein, he was appointed by the emperor as duke and had to be confirmed by the nobility and was as such vassal of the emperor, but independent in relation to the Danish royal councils. This situation became even more muddled when in 1481 two brothers were elected or appointed as dukes of both Schleswig and

---

16. Nicolai Rubenstein: "The history of the word *politicus* in early-modern Europe", in *The languages of political theory in early-modern Europe*, ed. Anthony Pagden, Cambridge 1987, pp. 41-56. For the use of these concepts for the Kalmar Union, see Erik Lönnroth: *Sverige och Kalmarunionen 1397-1457*, Göteborg 1934.
17. Carsten Jahnke: "'"dat se bliven ewich tosamende ungedelt". Neue Überlegungen zu einem alten Schlagwort,"in *Zeitschrift der Gesellschaft für schleswig-holsteinische Geschichte* 128, 2003, pp. 45-59.

Holstein and divided the duchies into minor areas, so they both had authority over some land in both areas.

Shared ducal authority

The main reason for this subdivision of Schleswig was a recurrent problem in princely circles in early modern times: how to support younger sons of a king and their sons again in a manner consistent with their station. Within the kingdom of Denmark, territorial subdivisions in that respect were – as mentioned – out of the question, whereas in the duchies of Schleswig and Holstein, where the legal, administrative and social structures were different from the ones in the kingdom, subdivisions were a possibility. Thus, in 1490 the duchies were subdivided between King Hans and his brother Duke Frederick. In 1544, another subdivision took place between King Christian III and his two half-brothers Duke Hans (the Elder) and Duke Adolphus and further subdivisions later took place between the sons of the dukes in question (apart from Hans the Elder, who died childless), and in 1581-1582 another subdivision took place between King Frederick II and his brother Hans (the Younger). The background for all this was, as mentioned, the need to support younger sons of kings, and what was divided was the ducal authority and the revenues of those areas divided between the princes in question. In order that each duke would get approximately the same share of the revenues, their respective, allocated territories were scattered criss-cross with areas in both of the duchies. Yet, Schleswig and Holstein remained two and only two duchies, only the ducal authority and the revenues were shared by more than one prince. Apart from this there were areas of the duchies ruled jointly by the sharing dukes. At the division of 1581-1582, it was stipulated that Duke Hans (the Younger) be allocated the revenues, yet not be given any say in the joint ducal government. Thus, even if he maintained some ducal rights, he was in many respects merely a landlord, yet one with extraordinary resources.

The local nobility jealously ensured that these subdivisions did not develop into several small sovereign duchies. And all the dukes were dukes of Schleswig and of Holstein. However, in order to distinguish the individual dukes and their families from each other they were often referred to by the name of the castle in which they were residing, for instance, the family of Duke Adolphus was named after the castle of Gottorp outside the city of Schleswig. Despite the attitudes of the nobility, the dukes tried to act as independent princes as much as possible, among other things by creating palaces and courts that might contribute to forming such an impression. In 1608, Duke Johan Adolphus of the Gottorp family line managed to introduce the right of primogeniture within his allocated territories thus preventing their further subdivision between his sons and their sons, etc.

Certainly, these scattered ducal territories and the shared or joint ducal authorities seem confusing, and studies on a micro level of how this system worked in practice in the daily life of the population of the duchies are needed. However, the dukes were not sovereign rulers but were sharing the ducal authority, and all of the dukes in Schleswig were vassals of the king of Denmark and the king of Denmark in his capacity as duke of Schleswig was thus a vassal of himself in his capacity as king of Denmark. In Holstein, the dukes were vassals of the German emperor. Furthermore, the duchies and the kingdom of Denmark constituted a defence union with a common foreign policy. Thus, even if the king of Denmark was only controlling those areas indirectly, their belonging to the composite Danish state was not put into question by these subdivisions.[18]

A hostile, sovereign duke: the Gottorp problem ca. 1625 till 1773

One of the ducal families, the one residing at Gottorp, felt let down by King Christian IV, who allegedly put the interests of himself and his children before those of the Gottorps, whose overlord he was. During the wars of Christian IV, the Gottorps had experienced that their overlord

---

18. Bregnsbo & Jensen: *Det danske imperium*, p. 120ff.; Gregersen: *Slesvig og Holsten*, s. 254-312; Gottfried Ernst Hoffmann & Klauspeter Reumann in Klose (ed): *Geschichte Schleswig-Holsteins*, bd. 5, pp. 1-200; Carsten Porskrog Rasmussen in Hans Schultz Hansen et al. (ed): *Sønderjyllands historie*, bd. 1, pp. 187-234; Carsten Porskrog Rasmussen, Inge Adriansen & Lennart S. Madsen (eds): *De slesvigske hertuger*, Aabenraa 2005.

and co-duke was unable to safeguard the Gottorp territories and their security. On the contrary, they were on several occasions occupied and pillaged by enemy troops. As a consequence of these experiences, the Gottorps actively joined sides with the Swedes during the Dano-Swedish War from 1657 to 1658 and were rewarded at the peace of Roskilde in 1658: they were released from their oath to their overlord, the king of Denmark and thus obtained sovereignty, but, only within their Schleswigian areas, whereas in the Holsteinian areas they were still subject to the German emperor as their overlord.

The Gottorp duke had thus been made an independent prince. His Schleswigian territories were situated inside the Danish state, and the king of Denmark now had a hostile state, allied with his Swedish enemy, inside his state. Certainly, the Gottorp territories were small, scattered and militarily weak in comparison with the Danish state. However, the problem as seen from the point of view of the king of Denmark was that the Gottorps were allied with and had married into the royal family of Sweden (and later into the Russian imperial house) and consequently, any one-sided military action from the Danish side against the Gottorps would immediately lead to serious diplomatic and military consequences against Denmark, not only from Sweden but from European great powers as well. Indeed, during the last decades of the 17th century, Denmark tried to solve the problem through military action several times. Militarily, the Gottorp territories could relatively easily be seized; however, international pressure each time forced Denmark to abandon these military actions and restore status quo ante. Thus, this sovereign and hostile duchy within the Danish state posed a most serious security problem for Denmark, a problem that she could not solve by herself.

It had to be solved slowly and through international agreements. After the Great Nordic War, where the Gottorp state once again sided with Sweden and thus was dragged down by her defeat, the Gottorp parts of the duchy of Schleswig (but not those of Holstein) were incorporated under "the crown of Denmark" as it was formulated. However, not all powers recognised this arrangement and the Gottorp family itself most certainly did not. This became all the more a problem as the Gottorp family soon after married into the Russian imperial family. These problems developed into a catastrophe when the head of the Gottorps became emperor of Russia in 1762 as Peter III and firmly decided to use his resources as a Russian ruler to rectify the wrongs that his family had suffered at the hand of the Danes, including regaining the Gottorp parts of Schleswig. It almost came to a Dano-Russian war in 1762 but this was cancelled at the very last moment due to a coup in St. Petersburg, in which Peter III was deposed by his wife, who was declared ruling empress under the name of Catherine II. As she was interested in an alliance with a Denmark turned against Sweden, she held out the prospect of a treaty of exchange through which the king of Denmark was to get the Gottorp parts of Holstein in return for ceding the north German counties of Oldenburg and Delmenhorst, which had belonged to the Danish state and the Gottorp family since the 1670s. Furthermore, the Gottorps were to be compensated financially in other respects. After long and protracted negotiations, the exchange treaty was finally ratified in 1773 and a century-old Danish security problem was thus finally solved. Still, even if the king of Denmark had been awarded the areas in question, ambiguity and confusion concerning the dynastic rules of succession remained and became a problem during the first half of the 19th century, when the male line of the Danish royal house was dying out.[19]

The centralising, interfering unitary state and local reactions: ca. 1780 till ca. 1820

As should be clear by now already, Schleswig used to be a contested place due to dynastic conflicts and as we already know, later on, national antagonism became the apple of discord. However, a phase in between can

---

19. Bregnsbo & Jensen: *Det danske imperium*, p. 143f. & 150ff.; Johanne Skovgaard in la Cour (ed): *Sønderjyllands Historie*, vol. 2, pp. 345-388, vol. 3, p. 3-152, Holger Hjelholt in la Cour (ed): *Sønderjyllands Historie*, bd. 3, pp. 155-389; Gregersen: *Slesvig og Holsten*, pp. 350-378 & 389-421; Carsten Porskrog Rasmussen in Schultz Hansen m.fl. (eds): *Sønderjyllands Historie*, vol. 1, pp. 311-332 & Lars Henningsen: ibidem, pp. 333-345 & 395ff.; Hermann Kellenbenz in Klose (ed): *Geschichte Schleswig-Holsteins*, vol. 5, pp. 203-400 & Klose i Klose (ed): vol. 6, pp. 1-159; Mette Skougaard (ed): *Gottorp – et fyrstehof i 1600-tallet*, Copenhagen 2002; Porskrog Rasmussen et al. (ed): *De slesvigske hertuger*.

be identified. In the dynastic state, the king had endeavoured to obtain and maintain the sovereignty of the duchies and of all other territories of which the state consisted. However, the fact that the legal, political, administrative, social, and economic structures had been most heterogeneous and that ducal authority within the duchies could even be shared was not considered any major problem as long as the king's sovereignty was not endangered. The core of the Gottorp problem was that here it was indeed endangered. During the last decades of the 18th century this heterogeneity increasingly became a problem. The problem can be described as arising from Denmark's transition from a conglomerate state to a unitary state, to use the concepts of the Swedish historian Harald Gustafsson. A conglomerate state means a state consisting of several territories and which is kept together by the ruling dynasty and few other factors if any at all. Each territory or rather the elites within each territory have their own relation to the ruling monarch, their own laws, privileges and their own system of administration and justice. The opposite of the conglomerate state is the unitary state, where all parts of the state have the same relation to the power centre, and the same laws and administrative and legal structures apply within all territories of the state. A unitary state might be a nation-state, but need not be.[20] It will be argued here that the conditions in the duchies during the late 18th and early 19th centuries and the relationship between the duchies and the government in Copenhagen should be seen as an attempt to create a unitary state which was not yet a nation-state.

The endeavours towards achieving a unitary state began in 1721, when the Gottorp parts of Schleswig were allocated to "the crown of Denmark". Furthermore, during the 17th century many of the small dukes, descendants of some of the dukes at the various subdivisions during the 16th century, either went bankrupt with their estates or passed away leaving no offspring and thus, their territories returned to the Danish crown. This development was further speeded up by the exchange treaty of 1773.

---

20. Harald Gustafsson: "Conglomerate States or Unitary States? Integration Processes in early Modern Denmark-Norway and Sweden,"in Thomas Fröschl (ed): *Föderationsmodelle und Unionsstrukturen. Über Staatenverbindungen in der frühen Neuzeit vom 15. bis 18. Jahrhundert*, Vienna-Munich 1994 and "Gesamtstaat oder Konglomeratstaat? Schleswig in Dänemark-Norwegen im 18. Jahrhundert," in Becker-Christensen (ed): Geschichte Schleswigs.

During the 1780s and 1790s radical reforms were introduced within the kingdom of Denmark, the agricultural reforms liberating the peasantry from the landlords and modernising agriculture in general being the best known example of this. The government sought to extend such reforms to the duchies, which, however, produced difficulties. In the kingdom, royal absolutism had ruled since 1660, and here there were no assemblies of estates still less any group of noblemen who had any say at all in political affairs who could thus have blocked these reforms. In the duchies, things were quite different. Here, the nobility was well organised. Officially, the government in Copenhagen maintained that royal absolutism also ruled at least in Schleswig and denied that the local nobility had any say at all. In practice, however, it recognised the executive committee of the nobility of the duchies, *Die Fortwährige Deputation*, as a negotiating partner. And due to the fact that the local nobility, unlike their colleagues within the kingdom of Denmark, had strong privileges and as a result of the many specific and heterogeneous legislative and administrative structures within the duchies, it was not as straightforward introducing ambitious reform schemes here. Nonetheless, this was what the government tried to do when in 1802 it imposed a tax without previously consulting the Fortwährige Deputation and this led to bad feelings and a crisis. An outstanding Holsteinian aristocrat who was a member of the government in Copenhagen, Cay Reventlow, chose to step down from his post in resentment.

When the Holy Roman Empire was dissolved in 1806 due to the Napoleonic Wars, the king of Denmark was declared master of the duchy of Holstein. As expressed in the official document: *"Mit dem gesammten Staatskörper der Unserm Königl. Scepter untergebenen Monarchie, als ein in jeder Beziehung völlig ungetrennter Theil derselben verbunden"*,[21] i.e. "As an in every respect fully inseparable part of the complete body politic of the monarchy that is subjected under our royal sceptre". One might assume that it was only meant as an act of bitter necessity on the part

---

21. Michael Bregnsbo: "Die Einverleibung Holsteins im Jahre 1806 und die dänische Reaktion auf die Auflösung des Alten Reiches," in Michael North & Robert Riemer (eds): *Das Ende des Alten Reiches im Ostseeraum. Wahrnehmungen und Transformationen*, Köln 2008; Christian Degn in Klose (Hg.): *Geschichte Schleswig-Holsteins*, vol. 6, pp. 297-302.

of the Danes in order to secure control of Holstein, which had been left politically masterless in consequence of the dissolution of the German Empire. Looking at the policy that was implemented in Holstein after 1806, however, it seems clear that the intention was more than to merely secure Holstein for the Danish state. Already before 1806 there had been endeavours on the part of the government to make Holstein part of the unitary state, but this had met with opposition and difficulties. However, after the king had become the master and sovereign of Holstein, this policy of centralisation could now be carried out. Thus, in 1807 it was decided that new laws for the duchies should be formulated both in Danish and German and that applicants for public offices in Holstein where Danish was not spoken should in their applications declare whether they had knowledge of the Danish language or not. The establishment of a chair in Danish language at the University of Kiel in 1811 should be seen in the same light. Further measures in order to strengthen the position of the Danish language within the duchy of Schleswig were considered, yet not implemented. The military academy in Rendsburg was closed; Holsteiners who wanted to become officers now had to go to the military academy in Copenhagen. Till then, both duchies had been administered from the German Chancery in Copenhagen, which was now renamed Schleswig-Holsteinian Chancery and appointed with a native Dane as head of it. If a Holsteiner from now on identified himself as German, it was considered unpatriotic. Certainly, these measures were merely tentative and by no means led to a unitary state. A harmonisation of the constitutional, legal, administrative, and social structures between the Kingdom of Denmark and the duchies of Schleswig and Holstein with the introduction of a single central bank with a single currency in 1813 was the exception that proved the rule. Still, the various, however tentative, homogenising measures caused resentment and irritation within the duchies. It is tempting to see this development as the beginning of nationalism, but this is probably too early in the day. Rather, it should be interpreted as the interference of the centralising unitary state encroaching on existing and centuries-old well-established privileges and structures. It was the nobility, not the population in general, that protested, and the reason for the dislike of a native Danish head of the Schleswig-Holsteinian Chancery was not that he was a Dane, but that unlike normal practice the head of the chancery was not a member of the Schleswig-Holsteinian nobility.[22]

Nationalism and/or historical legitimism: ca. 1820-1955

Even if antagonisms of the late 18th century and during the Napoleonic Wars should not be interpreted as national, there is no doubt that later during the 19th century national tensions and antagonisms between the Danish and the Germans within the duchies certainly emerged. However, things were perhaps not that simple after all. The problem was that both sides of this nationality conflict were stuck in historical-legitimistic ways of thinking from the age of the dynastic, conglomerate state. In the argumentation on the German (or rather Schleswig-Holsteinian) side, the Ribe Treaty of 1460, which stated that the two duchies should remain "up ewich tosammende ungedeelt" (undivided for all time), was invoked, whereas on the Danish side it was maintained that the duchy of Schleswig was not and had never been a member of the German Empire or the German Federation, but was an originally Danish territory. The problem was that the population of Schleswig was linguistically divided: to the north overwhelmingly Danish, in the middle mixed but with the German language in the offensive, and in the south overwhelmingly German. The logical solution would have been to divide Schleswig along linguistic lines, but historical-legitimistic ways of thinking were too much ingrained on both sides and their nationalism was too inconsistent to opt for such a solution. Certainly, the idea of partitioning Schleswig was discussed during the wars of 1848-1850 and 1864, but when the German side was in the defensive and suggested a partition as a solution, the Danes said no and vice versa. It must, however, be emphasised that partition in accordance with the nationality principle would not have been that simple, since it would have meant that existing

---

22. Bregnsbo & Jensen: *Det danske imperium*, pp. 159-162; Holger Hjelholt og Johanne Skovgaard in la Cour et al. (eds): *Sønderjyllands Historie*, vol. 3, pp. 390-484 and vol. 4, p. 1-92; Gregersen: *Slesvig og Holsten*, pp. 422-465; Christian Degn in Klose (ed): *Geschichte Schleswig-Holsteins*, vol. 6, pp. 163-398.

economic, commercial, individual and family ties traversing the national differences would thus have been cut.

That it was more than merely a nationality conflict can also be seen from the fact that dynastic interests were strongly involved. By the 1830s it seemed clear that the male line of the Danish royal family would die out with Prince Frederick (later Frederick VII), which was indeed what later happened. The problem was that the rules of succession in the kingdom and in Holstein were not the same, and there was no agreement on which rules of succession applied in Schleswig. Thus, the integrity of the state was threatened. The Augustenburg family, a ducal family descending from Duke Hans the Younger with no inherited political rights, considered itself to be entitled to succeed in both Holstein and Schleswig and maybe even in the kingdom, something which was not recognised and was considered unacceptable on the Danish side. True to their convictions, the Augustenburgs placed themselves at the head of the Schleswig-Holsteinist separatist movement that emerged in 1848, and shortly afterwards it came to an armed conflict between the kingdom of Denmark and the Schleswig-Holsteinist separatists. The latter wanted to secede from the Danish state and wanted Schleswig to also join the German Federation and the new central German state which was being planned, something that was totally unacceptable from a Danish point of view, due to both the historical-legitimistic status of Schleswig and the fact that a large part of her population was Danish-minded.

Both within the kingdom and within the duchies the national antagonisms tended to overshadow the traditional political, ideological and social antagonisms in 1848 – at least for a while. In March 1848, new governments were formed both in Copenhagen and in Kiel, and both governments were broadly composed coalitions of conservative aristocrats, bourgeois liberals and left-wing democrats. For instance, the brother of the Augustenburg duke, Prince Frederick of Nør, became a member of the Schleswig-Holsteinian ministry. Almost everywhere else in Europe of 1848, aristocrats, conservatives, liberals and democrats stood fiercely against each other and were bitter and irreconcilable enemies, but both in the kingdom of Denmark and in Schleswig-Holstein they sat in the government together.

The armed conflict between 1848-1850 (which should rightly be seen as a civil war within the Danish state, in which the Schleswig-Holsteinian side was supported by the German Federation) did not solve the problems. The great powers interfered and dictated that the Danish state from before the civil war should be re-established in order to avoid the valuable naval harbour of Kiel coming under Prussian control. The 1850s were characterised by attempts to create a single constitution for both the kingdom and the duchies. It was not the intention to create a fully developed unitary state. However, the single constitution was intended as an umbrella over the separate political entities consisting of the Kingdom of Denmark and the duchies of Schleswig, Holstein and Lauenburg respectively. It could be compared with a federal state where the single constitution was the federal constitution and the kingdom and the duchies were the member states. These efforts did not succeed, however, due to mutual distrust and bitterness and negativity from Schleswig-Holstein and the German federation. In 1863, the Danish government and public lost patience and decided to incorporate Schleswig in the kingdom and separate out Holstein and the small duchy of Lauenburg. This was clearly against international agreements and led to the Danish defeat in the war of 1864, with Denmark having to cede Schleswig, Holstein and Lauenburg. The defeat was a trauma of far-reaching impact for Denmark.

After 1864 a Danish minority in Schleswig lived under German rule but felt Danish and wanted to be under Denmark. This eventuated 56 years later in 1920 as part of the Versailles Treaty. A plebiscite was implemented and the northern part of Schleswig, where there was a clear Danish majority, was turned over to Denmark. This event is usually called The Reunification (in Danish: Genforeningen), but it would be more correct to call it the incorporation of Northern Schleswig into the kingdom of Denmark. As Schleswig had not formerly been part of the kingdom, it was not really a *re*unification. The Reunification meant recognition of the nationality principle and the right to self-determination. Still, there was bad feeling, as the plebiscite meant that there would from then on be national minorities on both sides of the border, the Danish minority south of the border being by far the larger one. Furthermore, the fairness of the principles concerning those who had been entitled to vote in the plebiscite were called into question and cases of alleged favouritism on both sides were pointed out. Add to this that there were those who spoke in favour of some kind of home-rule for Northern Schleswig/Southern Jutland in order to respect that the area had never been an ordinary Danish province before. What is more, the principle of historical legitimism had not died out as there were voices that spoke in favour of Denmark's legitimate right to the whole of Schleswig, irrespective of the opinions of the population there.

After the Nazis came to power in Germany in 1933, there was growing fear in Denmark that the German government would demand a revision of the Versailles Treaty for Schleswig as well. This, it did not do, not even during the German occupation of Denmark from 1940 to 1945. Even immediately after 1945 voices were raised in Denmark about Denmark's historical right to the whole of Schleswig. Furthermore, there was fear concerning the fate of the Danish minority, as the population of Schleswig-Holstein strongly increased with refugees from the eastern parts of Germany now under Soviet or Polish rule, thus decreasing the percentage of the population of Schleswig identifying itself as Danish.[23]

From separate, national identities towards a common regional identity: 1955-

The minority problems in the Dano-German borderland found a durable solution in the Copenhagen-Bonn declarations of 1955. This arrangement was a Danish desire (but not an outright condition) and it was considered that it would make Danish acceptance of the Federal Republic of Germany joining the NATO alliance easier. It was expressly not a Dano-German treaty, but two unilateral (yet in practice coordinated in advance) governmental declarations, each one later passed by

---

23. Bregnsbo & Jensen: *Det danske imperium*, pp. 173-190, pp. 192-199, pp. 209-218; Knud Fabricius and Hans Lund in la Cour (ed): *Sønderjyllands Historie*, vol. 4, pp. 93-512 and vol. 5, pp. 3-304; Schultz Hansen et al. (eds): *Sønderjyllands historie*, vol. 2; Alexaner Scharff, Oswald Hauser, Jürgen Hartwig Ibs, Kai Detlev Sievers and Erich Hoffmann in Klose (ed): *Geschichte Schleswig-Holsteins*, vol. 7, pp. 3-155, vol. 8, part 1, pp. 1-124 & 125-198, vol. 8, part 2, pp. 1-198 and 199-335; Rerup: *Slesvig og Holsten*.

the respective national parliaments, aimed at recognising the minorities within their own states and committing themselves to securing their rights and privileges. Thus, the Danish declaration was about the rights and privileges of the German minority in Denmark, and the German one about the Danish minority in Germany. Formally seen, the declarations were not mutually binding but in practice they soon became so. Thus, a centuries-old, bitter and traumatic nationality conflict had been efficiently dismantled and historical legitimism as a valid political argument was made null and void.[24]

During recent decades, the political party of the Danish minority within the German Land Schleswig-Holstein, SSW (in German: Südschleswigscher Wählerverein, in Danish: Sydslesvigsk Vælgerforening) has enjoyed increasing success, also among German-minded voters outside the Danish minority, and has even begun to establish itself in Holstein, where there is no Danish minority worth speaking of and where the SSW does not even nominate candidates within the constituencies or do any electioneering. Thus, in 2011 the largest city of Schleswig, Flensburg, for the first time instated a mayor belonging to the SSW, and the general election in Schleswig-Holstein in May 2012 resulted in a coalition government between the Social Democrats, the Green Party and the SSW, with the latter being represented for the first time ever with one member. There are, of course, many reasons for this electoral behaviour. It hardly means that more and more citizens of Schleswig-Holstein want to be part of Denmark, but it may have been a form of protest against the established federal-wide parties, a show of sympathy for particular candidates or expression of agreement on specific political issues (e.g. the liberal Danish educational tradition). The SSW is increasingly stressing itself as being a Scandinavian-oriented, regional party intent on furthering regional economic, social, health care, educational and cultural interests across national divisions, while at the same time emphasising the fact that Schleswig and Holstein used to be duchies under the king of Denmark

---

24. Bregnsbo & Jensen: *Det danske imperium*, p. 216ff.; Schultz Hansen et al. (eds): *Sønderjyllands historie*, vol. 2; Lars N. Henningsen (ed): *Zwischen Grenzkonflikt und Grenzfrieden. Die dänische Minderheit in Schleswig-Holstein in Geschichte und Gegenwart*, Flensburg 2011; Thaler: *Of Mind and Matter*.

and that the population of Schleswig and even Holstein thus have a common identity, history and heritage.[25] So perhaps the identity of the SSW as a regional party in contrast to the federal-wide established parties is one of the important reasons for its electoral success.

Indeed, a kindred development can be seen for *Slesvigsk Parti*, the party of the German minority in Denmark. Since 2006, Southern Jutland is no longer an independent administrative unit but has been merged together with Funen and Vejle Amt to form The Southern Danish Region. In Southern Jutland, this has partly caused fear of obliteration of the special southern Jutish identity and heritage and fear that the financial, educational, economic, health care and transport needs of Southern Jutland will not be properly and sufficiently considered by the Southern Danish Region. Just like the SSW south of the border, the *Slesvigsk Parti* has begun to identify itself and campaign as a regional party emphasising the common identity and cultural heritage of the Southern Jutish population, even characterising itself as a "bulwark for the Southern Jutish identity".[26]

---

25. http://ssw.de (June 18th 2012).
26. The newspaper *Jydske Vestkysten* 16 November, 2009. Furthermore: www.slesvigsk-parti.dk. This by no means suggests that national tensions and disagreements in Southern Jutland/ Schleswig have vanished completely. In 1997, the creation of a Euroregion Schleswig by the local political authorities on both sides of the border in order to further closer regional cooperation and integration caused a great public outcry north of the border and among Danish-minded (Southern) Schleswigers. The name of this project consequently had to be changed from "Euroregion Schleswig/Slesvig" to "Euroregion Sønderjylland/Schleswig" (Southern Jutland/Schleswig) in order not to hurt Danish feelings too much. Still, this project was eventually established and has developed peacefully and harmoniously ever since. The original opposition to the Euroregion was probably due rather to scepticism towards the high-flown declarations and large-scale plans initiated politically in a top-down way, which in some respects characterises the way the project evolved during the initial phase. After it had been established, however, it concentrated its activities on practical projects initiated and grown from below, the use of which is clear and obvious for almost everyone. Cp. Martin Klatt: *Fra medspil til modspil? Grænseoverskridende samarbejde i Sønderjylland/Schleswig 1945-2005*, Aabenraa 2006. As late as in 2011 at the annual marking of the Danish defeat at Dybbøl in the war of 1864, the fact that *armed* German military representatives participated in the ceremonies for the first time caused protest and debate in the media. Still, such protests only seem to be raised when what is seen as emotionally charged symbols of the former nationality conflicts are felt to be violated. On the practical, down-to-earth, daily-life level, Southern Jutland/Schleswig is no longer a nationally contested place.

Conclusion

Over more than a thousand years, Schleswig and Holstein have either together or separately been contested areas. However, as can be seen from the chapter, the reasons for the areas being contested have at different times been motivated by different conditions and factors: economic, political, religious, feudal, and dynastic factors, as well as sovereignty and national issues, but the latter now seem inclined to develop into a move toward regionalism across the nationalities.

Finally one could share the take of the American literary historian Hayden White and characterise the history of Schleswig as a comedy, meaning a narrative where the antagonisms and conflicts are finally dissolved in the end.[27] In other words: a story with a happy ending. Maybe. But one could also argue that new antagonisms have arisen, namely between centre and periphery, or between the capital of Copenhagen and Periphery-Denmark (Udkantsdanmark is the expression in Danish) and possible antagonisms of a similar kind on the German side. In the same way as political, ideological and social antagonisms were being overshadowed by the national ones in 1848, today it is perhaps the case that a common regional identity is overshadowing old national identities.

---

27. Hayden White: "Historical Emplotment and the Problem of Truth," in Saul Friedlander (ed): *Probing the Limits of Representation*, Cambridge, Mass. 1992.

Enclaves as Contested Places

Per Grau Møller

"Borders" is used as a word to indicate areas situated between something. Normally, boundaries will distinguish these areas of interest for different nations, institutions, organisations or owners. The interests may be of different kinds: national-political interests, property rights, social and/or cultural traditions. In particular the concepts of national-political interests and property rights need a solid demarcation in space as a boundary of the interests. Posts in the soil, ditches and/or dikes may visualise the boundary very solidly. Boundaries of norms and cultural traditions do not need such solid manifestations and are traditionally not a problem for the population but more of a problem for researchers to register and gain a grasp of this landscape.

Even if borders do have different meanings, and even if boundaries may be solid or do not exist, borders may be contested. The interests lying behind may cause great clashes between different people belonging to nations or cultural 'groups'. The clashes may range from intellectual debates to militant wars.

Another principal issue approached in this paper is the place-space relation. Place is traditionally a spot of specific interests, 'defined in part by the existence and value of insiders, landscape being regarded as the environment perceived and place consisting in part of social networks'.[1] In line with this definition, the European landscape convention defines landscape as 'an area, as perceived by people, whose character is the result of the action and interaction of natural and/or human factors' (European

---

1. Richard Muir: *Approaches to Landscape*, Hampshire 1999, p. 271.

council 2000).[2] Historical research has traditionally focused on places in a wider sense, where specific people are living and acting. In contrast not much focus has been placed on space and the total aspects of landscape surrounding specific people – except in specific landscape or local historical research.

The borders in focus in this paper are of a very special kind as they involve distinctions based on feudal property rights being developed into borders of national-cultural character. It deals with the so-called Enclaves in the Duchy of Schleswig (or South Jutland), also named 'mixed districts'. They existed until 1864, when Denmark lost the war against Prussia-Austria and as a peace condition had to give up most of the duchy to Prussia, later the German Empire, which by one stroke solved the complicated situation of the enclaves. The existence of the enclaves is well known in historical research and taken for granted as a historical idiosyncrasy. The traditional reasons behind their existence are mentioned, but the implication of their later existence has not been investigated, and they are not conceived of as contested areas.[3] This chapter will investigate whether the place or space dimension is needed to explain why this phenomenon was constructed, and whether the time dimension is necessary to explain why the problems connected with the enclaves accelerated and made them even more contested.

---

2. *European Council. Landscape Convention of 2000* http://conventions.coe.int/Treaty/en/Treaties/Html/176.htm (July 30, 2012).
3. Carsten Porskrog Rasmussen in Schultz Hansen, Hans et al. (ed.): *Sønderjyllands historie* vol. 1-2, Aabenraa 2008-09, vol. 1, 2008 p. 198.
   Johanne Skovgaard in La Cour, V. et al. (ed.): *Sønderjyllands historie – fremstillet for det danske folk*, vol. 1-5, Copenhagen 1930-43, vol. 2 1937-39 p. 355.
   Gerret Liebing Schlaber: *Hertugdømmet Slesvigs forvaltning. Administrative strukturer og retspleje mellem Ejderen og Kongeåen ca. 1460-1864*, vol. 1-2, Studieafdelingen ved Dansk Centralbibliotek for Sydslesvig, Flensborg 2007 p. 16, 51.
   Gerret Liebing Schlaber in Adriansen, Inge et al. (eds): *Sønderjylland A-Å*, Historisk Samfund for Sønderjylland 2011, pp. 94-95.

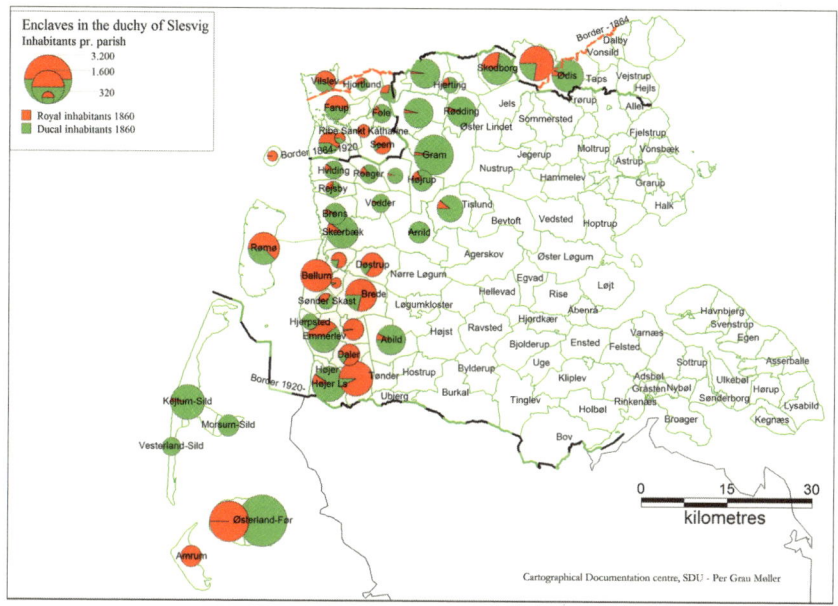

Figure 1 shows a map of the Enclaves illustrated as the share of population of the total number of people in the parishes in South Jutland. The map reflects the situation around 1860 at the end of their existence, and they are situated in the north-western part of Schleswig and in the part of the duchy that after 1920 became part of the Danish state. Included in the map are the islands of Amrum, Föhr, Sylt in the Wadden Sea, of which the whole of Amrum, the western part of Föhr and the Northern part of Sylt belonged to the Enclaves (these islands today belong to Germany). (Source: Trap, J.P. Statistisktopografisk Beskrivelse af Hertugdømmet Slesvig, Copenhagen 1864, vol. 1-2)

The origin of the Enclaves

The origin of the mixed districts derives from estates belonging to the Bishop of Ribe or the Chapter of Ribe. The bishop had his seat in the town of Ribe, which traditionally belonged to the kingdom of Denmark, even if it was actually an enclave in itself in the Duchy of Sønderjylland/Slesvig (Schleswig). Most of the diocese was therefore located to the north of the town and the cathedral. The kingdom played a special role in the development of this particular property relationship, as in the year 1407 Queen Margrethe I acquired the estate Trøjborg near Tønder from the Limbek family and gave it as lien to the Bishop of Ribe, who also owned the other powerful estate near Tønder called Møgeltønderhus. Her interest in this area must be seen as an endeavour to get a strong foothold against the Holsteinian dukes in Schleswig in their contest of the Duchy of Schleswig. Moreover in the year of reformation, 1536, the belongings of the bishop, like other clerical possessions, passed over to the kingdom, which thereafter was in charge of the estate, whether it was situated north or south of the Kongeåen, which was the traditional boundary between the kingdom and the Duchy of Schleswig.

Another aspect may be in focus when looking at the islands in the Wadden Sea. Traditionally all or part of them had belonged to the Danish king. The reason why the islands (or part of them) and areas near the coast (long before these areas were reclaimed) were of such great interest to the king may be because strategic interests were connected to them. These interests were not so much military-political, but rather economic-political from the point of view of taxation of trade and shipping.[4] In the medieval period the areas were therefore highly contested.

The implication of the Enclaves

Generally, a landowner in a feudal society had specific rights to his tenants. These rights were of economic, social and judicial character. The peasant had to pay rent to his landowner and probably do villeinage on his farm; the peasant had to obey his landowner in all essential relations. And the peasant might be subject to the district court of the landowner (birketing), if the latter was allowed to establish one, appoint the judge, set the judicial norms among his tenants, and keep the fines eventually imposed on his tenants. The alternative was to use the local district court. This means that peasants in a village involved in the same open field system of a village might belong to different landowners and therefore be subject to different economic, social and judicial treatment, as their relationship to the landlord determined.

---

4. N.H. Jacobsen: "De gamle kongerigske enklavers oprindelse," in *Geografisk Tidsskrift*, 41, 1938. 171-89, here p. 177ff.

The question of the right to establish a special court (birketing) was complicated and closely connected to the type of landowner. The king naturally had special rights and could establish such courts where appropriate. Likewise the church and its institutions (monasteries) had this right and many of these courts passed to the kingdom when the reformation abolished the clerical estate. This was valid in both the kingdom and the Duchy of Schleswig. Concerning the noblemen, it seems that they were not given the right to establish their own courts unless they acquired an estate from either of the two parties mentioned or they had personal privileges. But in the Duchy of Schleswig (and Holstein) this right was given as a general right to noblemen in 1524, earlier than in the kingdom. In the county of Holstein, which was a fief under the German emperor, the noblemen had more privileges than in the kingdom, including the Duchy of Schleswig; this also included the right to establish a court for their peasants.[5]

The right of 1524 to establish an individual court had a special importance when the estate was big, and included numerous tenants who were located close to the estate. For most of the noblemen in Schleswig this was seldom the case, except in the south eastern part where noblemen of Holstein origin had established large estates as in Holstein. In the kingdom of Denmark (north of Kongeåen) such large estates were generally established after the law of 1671, which gave special privileges to counts and encouraged the establishment of large estates.

Besides judicial and temporal matters, peasants were also involved in ecclesiastical issues like payment of tithe, general church matters – and when developed, matters of schooling and charity (which were matters of the church). To make things complex the temporal and ecclesiastical lines of jurisdiction did not necessarily comply with each other. This means that if a peasant belonged to the enclave and the kingdom in temporal cases, he might be a subject of the Diocese of Schleswig and its jurisdiction in ecclesiastical questions, and by the same token, in temporal cases be subject to the duke and in ecclesiastical questions to the Danish bishop

---

5.   Henrik Lerdam: *Birk, lov og ret. Birkerettens historie i Danmark indtil 1600*, Copenhagen 2004, p. 61 ff.

(in Ribe).[6] Nielsen claims that the physical location of the church was the reason behind the differentiation between being subject to either ducal or royal church legislation.

In 1576 it became apparent that things had become too complicated, so negotiations took place in Kolding between delegations from King Frederick II and the Duke of Gottorp, Johannes Rantzau representing the duchy. One of the issues was peasants around Ribe formerly belonging to the bishop and now to the king and the county of Ribe: where did they have to go to court – at a special birketing situated in Ribe? The resolution was made that the royal peasants in this area had to go to court in line with the other peasants in the area, namely the local district court, even if it was under ducal legislation and rules. This was in contrast to the areas around Trøjborg and Møgeltønderhus (near Tønder) where there was a specific court (birketing) to solve issues for peasants belonging to the king, namely the district court of Lø (Lø herredsting).

In the case of the enclaves, judicial relations became even more complicated. In the beginning the overall legislation was the same in the whole of Jutland (including South Jutland or Schleswig), namely a regional set of laws called Jyske Lov, which was in place, whether a peasant belonged to the kingdom or to the duchy. But this changed in 1683, when a new central law codex was introduced in the kingdom by King Christian V, called the Danish Law (Danske Lov); in the duchy the medieval Jyske Lov was still in use – and in Holstein the German-inspired Sachsenspiegel. This meant that judicial elements might be different and of some importance.

In any case, the landowners took care of their peasants and the resolution of 1576 showed that this was a matter of great importance to them. Concerning peasants in the enclaves, the relationship between the landowner and the peasant was not a strong relationship involving much or strong villeinage and did not develop into one. They generally lived in a formal copyhold relationship, which involved paying the annual fees and duties and submitting them to the court of the landowner. But in several ways the situation of their peasants was more like that of freeholders.

What did all this mean to the peasants in their daily life? A peasant

---

6. M. H. Nielsen: "De kongerigske Enklaver," in *Fra Ribe Amt* 5, 1922, pp. 485-551 here p. 516 f.

would normally live in a village and belong to an open field system – this system operated independently from the landowners of the peasants (except that big estates might standardise the village statutes in a bigger area[7]) – the peasants had their own internal organisation deciding on cultivation matters and conviction of fines in smaller cases. When the peasant had to pay his rents to the landowner he had to go to his specific owner once a year and deliver money and/or goods. This organisation might be in a town, as in the case of Ribe, and might guide the peasants of this specific landowner to go to the market of this town, perhaps in contrast to other peasants.

Going to court was a decisive event distinguishing peasants of the enclaves from the others. But how often was a peasant brought to court? Maybe once in a lifetime, on average? This means that the importance of the enclaves was limited in daily life.

Another question is whether different courts might produce different results. Only few investigations have tried to solve this problem, and none is exactly suitable for the case of the enclaves. In a comparison between two noblemen's courts (Tåsinge and Skjoldnæsholm, both in eastern Denmark) and the court of the royal estate of Falster, the result is that there are differences and that particularly the role of the noblemen in specific cases may have been decisive (Johansen 2009). Generally, there is a humorous saying which probably contains a grain of truth, at least in the conception of people: "Thank god, my son, said the woman, that you were not convicted at the court of Ribe" – when she saw him hanging in the gallows of Varde at Tinghøj.[8] This kind of black humour might actually indicate that the courts were handing down different convictions for similar crimes – and in this case it is the court of Ribe which is seen as the harsher court.

Another matter of importance for historians who want to investigate the resulting complexity of issues in areas where the enclaves were active is that original sources have to be found in the respective files of

---

7. Martin Rheinheimer: *Die Dorfordnungen des Herzogtums Schleswig*, vol. 1-2. Quellen und Forschungen zur Agrargeschichte 46/1, Stuttgart 1999, here vol. 1 p. 183ff.
8. E.g. *Ordbog over det danske sprog* – see "hænge 1.3": http://ordnet.dk/ods/ordbog?query=-h%C3%A6nge (January 26, 2013).

the landowners or of district courts. This may in practice also mean that the files of one landowner may have been preserved, but not for another, which makes it difficult to complete regional studies. To facilitate the heuristic process of finding files of specific areas the project DIGDAG (Digitalisation of Danish Administrative Geography) has been established by the Danish National Archive in cooperation with other research institutions.[9] The enclaves are one parameter involved in the database of the project.

As stated earlier the essential issue of the enclaves was the ownership of the peasant, whether he belonged to an owner in the kingdom (the bishop or the king) or was a tenant with an estate belonging to the duchy. During the time of the open field system, this relationship meant that the peasant with his rights, also in the open fields of the village, was central to understanding the use of landscape. One or several farms in the village had the status of belonging to the enclaves, but this was not marked in the fields of the village; only the position of the farms(s) in the settlement was 'highlighted'. Enclosure changed the conditions: enclosure was a redistribution of all land of a village with the aim of consolidating the areas of the farm in one place surrounding the farm. This meant in practice a territorialisation of the landholdings. Before enclosure it was a question of shares of the resources of the village – the number of individual cultivation fields or number of cattle to put on the common fields for grazing. When illustrating the possessions of peasants after enclosure, the distribution of the peasants' land in the enclaves shows a very complex picture – more complex than it really was before enclosure when the enclaves were established (see illustration in Figure 2). But the peasants were able to keep a record of their land both before and after enclosure – it is only more complex to external and later audiences. What was more complex was which court they had to go to when appropriate – or rather it was more complex for the officials to decide this. Officials on both sides often quarrelled, taking the side of their masters.[10]

---

9. See the homepage of the project http://www.digdag.dk/index.php?lang=en (July 30,2012).
10. Nielsen: "De kongerigske Enklaver," p. 517.

Figure 2. A map showing the village of Harrits (in the parish of Brede) and its nearest fields after enclosure. 8 farms are Danish (marked red) while 5 belong to the duchy (marked dark grey) and a corresponding number of smaller houses likewise. The buildings are mixed up in the village (before and after enclosure) and the land shows the mixed situation after enclosure in 1774. Parcels belonging to royal farms have a cadastre number, a figure of soil quality (scale 0-24) and a calculation of the area (the basis of the so-called "hartkorn tax" in corresponding books). Parcels belonging to duchy farms only say 'plovtaxt', meaning that they still had the traditional taxation based on the number of ploughs. The illustration is a selection of the village map from 1839, made due to the Danish land register of 1844 (© Kort- & Matrikelstyrelsen, København).

An instance of how complicated things were with different jurisdictions was the right for ducal peasants and citizens to negotiate in the royal town of Ribe, which was a privilege to citizens in royal towns.[11] In line with this, in 1747 it was reported that peasants belonging to the Duchy of Schleswig (county of Haderslev) negotiated and had booths quite close to Ribe, whereas there was a zone of two miles around towns in

---

11. Nielsen: "De kongerigske Enklaver," p. 518.

the kingdom forbidding this activity. Likewise in the same report royal peasants in the enclaves were not allowed to brew their own beer, keep an inn and so on – in contrast to ducal peasants. The town of Ribe wanted a solution to this problem, which came in 1769, also allowing royal peasants to brew their own beer and keep an inn; this solution was contrary to what the town had wanted.[12]

A specific annoyance to the local population and travellers was the question of roads and their maintenance – this was regulated by the landowner. If one peasant was asked to carry out road repairs while his neighbour belonging to another landowner was not, the result might be negative: the road was not repaired.[13]

Questions of property rights in relation to land and to rights to the resources were normally part of the functions of a village, but the special circumstance was that the peasants and their landowners might draw the rights from different legislations. As mentioned, the difference between temporal and ecclesiastical legislation and administration caused troubles for officials and the population even if attempts were made to solve these issues. A solution was found in 1721 when the Danish king became duke of the whole of Schleswig, but he still had a different status as king and duke, and this did not solve the question of the enclaves.

Solutions

Occasionally an attempt was made to find a solution to the complicated situation which the enclaves enforced on the inhabitants in the parishes. In 1798 a commission was established to try to establish clear lines, but it was so complicated that it was given up again; it was impossible to make a just solution to suit both parties – for instance part of the suggestion was that all the islands in the Wadden Sea should belong to the duchy and likewise the areas around Møgeltønder, both of which had a long tradition of belonging to the royal possessions. Again in the 1840s

---

12. Jørgen Mikkelsen: "Økonomi og erhverv 1660-1850," in Søren Bitsch Christensen (ed.) *Ribe Bys Historie* 2, Esbjerg 2010, pp. 219-247, here p. 228f.
13. Nielsen: "De kongerigske Enklaver," p. 520f.

attempts were made according to which the majority of the number of people in a parish should decide where to belong. But generally people were conservative and unwilling to give up their rights, and the project was given up.[14]

Again in the 1850s an attempt was made to find a solution. Things were developing, and within agricultural affairs different jurisdictions hindered solutions to problems of improving enclosure and regulating dams. In 1856 a commission was established, and an effort was made to draw up common laws on specific areas such as the police, commerce, roads, agriculture and municipality (the law of communes of 1841 was only valid in the kingdom). The proposal was put forward in the Danish Parliament and accepted in the Upper House (Landstinget), but when negotiated in the Lower House (Folketinget) it was rejected. Among the opponents was the priest, poet and politician N.F.S. Grundtvig. One of his arguments was that people belonging to the royal areas would lose too much if they were to give up the rights they had been given by the constitution of 1849, like political rights, freedom of speech, freedom of religion and the right of assembly. The situation was that the constitution was not valid in the duchies, but only in the kingdom, and that a solution was pending for the duchies. Therefore in 1863 the Danish Parliament decided on a common constitution for the kingdom and the Duchy of Schleswig.

The common constitution of 1863 was enacted under Danish nationalistic policy and provoked the German nationalistic movement in Schleswig-Holstein, who wanted to keep the two duchies united. They were supported by Bismarck in Prussia, which led to the war in 1864 and the defeat of the Danish troops at Dybbøl and on the island of Alsen. In addition, the Danish delegation lost at the negotiating table as no compromise was possible. The solution was therefore that officially from the beginning of 1867 the Duchies of both Schleswig and Holstein were incorporated into the Prussian state, and later the German Empire.[15] A regulation of the borders was made so that an area around the town of Ribe and eight parishes south-east of Kolding were to belong to the Danish kingdom, as well as the island of Ærø. But the former royal areas

---

14. Nielsen: "De kongerigske Enklaver," p. 522ff.
15. Schlaber vol. 1, 404.

in the south-western part of Schleswig around Tønder and the islands in the Wadden Sea were now Prussian/German. The enclaves were included in the surrounding area and the complicated jurisdictional situation was solved at one stroke. This was especially appreciated by a German judge, Mackeprang, in Tønder who thought that this disorder had been unacceptable but also that injustice was committed when the areas south of Kolding (the 8 parishes) were given to Denmark when they had formerly belonged to the duchies.[16]

Perspectives

Even if the complex situation of the enclaves was solved in 1864, it might be possible to track some traces of its aftermath showing the inertial energy of history based on space. A good comparison is the situation in 1920, when as a result of the Paris peace after World War I the population had to decide by referendum whether they wanted to belong to Denmark or Germany. The question was whether the vote for Denmark would be higher in the parishes of the former duchy that had been to a large extent royal possessions or whether enclave-parishes that had largely been ducal possessions surrounded by parishes with royal affiliation would vote for Germany. Statistically the correlation in all enclave parishes is not significant at all, but Figure 3, showing the situation in 1860 and 1920, nevertheless shows some significant examples. First of all the enclave-islands to the South, Amrum and Vesterland-Föhr, do not show a specifically high vote for Denmark in 1920. The importance of these islands to the Danish king back to the Middle Ages did not reflect significantly in the votes of 1920. Another interesting area is the parish of Højer, west of the town of Tønder. This parish was, in contrast to other enclaves in this corner, dominated by ducal possessions – and the result in 1920 was a majority of German votes. In this case there is a clear connection to its former situation as an enclave with less royal affiliation and the fact that a township developed in the par-

---

16. Mackeprang: "Über den Ursprung der vormals Dänischen Landestheile Schleswigs und ihre Wiedervereinigung mit dem Herzogthum," in *Zeitschrift der Gesellschaft für Schleswig-Holstein-Lauenburgische Geschichte* 1888 vol. 18: pp. 305-14, here p. 313f.

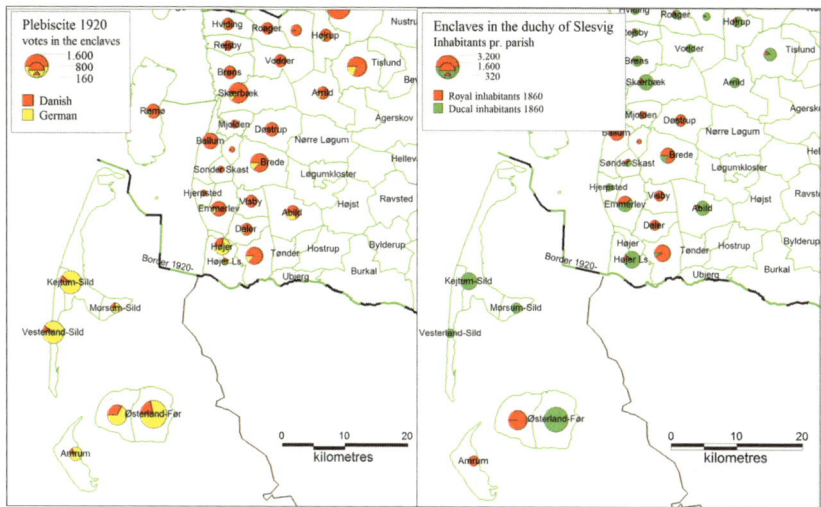

Figure 3. Illustration showing the south-western part of the Duchy Schleswig, showing to the right an excerpt from Figure 1 and to the left the distribution of votes at the 1920 plebiscite, in zone 1 (north of the 1920 border) on 10 February, 1920 and on 14 March, 1920 in zone 2. (Source: Franz von Jessen: Haandbog i det slesvigske spørgsmåls historie 1900-1937, *vol. 1-3. Copenhagen 1938, here vol. 2. Tables.)*

ish, a so called 'flække' with the name of the parish; the township might mean that specifically German craftsmen and merchants settled there. This is in contrast to the two parishes to the North, Emmerlev and Hjerpsted, showing ducal majority as an enclave, but an overwhelming majority of Danish votes. But even if there was a German majority in Højer (and actually the town of Tønder), these areas were included in the Danish state as they belonged to zone 1, which voted en bloc, and as a consequence of the Danish majority the whole area became Danish. This was in contrast to zone 2, the middle part of Schleswig, where the result was effected parish by parish, but here all parishes had a German majority.

Conclusion

Looking at the enclaves in South Jutland in a spatial perspective underlines the differences between the areas constituting the enclave areas and the surrounding areas. The differences were of judicial, administrative and economic character, but probably did not affect the peasants in daily life, except on particular occasions, when they had to go to court or to markets in towns. Including the temporal aspect, differences became enhanced. Legislation, administration and political systems developed differently on both sides of the invisible borders of the enclaves. In the Danish kingdom, the new law book of 1683 meant a different judicial basis. The introduction of municipalities in 1841 and finally the introduction of democracy and the constitution in 1849 widened the differences. In fact, the constitutional question meant a solution to the enclave problem, as it was the trigger for the war between Denmark and Prussia/Austria, which ended in a Danish military and diplomatic defeat in 1864. So time enhanced the differences and solved the problem. But structures concerning the habits and feelings of the population as expressed in the national referendum in 1920 underline that the time factor is inertial and essential to explaining the development, here in combination with the space to underline the differences.

Future research issues might focus on investigations of the empirical differences between peasants belonging to different jurisdictions. This will involve sources from different authorities in order to fulfil a spatial or landscape perspective which is untraditional. Normally research takes place in places corresponding to specific sources and jurisdictions, which is much easier and more realistic to fulfil than the desired landscape perspective. Research of this kind is very much in line with regional historical research, where regions are seen in a wider perspective.

The perspective of the enclaves has not been very much elucidated as only few references to this kind of investigation have been found in international literature, whether the perspective is the political implications, judicial aspects or social cultural history. Therefore the field is also open to specific enclave studies.

MEMORY SITES

The Ground Zero Mosque: A Clash Over (Civil) Religion and Freedom

Jørn Brøndal

In the late spring of 2010, just as the midterm election campaign season was beginning to warm up, a controversial story flashed across the US news media: a one-hundred-million-dollar, fifteen-story Muslim community center was being planned for construction only two blocks from the site where two hijacked passenger planes had slammed into the twin towers of the World Trade Center on September 11, 2001. Indeed, the proposed construction site was so close to Ground Zero that an existing 1850s structure on the address – Park Place 45-51 – had been hit by debris from the planes and severely damaged, causing the Burlington Coat Factory, a discount department store, to close down its business on the premises. The community center was to feature a wide array of modern facilities, including a five-hundred-seat performing arts center, a swimming pool and other sports facilities, a culinary school and a food court specializing in *halal* cuisine, as well as a bookstore. Above all, a large prayer space was to occupy fully two stories of the building.[1] Kuwaiti-born Imam Feisal Abdul Rauf, a graduate of Columbia University, suggested that the new center be named "Cordoba House" after the city in Spain which for centuries – so it was argued – had served as a model of peaceful co-existence between Muslims, Christians, and Jews. He claimed that with this project he was hoping to push back the extremist element within Islam and promote interfaith understanding.[2] Other proponents,

---

1. *New York Times*, May 26, 2010; *Washington Post*, August 17, 2010.
2. *Christian Science Monitor*, September 10, 2010; *The Economist*, August 5, 2010; *New York Times*, March 30, 2011.

including New York-born real-estate investor Sharif El-Gamal, preferred the more neutral "Park51" to "Cordoba House."[3] Quickly, however, its detractors dubbed the proposed building the "Ground Zero mosque."

Thus, in the spring and summer of 2010 Ground Zero became a contested place. A public controversy developed that attained national dimensions when several prominent politicians stepped into the melee, including not only former Republican vice presidential candidate Sarah Palin, former Republican Speaker of the House Newt Gingrich, and present New York City mayor Michael Bloomberg but also president Barack Obama. As far as Ground Zero was concerned, it turned out to be difficult, literally, to find common ground. On the one hand were the critics of the proposed site. On Twitter, Sarah Palin urged, "Ground Zero Mosque supporters: doesn't it stab you in the heart, as it does ours throughout the heartland? Peaceful Muslims, pls. Refudiate [sic!]." On another tweet Palin added, "Twin Towers site is too raw, too real."[4] More dramatic, if linguistically less inventive, was the appeal by Newt Gingrich, the Georgia politician – and historian – who back in the mid-1990s had been one of president Bill Clinton's main political foes (and who in 2012 would make a bid for the Republican nomination for the presidency): "Nazis don't have the right to put up a sign next to the holocaust museum in Washington. We would never accept the Japanese putting up a site next to Pearl Harbor." Maybe Gingrich even counted on his audience recalling that just one year previously a guard at the Holocaust Museum had actually been killed by a white supremacist?[5]

On the other hand were the defenders of the Muslim community center. Prominent among these was New York City mayor Michael Bloomberg, a financial-data service billionaire of Reform Jewish background who in running successfully for the mayoralty in 2001 had switched his lifelong Democratic allegiances for Republican ones before emerging as an independent in 2007.[6] "I think it's fair to say if somebody was going to

---

3. *New York Times*, January 15, 2011; *The New Yorker*, August 16, 2010.
4. Stephanie Condon: "Palin's "Refudiate" Tweet on Mosque Near Ground Zero Draws Fire (For Substance and Style)," http://www.cbsnews.com/8301-503544_162-20010892-503544.html (May 3, 2011); *The Economist*, August 5, 2010.
5. *Washington Post*, August 16, 2010.
6. *New York Times*, June 19, 2007.

try, on that piece of property, to build a church or a synagogue, nobody would be yelling and screaming," Bloomberg asserted in late May of 2010. "And the fact of the matter is that Muslims have a right to do it, too."[7] On Friday, August 13, president Obama entered the debate. Like George W. Bush, his predecessor – indeed, like Thomas Jefferson, the third president of the United States (1801-1809) – Obama decided to follow a not fully developed tradition of celebrating the Muslim month of *Ramadan* at the White House by holding an *iftar*, a sunset supper breaking the day's fast. "I understand the emotions that this issue engenders. Ground zero is, indeed, hallowed ground," Obama said. Still, he insisted, "as a citizen, and as president, I believe that Muslims have the same right to practice their religion as anyone else in this country. That includes the right to build a place of worship and a community center on private property in Lower Manhattan, in accordance with local laws and ordinances." Even though Obama backtracked a bit the following day by claiming that he was not commenting on the *wisdom* of placing a mosque there, his standpoint in favor of letting the building project proceed was clear.[8]

What was truly at stake in the heated controversy over the "Ground Zero mosque"? As it turns out, the political rhetoric revolved around two central conceptions of what it means to be American. Both are rooted in what Robert N. Bellah back in 1967 dubbed America's "civil religion."[9] But whereas one is based on a ritualistic celebration of the symbols of the creed, the other places a strong emphasis on a literal understanding of a central tenet of that faith: American freedom. A further study of the concept of civil religion and specifically of America's freedom tradition – notably freedom of worship – promises to shed more light on the controversy over the "Ground Zero mosque" and to ground it in its historical context.

There is no state church in the United States. As the First Amendment to the Constitution decrees, "Congress shall make no law respecting an

---

7. *New York Post*, May 29, 2010.
8. *New York Times*, August 13, 2010; *New York Daily News*, August 14, 2010.
9. Robert N. Bellah: "Civil Religion in America," in *Daedalus* 91, 1 (Winter, 1967), 1-21.

establishment of religion, or prohibiting the free exercise thereof..."[10] Despite this proscription of religion from the public affairs of the state, in many ways the United States remains a strongly religious nation. In fact, according to a 2007 survey by the Pew Forum on Religion and Public Life, 56 percent of Americans said that religion is very important in their lives.[11] "Religion," however, refers to a welter of different faiths. More than three-quarters of the American population (78.4 percent) affiliate with some Christian faith, with a bare majority (51.3 percent) belonging to one of the many Protestant sects and another major chunk (23.9 percent) associating with the Catholic church. Outside Christianity, the Jewish group is the largest (1.7 percent), followed by Buddhists (0.7 percent), Muslims (0.6 percent), and Hindus (0.4 percent). One in six Americans (16.1 percent) affiliates with no church in particular, including a number of atheists and agnostics (4.0 percent).[12]

Despite the separation of state and church, America does in fact practice a "civil religion." Devout followers of the Christian faith like presidents Jimmy Carter and George W. Bush never alluded to "Jesus Christ" in their official rhetoric but they did, as all the other presidents, refer to an unspecified "God." Moreover, even though state and church are strictly separated, "In God we trust" has since 1956 been the official motto of the nation (a fact that president Obama apparently was unaware of when in a speech in Indonesia in 2010 he claimed that the nation's motto was *E Pluribus Unum*, i.e., "Out of Many, One").[13] Likewise, the Pledge of Allegiance, recited by millions of American school children on a daily basis since its adoption by Congress in 1942, includes the phrase, "one nation under God." American civil religion, as it turns out, does in fact rely on scripture of sorts, but it is neither the Holy Bible, the Torah, nor the Qur'an.

---

10. The First Amendment here quoted from Eric Foner: *Give Me Liberty! An American History*, New York 2011, A-9.
11. The Pew Forum on Religion and Public Life, "How Religious is Your State?" December 21, 2009 http://pewforum.org/How-Religious-Is-Your-State-.aspx (May 3, 2011). This particular statistic is based on the Pew Forum's 2007 U.S. Religious Landscape Survey.
12. The Pew Forum on Religion and Public Life, "U.S. Religious Landscape Survey: Summary of Key Findings" http://religions.pewforum.org/reports# (May 3, 2011).
13. *New York Times*, November 1, 2011.

What makes the United States different from so many other nations in Western society is that originally it was conceived on the basis of a number of ideas, rather than on a history reaching back, as it seemed, to time immemorial. As early as 1944, Gunnar Myrdal, the Swedish economist and later Nobel Prize winner, referred to those ideas as "the American Creed." This faith was based on a body of scripture comprised by the Declaration of Independence (1776), the Preamble to the Constitution (ratified in 1788), and a number of the early state constitutions.[14] A central tenet of the faith was expressed in the most famous sentence of the Declaration of Independence: "We hold these truths to be self-evident, that all men are created equal, that they are *endowed by their Creator* with certain unalienable Rights, that among these are Life, Liberty and the pursuit of Happiness" (italics added). The belief in equality and those rights – underwritten by an unspecified "Creator" – indeed formed the core of this American faith which at the same time, Myrdal maintained, rested on a Protestant nonsectarian basis. One might easily argue that later additions to the creed would include not only the Bill of Rights (1791) but also Abraham Lincoln's Emancipation Proclamation (1863), freeing most slaves, and the Thirteenth (1865), Fourteenth (1868), and Fifteenth (1870) Amendments to the Constitution, respectively abolishing slavery, promising citizenship to all persons born or naturalized in the United States (i.e., irrespective of color), and ensuring that the right to suffrage not be limited by racial factors.[15]

Numerous speeches by prominent Americans – including several presidents – may at the same time be viewed as sermons in the spirit of the creed, with the speaker envisioning an American future only by dwelling on the nation's past and its founding ideals. Most important among these sermons are two addresses, Abraham Lincoln's Gettysburg

---

14. Gunnar Myrdal: *An American Dilemma: The Negro Problem and Modern Democracy*, New York 1944, pp. 4-5, and pp. 9-13. Myrdal was no admirer of the American Constitution as a whole, considering it in many ways "impractical and ill-suited for modern conditions." Excepting the Preamble, he viewed its "worship...a most flagrant violation of the American Creed." *Ibid.*, pp. 12-13.
15. Myrdal: *An American Dilemma*, p. 13, argued, however, that the Fourteenth Amendment in practice had been used "more to protect business corporations against public control" than to protect the civil rights of African Americans. That, however, is no longer the case.

Address (1863), which opens by invoking the Declaration of Independence and later pledges that "this nation, *under God*, shall have a new birth of freedom," and Martin Luther King, Jr.'s, "I Have a Dream," with King intoning, "I have a dream that one day this nation will rise up and live out the true meaning of *its creed* – "We hold these truths to be self evident, that all men are created equal"" (italics added).[16] As with so many other religions, special days have been marked for celebrating America's civil religion. Those dates include Thanksgiving Day (in thanks to God for allowing the Pilgrims to survive the first harsh winter at Plymouth Colony in present-day Massachusetts in 1620-21), the Fourth of July (the date of the Declaration of Independence and thus of the founding of the nation in 1776), Memorial Day (growing out of the Civil War 1861-65 to commemorate US soldiers dying in the service) but also the birthdays of George Washington, Abraham Lincoln, and Martin Luther King, Jr.[17]

If America's civil religion thus includes both scripture, a creed, sermons, and dates of ritualized celebration, several holy places – if not outright churches – were built in its honor. Among the most obvious is the Washington Monument (1885) in the nation's capital, which at the time of its dedication was the tallest man-made structure in the world, an impressive obelisk reaching, almost literally, into the heavens. Another sacred symbol that easily springs to mind is the Statue of Liberty (1886) in New York City's harbor, representing a goddess who cannot be found in the Bible but who fits perfectly into the American creed. Later shrines to America's civil religion include the Lincoln Memorial (1922) in Washington, D.C., a large Doric temple featuring an imposing and godlike statue of Abraham Lincoln – the Great Emancipator – sitting majestically on his throne inside, and Mount Rushmore National Memorial (1939) in South Dakota where the faces of presidents George Washington, Thomas Jefferson, Abraham Lincoln, and Theodore Roosevelt were carved directly into the rock by Danish-American sculptor Gutzon Borglum.

If American civil religion is based on the ideals of freedom and equality, death and hopes of redemption add depth to the faith. Abraham

---

16. On the significance of the Gettysburg Address, see also Bellah: "Civil Religion," p. 10; Lincoln quoted from Foner: *Give Me Liberty!* A-22; King quoted from *ibid.*, A-30.
17. See also Bellah: "Civil Religion", p. 11.

Lincoln died for the sins of his nation and has been equated symbolically with Jesus Christ. The death of Martin Luther King, Jr., is often viewed in a similar light. One prominent King biographer titled his book on the slain civil rights leader, simply, *Bearing the Cross*.[18] Nowhere is death more present than at the Vietnam Veterans Memorial (1982) in Washington, D.C., arguably the wailing wall of American civil religion. Here visitors, many of them moving along solemnly and contemplatively as if on hallowed ground, can identify the names of the more than 58,000 US soldiers who perished in the Vietnam War while at the same time viewing their own reflection in the black stone and perhaps meditating on the complex meaning of dying for what was supposed to be the ideals of the nation.

In sum, it may fairly be stated that American civil religion, while definitely based on Christian values, is clearly also built around the ideals of freedom and equality. This view, it should be added, is not in complete agreement with the opinion aired by Robert Wuthnow in his important 1988 discussion of civil religion. Back then he suggested that even though "the idea of freedom cannot in any way be regarded as a strictly secular ideology in conflict with religious myths of America," still, freedom is somehow external to the creed proper, being "often *combined* with some version of American civil religion" (italics added). To the contrary, in the view of the present writer, freedom makes up a central and defining tenet of the faith. That being said, it should be emphasized that I agree with one of Wuthnow's main propositions: that even though they share a number of common symbols, two competing understandings of America's civil religion co-exist, the one conservative in orientation, the other liberal.[19]

Ground Zero fits well into notions of American civil religion. Here large numbers of innocent Americans – including many firefighters attempting to save other people's lives – saw death as the result of an attack on the American nation by Islamic terrorists. Whereas the World Trade Center originally figured as a powerful symbol of capitalist America, after the attacks it became a place of mourning and redemptive hope.

---

18. David J. Garrow: *Bearing the Cross: Martin Luther King, Jr., and the Southern Christian Leadership Conference*, New York 1999; Bellah: "Civil Religion," pp. 10-11.
19. Robert Wuthnow: *The Restructuring of American Religion: Society and Faith Since World War II*, Princeton, New Jersey 1988, pp. 244-245 and p. 259.

The mourning aspect is reflected in the National September 11 Memorial and Museum at Ground Zero that opened on the ten-year anniversary of the terrorist attacks (September 11, 2011). The museum is located underground, reflecting the tremendous impact of the falling of the towers but also adding a dimension of death to the edifice. The memorial likewise points downward. Designed by architects Michael Arad and Peter Walker, it features a wooded plaza with two huge pools, one placed in each footprint of the original Twin Towers, with a square void receding further down from the center of the respective pools. Each void represents the absence of the people who were killed. The sound of the cascades of water feeding the pools and vanishing into the voids is intended to keep out the noise of the city and to put the visitor in a reflective mood. Indeed, the architects named the memorial, simply, "Reflecting Absence." The names of the victims – ordered by their "meaningful adjacencies" on the day of their deaths – are inscribed into bronze parapets along the perimeter of each pool. Included here are also the names of the six people killed during a previous terrorist attack on the World Trade Center, on February 26, 1993, when a truck bomb exploded beneath the North Tower.[20] Daniel Libeskind, the main Ground Zero architect, suggested that the memorial site would have a sacrosanct dimension to it: "We have to be able to enter this hallowed, sacred ground while creating a quiet, meditative and spiritual space."[21]

Yet there is also an assertive quality with redemptive overtones to the Ground Zero design, reflecting, as it were, president George W. Bush's declaration on September 11, 2001, that "our very freedom came under attack in a series of deliberate and deadly terrorist acts," and his further vow that the United States would stand up to the terrorist challenge.[22]

---

20. Michael Arad and Peter Walker: "Reflecting Absence," 2003, http://www.wtcsitememorial.org/fin7.html (May 5, 2011); Elizabeth Shell: "The Complexity of 2,982 Names on the September 11 Memorial," *PBS Newshour*, September 11, 2011, http://www.pbs.org/newshour/rundown/2011/09/the-mathematical-complexity-of-2982-names.html (February 9, 2012).
21. Daniel Libeskind: "New World Trade Center Site Designs: Introduction," http://www.renewnyc.com/plan_des_dev/wtc_site/new_design_plans/firm_d/default.asp (May 5, 2011).
22. Quoted from Peggy Noonan and Jay Nordlinger (eds.): *We Will Prevail: President George W. Bush on War, Terrorism, and Freedom*, New York 2003, p. 2.

"Freedom and fear are at war," Bush claimed nine days later, adding that the enemies "hate our freedoms, our freedom of religion, our freedom of speech, our freedom to assemble..."[23] One World Trade Center, the new skyscraper conceived by Daniel Libeskind that is presently under construction, reflects this national self-confidence while simultaneously placing the skyscraper squarely in the tradition of American civil religion. Pondering the survival of the slurry walls adjacent to the Twin Towers – designed to keep back the Hudson River – Libeskind himself argued in December 2002, "The foundations withstood the unimaginable trauma of the destruction and stand as eloquent as the Constitution itself asserting the durability of Democracy and the value of individual life." One block removed from the original Twin Towers, Libeskind proposed to create his high-rise, still colloquially known as "Freedom Tower." It was decided to let the new structure have a height that measured in feet would tally with the year of the Declaration of Independence: 1776. As Republican governor George E. Pataki of New York argued in 2003, "This is not just a building. This is a symbol of New York. This is a symbol of America. This is a symbol of freedom."[24]

If notions of civil religion were at stake in the controversy over the "Ground Zero mosque," so were – as several of the above quotes have already made clear – ideas specifically about one of the creed's central tenets: freedom. Even though the Declaration of Independence counted liberty among the rights of man, and notwithstanding that the Preamble to the Constitution held out the promise of securing "the Blessings of Liberty" to posterity, freedom, of course, has remained a hotly contested concept down through American history. One need only reflect on the fact that Thomas Jefferson, who wrote the Declaration of Independence, was a slaveholder. Indeed, it may be argued, roughly, that the history of American freedom is the tale of how what was originally a privilege reserved for propertied white men gradually evolved into a universal entitlement that all men and women of every shade and color could claim for themselves.[25] As noted, a central document in the history of

---

23. Here quoted from Eric Foner: *Give Me Liberty!*, pp. 1174-1175.
24. *New York Times*, December 20, 2003.
25. Eric Foner: *The Story of American Freedom*, New York 1999, p. 15 and p. 303.

American liberty is the Bill of Rights, i.e., the first ten amendments to the Constitution (1791). Especially the First Amendment is important, underwriting not only freedom of speech and of assembly but also freedom of worship.

From an early date, doubts about the effectiveness of the Bill of Rights in protecting individual liberty from encroachment by the state surfaced. Already James Madison, the main architect behind the Constitution, decried the first ten amendments as just so many "parchment barriers" to the abuse of power. On numerous occasions history proved him right. Thus, during World War I the civil liberties of German Americans and of people critical of the war came under severe strain; during World War II 110,000 Japanese Americans were interned in camps; during the early phase of the Cold War would-be Communists were scapegoated; and during the War on Terror the Bush administration not only engaged in controversial maneuvers to enhance the president's executive authority but also condoned the use of coercive techniques against prisoners that critics labeled torture.[26]

Ever since the Bill of Rights was adopted in 1791, the United States has practiced freedom of worship. Even before that point and until the 1920s – when a number of restrictive immigration laws were enacted – America served as a haven for many religious refugees escaping harassment or downright persecution. Despite the absence of persecution by the state, however, the dominant white Protestant culture oftentimes made life tough for members of religious minorities. Thus, down through its history the United States experienced several outbursts of anti-Catholicism. This was the case during the 1830s when angry Protestants of mostly Scotish-Presbyterian background burned down the Ursuline Convent in Charlestown outside Boston (1834), and when Maria Monk's tract, *Awful Disclosures of the Hotel Dieu Nunnery* (1836), supposedly describing the sexual escapades among nuns in Montreal, became a bestseller in the United States, to be outsold in the nineteenth century only by *Uncle Tom's Cabin*. It later came out that Monk had a past as a prostitute

---

26. Foner: *The Story of American Freedom*, p. 25; James Pfiffner: "Constraining Executive Power: George W. Bush and the Constitution," in *Presidential Studies Quarterly* 38, 1 (March, 2007): pp. 140-141.

and had never lived in the nunnery (but for a while at the Magdalen Asylum for fallen women).[27] Another round of anti-Catholic sentiment arose in the mid-1850s when a new political party, the American Party, aimed its main wrath at incoming Catholic immigrants from Ireland and German-speaking areas. By the late 1850s, the party – also known as the Know-Nothing Party because members of this originally semi-secret organization were instructed to say, "I know nothing," when questioned about the party's activities – had disappeared from view again.[28] A later nativist outburst occurred during the World War I era and lasted into the 1920s when it subsided with the enactment of immigration restriction. Those years saw the revival of the Ku Klux Klan, an organization that originally had directed its anger at African Americans living in the South in the post-Civil War years. In the World War I era, however, the Klan expanded its activities, setting down roots in many states outside the South and seeking out targets not only among blacks but also among Catholic and Jewish immigrants who since the final decade of the nineteenth century had been arriving in large numbers to the United States from Southern and Eastern Europe.[29]

Arguably, anti-Catholicism in the United States lasted until the outbreak of the Cold War when many American Catholics got the chance to prove their American loyalties by posing as staunch anti-Communists. It was only in 1960 that America elected its first – and thus far only – Catholic president, John F. Kennedy. Reflecting on how anti-Communism had replaced anti-Catholicism, one historian argued in 1965, "the Whore of Babylon now sits in Moscow, not Rome..."[30] Democratic presidential nominee John Kerry's defeat to George W. Bush in the election of 2004

---

27. Jenny Franchot: *Roads to Rome: The Antebellum Protestant Encounter with Catholicism*, Berkeley 1994, pp. 154-155.
28. David H. Bennett: *The Party of Fear: From Nativist Movements to the New Right in American History* (second edition), New York 1995, p. 112.
29. John Higham: *Strangers in the Land: Patterns of American Nativism, 1860-1925*, New Brunswick 1988, p. 297; David M. Chalmers: *Hooded Americanism: The History of the Ku Klux Klan*, Chicago 1968, p. 170; Kenneth T. Jackson: *The Ku Klux Klan in the City, 1915-1930*, Chicago 1992, pp. 155-156.
30. Richard Hofstadter: *The Paranoid Style in American Politics, and Other Essays*, New York 1965, p. 80.

thus had little to do with his Catholic background. Nor did it play any major role in the election of 2000 that Democratic presidential candidate Al Gore's running mate for the vice presidency was the Jewish Joe Lieberman, even if Jews historically have encountered levels of harassment in the United States that match the Catholic experience. On the other hand, in the spring of 2012 it seemed to constitute a certain problem for the Republican presidential candidate Mitt Romney that he is a Mormon, not least because the Republican grassroots comprise a much larger fundamentalist evangelical element than do the Democratic ones (whereas few people seemed to reflect on the fact that Newt Gingrich, one of Romney's main rivals, actually converted from the Southern Baptist faith to Catholicism in 2009, or that Rick Santorum, an outspoken representative of the religious right, likewise is a Catholic).

Thus overall, despite First Amendment protections of freedom of worship, belonging to groups other than the Protestant majority oftentimes proved troublesome in American history. If this was the case for such Christians as Catholics and Mormons and for such non-Christians as Jews, it was also so for people practicing the Muslim faith. Originally, the number of American Muslims was limited. There are examples of Muslim slaves from Africa being shipped to America in the eighteenth and early nineteenth centuries and attempting to cling to their faith for years. Thus, even though America's international slave trade ended in 1808, some slaves along the Georgia coast were still practicing their Muslim faith in the years leading up to the Civil War.[31] Likewise, there are a few examples of white Americans converting to Islam in the late nineteenth century, and of Muslim missionaries from South Asia arriving to the United States in the early twentieth century, along with Muslim immigrants from India and the Ottoman Empire.[32]

During the 1920s and into the 1930s, however, Islam as a religion began to grow in the United States, first of all among African Americans, due both to the activities of the Indian missionary Muhammad Sadiq, who arrived in New York in 1920, and to a number of homegrown Black

---

31. Edward E. Curtis IV: *Muslims in America: A Short History*, New York 2009, pp. 17-21.
32. Curtis: *Muslims in America*, 25-29; Jane I. Smith: *Islam in America* (second edition), New York 2010, p. 66.

Muslim movements. The latter included the Moorish Science Temple, established in Chicago in 1925 by Noble Drew Ali (formerly Timothy Drew), and the Nation of Islam which was founded in Detroit in 1930 by W. D. Fard, or Farad Muhammad. Among African Americans settling in the ghettos of America's northern cities during the World War I era and the following decades, converting to Islam sometimes became a means of racial self-expression in hostile white surroundings. The potential of a link between black pride and Muslim identity was suggested, if only tentatively, by the rise of Jamaican-born Marcus Garvey to national prominence in the United States in the years immediately following World War I. During those years, Garvey's Universal Negro Improvement Association (UNIA) flourished on the basis of a message of black self-help and total separation from whites. Soon, the organization's leadership was approached by Muslim preachers who attempted to persuade the UNIA to choose Islam as its official religion. Even though this never happened, several individual members of the UNIA did in fact convert to Islam before the organization disintegrated following Garvey's conviction in 1923 on charges of mail fraud and his subsequent deportation in 1927.[33]

The combination of black nationalism and Islam truly came to the fore with the expansion of the Nation of Islam under the leadership of Elijah Muhammad (born Elijah Robert Pool) following the disappearance of Farad Muhammad in 1934. The growth of the Nation accelerated during the 1950s and early 1960s when Malcolm X (born Malcolm Little) emerged as the movement's magnetic spokesman, known for his razor-sharp one-liners ("if someone puts his hand on you, send him to the cemetery") that contrasted sharply with Martin Luther King's simultaneous pleas for nonviolent civil rights protest.[34] Elijah Muhammad stressed the separatist message when telling his followers not to serve in the American military and not to vote in U.S. elections.[35] At the same

33. Curtis: *Muslims in America*, pp. 32-33; Smith: *Islam in America*, pp. 80-81; Judith Stein: *The World of Marcus Garvey: Race and Class in Modern Society*, Baton Rouge 1986, pp. 61-88, 90, 97, 108-127, and 153.
34. George Breitman, ed.: *Malcolm X Speaks: Selected Speeches and Statements*, New York 1989, p. 12.
35. Curtis: *Muslims in America*, p. 39.

time, however, Elijah Muhammad's version of Islam did not mesh well with either the Sunni or Shi'ite traditions (with the Sunni faith representing some 80 percent of Islam worldwide and Shi'ites the main part of the remainder).[36] Among other things, the Nation of Islam maintained that Yakub, a malicious scientist of the Shabazz tribe, had invented the white race – portrayed as evil, blue-eyed devils – by dabbling in cross-breeding after his exile from Mecca. The Nation likewise claimed that W.D. Fard in fact was God, and that Elijah Muhammad was a prophet like Muhammad.[37]

Following accusations against Elijah Muhammad for adultery, Malcolm X left the Nation of Islam in March 1964 and joined the Sunni faith, only to be gunned down in New York City on February 21, 1965, by assassins affiliating with the Nation.[38] With the death of Elijah Muhammad ten years later, the Nation of Islam split in two. W.D. Muhammad, a son of Elijah Muhammad who had been exposed to Sunni teachings, rejected most of his father's special theology and not only introduced the American flag into Nation of Islam mosques but renamed his organization the World Community of al-Islam in the West. In 1978, however, his leadership was challenged by Louis Farrakhan who stuck to the teachings of Elijah Muhammad and attempted to rebuild the movement using its original name. His teachings are today rejected by mainstream Muslims as heresy or blasphemy.[39]

With the passage of new immigration legislation in 1965 – and again in 1990 – the regime of immigration restriction came to an end as the United States once again opened its doors to large numbers of newcomers. Now family reunification and technical skills – in that order of priority – formed the main basis for the admission of immigrants. Today, the United States has thus once again become a magnet for immigrants, attracting on average approximately one million newcomers each year – or twice the population of Denmark in a decade. These days, however,

---

36. Smith: *Islam in America*, p. xiv.
37. Malcolm X and Alex Haley: *The Autobiography of Malcolm X*, New York 1966, pp. 167-169; Curtis: *Muslims in America*, pp. 78-79.
38. Taylor Branch: *Pillar of Fire: America in the King Years, 1963-65*, New York 1998, p. 201, 319, 328-329, and 596-597.
39. Curtis, *Muslims in America*, 78-79; Smith, *Islam in America*, 83-84.

the main groups of immigrants arrive not from Europe but from Latin America and Asia.[40] Over the past decades, many immigrants and refugees of Muslim background journeyed to America from the Middle East and Asia, in one estimate 1.1 million between 1966 and 1997.[41] Thus, by way of chain migration some communities in the United States are today colored quite strongly by an immigrant Muslim presence. Today, the Midwestern state of Michigan thus boasts substantial Muslim communities, with concentrations both in Detroit and in Dearborn. In fact, in the latter city the Muslim presence antedates the arrival of the Ford Motor Company in the 1920s and today includes people of Lebanese, Palestinian, and Yemeni background, as well as two Sunni and three Shi'ite mosques. Other areas with substantial immigrant Muslim concentrations include New York City and Chicago, as well as San Francisco and Los Angeles.[42] As president Obama argued, correctly, in a speech in Cairo in 2009, "there is a mosque in every state of our union and over 1,200 mosques within our borders."[43]

Thus, Islam in America has double roots. On the one hand as a substantial African-American community of Muslims dating back to the 1920s and 1930s (even if by far the majority of American blacks remain Christians). On the other hand as an immigrant community of more recent date, and divided into its Sunni and Shi'ite constituent parts. Notably, very few white Americans of traditional Protestant background – the group that historically was the politically and culturally dominant in the nation – have converted to Islam.[44] Thus, Muslims in America remain a minority not only in a religious sense but also in racial and ethnic terms. This may help explain why, following the terrorist attacks on September 11, 2001, some representatives of the dominant culture turned their suspi-

---

40. Jørn Brøndal: "Immigration and Immigration Law," in George T. Kurian et al. (eds.), *Encyclopedia of American Studies*, vol. 2, New York 2001, pp. 338-339.
41. Curtis: *Muslims in America*, p. 73.
42. Smith: *Islam in America*, pp. 56-62.
43. Obama here quoted from Foner: *Give Me Liberty!*, p. 1179; see also *Christian Science Monitor*, August 20, 2010.
44. Smith: *Islam in America*, p. 66, suggests that the number of "Anglo-Muslims" in the United States may amount to somewhere between 20,000 and 50,000, including Anglo-women who have married Muslim men.

cious and frightened eyes on the Muslim population group, the celebration of freedom of worship notwithstanding. In 2001, anti-Muslim hate crimes in the United States were reported to have increased by 1,700 percent, and the USA PATRIOT Act that was enacted that same year as a security measure in the "War on Terror" was soon criticized for singling out men of Arab, South Asian, and Muslim background and denying them the usual protections of their liberty. Recent polls likewise made it clear that not only do many Americans continue to feel uncomfortable with Islam but they are also "somewhat" or "very" worried about a radical Islamic presence in the United States.[45] At the same time, nearly one in five Americans mistakenly thinks that president Obama is a Muslim, a view promoted by leaders of the American chapter of the Stop Islamization organization (a hate group originating in Denmark which was very active at grassroots level in the agitation against what was sometimes dubbed the "victory mosque").[46]

That being said, in a global perspective it should be emphasized that comparing with recent debates over Islam in many European countries, the American tone remained generally somewhat more subdued and civil, a result no doubt both of the nation's strong multicultural and civil rights traditions and of the fact that Muslims even today make up only a relatively small share of the total number of immigrants in the United States, with Latinos outnumbering them by far. Whereas in recent years many European countries saw the rise of large, nativist political parties, nothing on a remotely similar scale happened in the United States. When Keith Ellison, a black Democrat of Minnesota, in 2007 became the first Muslim to be elected to the U.S. House of Representatives, he insisted on being sworn in by Thomas Jefferson's copy of the Qur'an, thus obviously endeavoring to place his faith in the tradition of American civil religion.[47] On the other hand, most Americans undoubtedly viewed extremists setting mosques on fire – notably at Murfreesboro, Tennessee, at the same time that the Ground Zero community center controversy was raging

---

45. Curtis: *Muslims in America*, p. 100; Smith: *Islam in America*, pp. 186-189.
46. *New York Daily News*, May 26, 2010; *Washington Post*, August 22, 2010; *Guardian Unlimited*, August 18, 2010; *New York Daily News*, February 26, 2011; *New York Times*, August 1, 2011.
47. Curtis: *Muslims in America*, p. 106.

– or burning the Qur'an – as happened at Gainesville, Florida, in early 2011 – as nutcases.[48]

The main theme in the controversy over the "Ground Zero mosque" was a paradoxical clashing of America's civil religion with notions of freedom itself – paradoxical in the sense that freedom plays such a vital role in the creed. To put it another way, the Ground Zero controversy saw a conflict between a symbolic understanding of what America stands for and a more literal interpretation of what American freedom entails.

The symbolists, conservative in orientation and led by figures like Sarah Palin and Newt Gingrich, viewed American freedom through the lens of a ritualistically oriented civil religion. In their view, an assault on the *symbols* of American freedom – as they perceived the plans to build the Muslim community center – constituted an attack on freedom itself. To them, Ground Zero – along with the Washington Monument, the Statue of Liberty, and so on – was a holy place and ought therefore not be besmirched by a place of worship to the very religion in whose name the terrorists had acted. Was it not, after all, al Qaeda that had started this war on symbols by picking the World Trade Center and Pentagon as targets, those structures serving as icons of American capitalist power and military might, respectively? Not surprisingly, many jubilant New Yorkers descended on Ground Zero in early May of 2011 to symbolically celebrate the sensational announcement that Osama bin Laden, the leader of the al Qaeda network, had been assassinated in his home near Abbottabad, Pakistan.[49]

On the other hand stood literalists – generally somewhat more liberal in political orientation – like mayor Bloomberg and president Obama. It is not that they did not acknowledge the existence of America's civil religion. As noted previously, Obama stated that "Ground zero is, indeed, hallowed ground." In fact, upon the death of Osama bin Laden, while president Obama visited Ground Zero, he decided not to give any speech there, apparently determining not to want to disturb the sacred atmosphere of the area with a triumphal message.[50] Instead, the literalists

---

48. *New York Times*, August 31, 2010, and April 1, 2011.
49. *New York Times*, May 3, 2011.
50. *New York Daily News*, May 6, 2011.

insisted upon keeping in mind what the freedoms enumerated in the Bill of Rights really stood for, notwithstanding the many challenges to those freedoms down through US history. If there be freedom of worship in America, then no government authority ought to infringe upon it. If there be respect for ownership of property in America, then no government agency should decide what the owner builds on that property – not even if this might well hurt the feelings of friends and relatives of the victims of the 9/11 tragedy. On the eve of September 11, 2010, a group of Park51 supporters tellingly calling themselves Neighbors for American Values held a candlelit vigil in support of the community center.[51]

The controversy over the Muslim community center at Ground Zero culminated in August 2010. By the end of the month, Feisal Abdul Rauf was complaining that the debate over the future of the Muslim cultural center had been hijacked by "radical voices" on all sides.[52] It was also in August that a poll conducted by the Pew Forum on Religion and Public Life showed that whereas less than one in three Americans (30 percent) had a "favorable" opinion of Islam, more than one in three Americans (38 percent) had an "unfavorable" view.[53] The following month, however, with the midterm and gubernatorial races now in full swing, the issue actually began to fade somewhat from view.[54] By that point it had long been obvious that a substantial majority of the American population opposed the center but also that a plurality of Manhattan dwellers in fact supported it.[55] As political commentator Hendrik Hertzberg noted acidly in *The New Yorker*, opposition to Park51 seemed to grow with geographical distance.[56]

In the end, the Ground Zero controversy became only a minor factor in the November 2010 gubernatorial election in the state of New York.

---

51. *Christian Science Monitor*, September 20, 2010.
52. *New York Daily News*, August 31, 2010.
53. Pew Forum on Religion and Public Life, "Public Remains Conflicted Over Islam," August 24, 2010, http://pewresearch.org/pubs/1706/poll-americans-views-of-muslims-object-to-new-york-islamic-center-islam-violence (February 9, 2012).
54. *New York Times*, September 20, 2010.
55. *New York Daily News*, July 1 and September 13, 2010; *Washington Post*, August 17, 2010.
56. Hendrik Hertzberg: "Zero Grounds," *The New Yorker*, August 16, 2010; also *USA Today*, November 2, 2010.

That election saw Democrat Andrew Cuomo roundly defeat his Republican rival Carl Paladino, even though Cuomo supported Park51 while Paladino, enjoying support from the right-wing Tea Party movement, loudly opposed it. Instead, the campaign revolved around other issues, including the perceived extremism of Paladino's views.[57] In the same election, Democratic Eric Schneiderman won the post as attorney general of New York, even though he had staked out a moderate position on the center and unlike several of his rivals had not called for an investigation into its funding, at least not unless concerns about terrorism arose.[58]

If agitation over the Muslim community center subsided somewhat towards the end of 2010, it did not disappear entirely. In March 2011, a former New York City firefighter decided to appeal to a judge the decision by New York City's Landmarks Preservation Commission to deny the existing 1850s building on Park Place landmark status, thus paving the way for the center. The firefighter argued that the Commission had been put under undue pressure by mayor Bloomberg and added that the plans for Park51 were "un-American." A Manhattan judge ended up dismissing the lawsuit, however.[59]

By then, the planners had run into their own problems. Following internal squabbles, in 2011 Imam Feisal Abdul Rauf and his wife Daisy Khan were forced out of the Park51 project by real-estate investor Sharif El-Gamal who, in turn, announced that he had not yet raised much of the money needed to build the community center.[60] Still, the latter – of part Egyptian Muslim, part Polish Catholic background – pressed ahead. On September 21, 2011 – ten days after the tenth anniversary of the terrorist attacks on the World Trade Center – the Park51 Community Center opened officially with a photo exhibition by Danny Goldfield, titled "NYChildren." Notably, Goldfield is of Jewish background.[61] Notwithstanding that

---

57. *New York Times*, September 28, 2010; *Washington Post*, October 15, 2010; *New York Daily News*, October 31, 2010.
58. *New York Daily News*, August 31, 2010.
59. *New York Times*, March 16 and 22, and July 10, 2011.
60. *New York Times*, March 16 and 30, 2011.
61. *Christian Science Monitor*, September 22, 2011; PBS Frontline, "The Man Behind the Mosque," September 27, 2011, http://www.pbs.org/wgbh/pages/frontline/religion/man-behind-mosque/transcript-8/ (February 10, 2012).

Park51 also soon featured its own website, the opening of the community center was more symbolic than real.[62] It took place on the old, damaged premises of the Burlington Coat Factory where American Muslims had in fact been convening for prayer at least since 2009.[63] Moreover, only one week before the opening, Consolidated Edison, a utility company owning part of the building, had served notice that if El-Gamal did not pay 1.7 million dollars in back rent within twenty days, he would be evicted. Even though a judge subsequently granted Park51 an injunction against the eviction, observing that the "[p]laintiff speculates as to whether defendant may be bowing to unspecified political pressure," by early 2012 the vision of a fifteen-story Muslim community center seemed distant indeed.[64]

Still, by this point in time the public controversy surrounding the "Ground Zero mosque" had definitely abated, if maybe only temporarily. With a presidential election looming, it might conceivably flare up again. By the spring of 2012, however, politicians of national renown were remaining silent on the issue. Were they accepting the claim that in reality Park51 was simply modeled on Manhattan's Jewish Community Center?[65] If so, most likely they did not buy the additional argument that being removed two blocks from Ground Zero proper – and out of sight of that location – Park51 was simply just another building in a less-than-sacred area also housing bars and strip joints.[66] They would doubtless find it hard to accept El-Gamal's assertion that "This project had nothing to do with Ground Zero," a contention flying in the face of Imam Rauf's point back in 2009 that a location so close to the World Trade Center, "where a piece of the wreckage fell," was vital, sending "the opposite statement to what happened on 9/11."[67]

---

62. Cf., http://park51.org/ (February 10, 2012).
63. *New York Times*, December 8, 2009.
64. *New York Times*, October 17, 2011; Joel Stashenko, "Ruling Blocks ConEd From Evicting Tenant Near WTC," *New York Law Journal*, November 29, 2011; *New York Post*, November 30, 2011.
65. *New York Times*, August 1, 2011.
66. Hendrik Hertzberg: "Zero Grounds," *The New Yorker*, August 16, 2010; *USA Today*, November 2, 2010.
67. PBS Frontline, "The Man Behind the Mosque;" *New York Times*, December 8, 2009.

Despite the relative calm, by early 2012 the "Ground Zero mosque" remained a contested place. At stake were still two understandings of what it meant to be American, understandings that historically had complemented each other but that in this instance clashed. One was based on a symbol-driven vision that accorded Ground Zero sacred status in America's civil religion, not to be disturbed by a mosque of an historically unpopular minority faith in whose name the September 11 attacks had been launched. In that view, constructing the community center amounted to nothing less than heresy and un-American behavior. The other conception of American identity, likewise claiming the mantle of American civil religion, was based on a more literal interpretation of the idea of liberty, with freedom to worship as one pleases and to do with one's property whatever one likes being emphasized. The wonder was, of course, that the opponents of the Muslim community center could write freedom out of their equation, even as they defended Ground Zero as a sacred space in a civil religion built around exactly that concept. One thing was certain: with America being deeply polarized between "red" states and "blue" states, between conservatives and "liberals," between evangelicals and Tea Party activists on the one hand and members of the Occupy Wall Street movement on the other, no easy resolution of the "Ground Zero mosque" controversy was in sight.

The Battle at Thermopylae and the Myth of Greek Unity

Jesper Majbom Madsen

The mountain pass Thermopylae, the Hot Gates, hosted one of the most idealised battles in the history of ancient Greece. It was here on a warm August day in 480 BCE that three hundred Spartans and a few hundred Greeks from cities in Central Greece fought and died in combat against the overwhelming Persian army that earlier the same year had invaded Greece to place the Greeks under Persian rule. The Battle at Thermopylae has it all. The tale of the three hundred Spartans' heroic struggle and glorious death is a story of great courage, discipline, honour and the readiness to die for the greater good. The Spartans and the other Greeks who remained behind were eventually defeated. King Leonidas and his contingent of three hundred were eliminated and the Persians could advance without challenge into central Greece and raze Athens to the ground. The attempt to stop Persia had failed. Athens was lost and the Greek coalition was on the brink of dissolution. In short, the campaign at Thermopylae was a military disaster that nearly handed victory to the Persians.

Since the age of Enlightenment philosophers, political thinkers, literati and Western scholars alike have theorised that a Greek defeat in the Persian Wars would have had significant implications for the Greek world, as the cradle of Western civilisation. Greece's war against Persia is presented as a clash of cultures, where the Greek underdog fought the larger, wealthier and demographically superior Persia. By their sacrifice the ancient Greeks saved not only their own, but also the entire Western civilization, which, according to many 18th-19th century political thinkers and modern scholars in ancient history and political scientists, never would have developed in the way it did had the Persian kings achieved their objectives. Consequently the Greeks who opposed the Persians have traditionally been seen as freedom fighters and each of the major battles as fundamental to the final victory.[1]

In this respect, the Battle at Thermopylae was no exception. Despite the defeat, modern scholars have described the battle, in particular the last stand, as the turning point in the Greek resistance to the Persian invasion and thereby as decisive for the later victories at Salamis and Plataea. In the 18th century, European intellectuals rediscovered the Greek past in a search for an alternative to Christian Rome. In turn, the accomplishment and values of the ancient Greeks became a significant and highly admired heritage of European culture. Western intellectuals travelled on a form of pilgrimage to the cradle of European civilisation to visit the core sites of Greek civilisation, its cities, temples and battlefields to experience the localities where the Greek and thereby Western civilisation was born, evolved and was defended.

Due to the dramatic events and the military advantages held by the force occupying the pass, Thermopylae soon gained the status of a place where legends were made. In 346 BCE during the war between Macedonia and a number of Greek cities, Philip II, the father of Alexander the Great, decided not to fight at Thermopylae against an army of Greek troops who had blocked the pass, presumably because the king wanted to avoid that a new battle at Thermopylae should awaken a historically motivated unity and determination among the traditionally divided Greeks.[2]

---

1. For 19th century thinkers see for instance Georg Wilhelm Friedrich Hegel: *Vorlesungen über die Philosophie der Geschichte*, Frankfurt am Main 1832-45, pp. 313-15; Stuart Mill: "Review of Grote, History of Greece [I]," in *The Collected Works of John Stuart Mill, Volume XI* – Essays on Philosophy and the Classics, Toronto 1846, p. 273; for literati see Byron: The Giaour 103-9; for modern historians see for instance Ernle Bradford: *Thermopylae: The Battle for the West*. Cambridge MA 1980, pp. 13-14, Rupert Matthews: *The Battle of Thermopylae. A Campaign in Context*, Gloucestershire 2006, p. x; Poul Cartledge: *Thermopylae: The Battle that Changed the World*, London 2006, pp. 202-203; Victor Davis Hanson: "Freedom – or "To Live as you Please" in *Why the West has Won: Nine Landmark Battles in the Brutal History of Western Victory*, New York 2001, p. 56; for an example of a modern social scientist see Anthony Pagden: *Worlds at War: The 2,500-Year Struggle between East and West*, New York 2008, pp. 29-30.
2. Richard Gabriel: *Philip II of Macedonia: Greater than Alexander*, Washington D. C. 2010, pp. 158-9.

Thermopylae, and in particular King Leonidas, was in Early Modern Europe also seen as a symbol of the virtue and excellence of European civilisation.[3] The interest in the battlefield of the Greco-Persian War became particularly powerful in the 18th century, when Western scholars and poets, such as Byron, started to see the Persian Wars and the deeds of Greeks who fought the battles as a symbol of liberty not only from the Ottoman empire but as a more abstract ideal of freedom in the thinking of the Enlightenment.[4] As part of this new interest in the Greek past, the European elite, who had previously travelled in Italy, was now drawn towards Greece to visit the core sights of the Greek civilisation. Serious expeditions to Ottoman Greece started to take place in the 17th century, where Western travellers focused on the collection of antiquities, but it was not until the beginning of the 18th century that the interest was directed towards the legendary battlefields.[5]

Due to geographical circumstances at Thermopylae the site saw dramatic changes from the 5th century to modern times; the place no longer resembled the accounts in the ancient texts. Alluvial deposits had widened the pass into a plain several kilometres wide, the ground level had risen in height and levelled the area so that the hill where the last stand had taken place was no longer 30 meters high but rather 10, and Mount Callidromos, which in antiquity towered over the pass and provided protection to the Greek forces, no longer offered a natural barrier.[6] As a result, the place was now difficult to find, which encouraged several expeditions of European intellectuals to visit the area in order to locate where exactly the Spartan 300 had stood and fallen against the mighty Persian army.[7] One of the most important attempts was the Wood-Dawkins-Stuart expedition, which in the middle of the 17th century made the first effort to analyse the geological changes at Thermopylae. Nothing was ever published from the expedition but the gathered information and

---

3. Ian Macgregor Morris: "Shrines of the Mighty: Rediscovering the Battlefields of the Persian Wars," in Bridges, Hall and Rhodes: *Cultural Responses to the Persian Wars. Antiquity to the Third Millennium*, Oxford 2007, p. 235.
4. Byron: *The Giaour*, pp. 103-9; Macgregor Morris, Shrines of the Mighty, pp. 231-2.
5. Macgregor Morris: Shrines of the Mighty, p. 238
6. Macgregor Morris: Shrines of the Mighty, p. 236.
7. Macgregor Morris: Shrines of the Mighty, p. 242.

the reputation of Wood and Stuart, as leading expects in classical Greek archaeology, made their observations interesting to other writers and cartographers, who used the drawing and diaries to conduct their own investigations.[8]

The new interest in Thermopylae and the focus on the courageous Spartans as a model of Western virtue inspired tales of battles in 19th and 20th century Europe. Among them was the Battle of Dybbøl, where the well-equipped numerically superior Prussian forces crushed what Danish romanticists saw as a brave but numerically inferior Danish army.[9] The Battle of Alamo in Texas in 1836, where a group of Texans barricaded themselves in the mission of Alamo and fought the superior Mexican army to the last man, has also been presented as the Thermopylae of Texas, both after the battle, where a memorial plate set up in Austin Texas compared Alamo with the Battle of Thermopylae, and today, where Ted Poe, a member of congress, on his official website, makes a parallel to Thermopylae, using both battles to underline the need to recognise those who sacrificed themselves in the fight for freedom.[10] A later, less obvious parallel is from the First World War, where the numerically superior Italian forces are celebrated as the Italian Thermopyleans for having blocked the Austrian offensive in 1916.[11]

Modern scholars have also traditionally described Thermopylae in an almost mythical way as a place where the heroic deeds of the Spartans played a vital role in the later victory. With references to 9/11, the Spartan specialist Paul Cartledge describes the defeat as an ideologically motivated suicide act, which inspired the Greeks to unite against the common enemy.[12] The historian Peter Green sees the battle as an act of inspiration, which mobilised the Greeks and in a sense made the

---

8. Macgregor Morris: Shrines of the Mighty, p. 240.
9. Inge Adriansen: *Nationale symboler i det danske rige 1830-2000* Vol. 2, Copenhagen 2003, pp. 252-3.
10. http://www.nationalcenter.org/Alamo.html (May 14, 2012); http://poe.house.gov/index.php?option=com_content&task=view&id=8141&Itemid=171 (May 14, 2012).
11. Nils Arne Sørensen: *Den Store krig: Europæernes første Verdenskrig*, Copenhagen 2005, p. 124.
12. Cartledge: *Thermopylae*, 202, 206-7. See also Poul Cartledge: *The Spartans. An Epic History.* London 2003, pp. 118-119.

later victories possible.[13] Other scholars have come to a similar conclusion. The military historian John Francis Lazenby, who holds that the Battle of Salamis was the military turning point, argues nonetheless that Thermopylae was a battle which acted as a source of inspiration to the Greeks, and the historian Nicholas Hammond, who doubts that Leonidas' decision to take a last stand made much military difference, holds that the Spartan sacrifice was essential to the later victory because it showed iron will and undaunted courage, which inspired others to follow their example.[14] In sum, there is a consensus to praise the battle as a moral victory decisive for the later success. The battle is presented as an act of bravery, which provided the demoralised and previously divided Greeks with a much-needed boost to morale, inspired by which they rallied and set aside various differences to continue the war in a more coherent and determined fashion.

Whether the Battle at Thermopylae lives up to its reputation is the theme for the present Chapter. The discussion opens with a re-examination of how the battle affected the political climate within the Greek coalition and challenges the general consensus that Thermopylae was significant for the later victories. Another question to be examined is why Thermopylae has achieved its legacy as the place where Greece stood up against Persian supremacy to fight and defend Greek culture and thus also Western civilisation from Persian destruction. A re-examination of the political implications following the defeat at Thermopylae is important because it puts to the test both the collective memory of Thermopylae as the battle that mobilised the Greeks to carry on the resistance as well as the entire notion of a united Greece.

It will be argued that the Greek cities continued to follow individual agendas and to join forces only when the alternative was less attractive. It was not a united Greece which stood up against the Persian threat – and as such not a war of civilisation – but a number of independent states pursuing individual strategies, which served their particular interests

---

13. Peter Green: *The Greco-Persian Wars*, Berkeley & Los Angeles 1996, p. 143.
14. John Lazenby: *The Defence of Greece 490-479*, Oxford 1993, p. 150; Nicholas Hammond: 'The expedition of Xerxes' in *The Cambridge Ancient History IV Persia, Greece and the Western Mediterranean c.525-479*. Cambridge 1988, p. 558.

best. To highlight the political and military implications of the no doubt courageous, self-sacrificial act, the analyses will be focused on the military situation and the political climate after the Persians' victory. But before turning to the situation after the battle, some consideration of the political manoeuvres before the occupation of Thermopylae is needed to give an idea of the various political interests which dominated Greek politics before the war.

Preparing for the Persians

When the news of Persian mobilisation first reached the Greek mainland in autumn 481, efforts were made to unite all Greeks for the coming war. According to the historian Herodotus, our primary source for the Persian War, Sparta called for a conference to discuss the Persian threat and how to prevent Greek cities from joining the Persian cause. Internal disputes between the Greek cities were postponed to save all available resources, and envoys were sent to Sicily on what should prove to be an unsuccessful attempt to persuade Galon, the tyrant of Syracuse, to join the mainland Greeks (Herodotus 7.157-164).

Several of the Greek states were in despair and uncertain of where to place their loyalty. Xerxes' overwhelming force made a Greek victory seem more than difficult, and various cities tried to delay their decision for as long as possible. The city of Argos stepped out of the coalition due to predictable disagreements over the command with Sparta, its mortal enemy, and Corcyra, modern Corfu, promised 60 ships but never made it further than the Peloponnesian West Coast.[15] Xerxes' envoys had managed to persuade the Aleuadai, a powerful family in the Thessalian city Larissa, to join the king, but as Xerxes prepared to move against Greece, other dynasties in Thessaly, who feared the family's growing power, managed to persuade the Greek coalition to send an army. And so a force of 10,000 Spartans, Athenians and presumably other Greeks took a stand at the pass of Tempe to the north of Thessaly to form a line of defence

---

15. Hammond: 'The expedition of Xerxes', p. 544; Green: *The Greco-Persian Wars*, p. 84

that would protect not only central but also northern Greece from the coming invasion (Herodotus 7.172-174).[16]

As the Greek commanders realised that the pass of Tempe could be turned and discovered more about both the Thessalian resilience and the size of the Persian army, the plan to meet Xerxes so far north was abolished.[17] Thessaly was abandoned and its political elite made an agreement with the Persians (Herodotus 7.174). Yet, the decision to send a joint force of 10,000 hoplites to defend Greece north of Thessaly demonstrates that the Greeks were prepared to meet Xerxes head on in a battle to keep Persia out of Greece – at least until the real threat was known.[18]

Despite Thessaly's siding with the Persians, the efforts to form a strong coalition against Persia continued. Both Herodotus and the Sicilian historian Diodorus, who wrote his narrative history in the 1st century BCE, describe how the negotiation continued at Corinth. Here it was decided to face the threat by sending a fleet to Artemision on the island of Euboea and a land army to the pass of Thermopylae to form a line of defence more to the south, but one that would still protect central Greece.[19]

> The point of view that won the day was that they should defend the pass at Thermopylae ... So they decided to prevent the Persians from entering Greece by defending this pass.
> (Herodotus 7.175)[20]

When reports reached the Greek delegates that the Persian forces were near, they voted for the immediate dispatch of the fleet to Artemision in Euboea. ... and of a strong hoplite force to Thermopylai, to occupy the

---

16. Herodotus 7.172.1; C. Hignett: *Xerxes' Invasion of Greece*, Oxford 1963, pp. 102-3; Hammond: The expedition of Xerxes', p. 545; Lazenby: *The Defence of Greece*, pp. 108-10; Green: *The Greco-Persian Wars*, p. 85.
17. Hignett: *Xerxes' Invasion*, pp. 102-3; Hammond: The expedition of Xerxes' 1988, p. 545; Lazenby: *The Defence of Greece*, p. 110, Green: *The Greco-Persian Wars*, pp. 85-7.
18. Lazenby: *The Defence of Greece*, p. 111.
19. Hignett: *Xerxes' Invasion*, pp. 113-15; Green *The Greco-Persian Wars*, p. 105.
20. Translation by Robin Waterfield in *Herodotus: The Histories*, Oxford 1998.

passes at their narrowest point ahead of the barbarians and thus block their further advance into Greece.
(Diodorus 11.4.1)[21]

It has been argued that the proposal to fight Xerxes at Thermopylae and Artemision was met with strong opposition by the Peloponnesian cities and Herodotus' remark that the proposal to fight at the Thermopylae-Artemision line got the most votes suggests that more than one strategy was on the table.[22] There are a number of reasons why the Peloponnesians were sceptical about fighting north of Central Greece. Having obtained more information about the size of the Persian army from the expedition to Tempe, the Peloponnesians may easily have started to doubt whether this was indeed their war and whether it was wise to prioritise the defence of Athens over the safety of the Peloponnesian cities. They may, and rightly so, have reasoned that a defeat at Thermopylae would leave their cities exposed and felt that the best strategy was to take a stand at the Isthmus between the Peloponnese and central Greece – leaving central Greece unprotected as an unfortunate but necessary price to pay. Some of the Peloponnesian delegates may therefore have had a mandate from home to argue for a defensive line at the Isthmus.

On the other hand, the strategy of meeting Xerxes at Thermopylae must have gained clear support from the Spartan delegation.[23] But to obtain most votes a fair share of the Peloponnesian representatives must have followed the Spartan delegation and voted in favour of a northern line of defence. As pointed out by Herodotus, the defence of the Peloponnese depended on the ability to prevent the Persians from landing troops on the peninsula, which was obtainable only as long as the Athenians invested most of their fighting power in the navy. The Spartan delegation may therefore have realised from early on that a defence of central

---

21. Translation by Peter Green in *Diodorus Siculus: Books 11-12.37.1: Greek History, 480-431 BC – The Alternative Version*, Austin 2006.
22. Hignett argues that Sparta's Peloponnesians were uneasy to fight at Thermopylae, which they regarded as too far to the north (in *Xerxes' Invasion*, 115). Also Green mentions the disagreement but argues that the plan of the Athenian general Themistocles to fight the Persians in a naval battle led by Sparta was met by Peloponnesian opposition (1996, p. 100).
23. Hignett: *Xerxes' Invasion*, p. 115.

Greece was the only way to keep the coalition together and the Persians away from Peloponnesian shores.

With Athens' naval power and Sparta's renowned army, the defence was organised so that each city committed to what they did best. But as the following events demonstrate, the plan to fight at Thermopylae was forcefully opposed in the cities. In Sparta the decision was delayed by deference to the Carneian festival, and the Peloponnesians, who from the beginning had questioned the plan and least of all wanted to go along without Sparta, used the Olympic Games as their reason to remain at home (Herodotus 7.206).

No doubt it is difficult to assess the religious importance of the Carneian festival and the Olympic Games. Still, the reluctance to send out the army suggests that the Spartans and Peloponnesians were divided on the strategy both within and between the individual cities. Here, the decision to use Peloponnesian forces in the defence of central Greece was met with understandable scepticism and fear.[24] As argued by Cartledge, the Peloponnesians were in panic, fearing that the Persians could not be stopped at Thermopylae and thereby preferred to stay at the Peloponnese ready to either defend their home or to make some sort of deal with Xerxes as hundreds of other cities had already done.[25] A point supported by Herodotus' claim that Leonidas left Sparta with his personal bodyguard of three hundred Spartans to prevent the Peloponnesians from making agreements with Xerxes (Herodotus 7.206).

By this initiative, Leonidas managed to raise an army of more than 6,000 hoplites from the Peloponnese and central Greece.[26] Had he remained in Sparta presumably the Peloponnesians would have followed the Spartan example and left Thermopylae and thereby central Greece undefended. If the Peloponnesians had failed to occupy Thermopylae, the coalition would have dissolved and the Peloponnese would soon have been without sufficient naval support to keep the Persian armada at

---

24. Green argues that the Peloponnesian reluctance was an attempt to sit out the situation. Expecting a final clash at the Isthmus, the Peloponnesian leaders were not ready to invest in the defence of central Greece before it was clear how the cities in central Greece would respond to the Persian threat (in *The Greco-Persian Wars*, p. 111ff).
25. Cartledge: *Thermopylae*, p. 124.
26. Hammond: 'The expedition of Xerxes', pp. 549-50.

bay. Leonidas' decision to move out was an attempt to pressurise Sparta and the other Peloponnesian cities to give up their passive strategy and engage in a battle necessary to the defence of not only Athens and central Greece but also of the Peloponnesian peninsula, which depended on the willingness in Athens to keep investing their resources on the sea.

It is, however, characteristic that the disagreement continued on arrival at Thermopylae, where several of the Peloponnesians, having realised what danger they were in, proposed a return to the Isthmus. Leonidas voted against the proposal and prevented a spontaneous withdrawal. But Spartan hesitation and the Peloponnesian proposal to vacate the pass underlines that the agreement between the delegations at Corinth never found support amongst the Peloponnesian public. When the army was able to meet Xerxes at Thermopylae, it was because Leonidas and a group of influential Spartans were determined to honour their promise to lead the land forces and defend Thermopylae – either because they chose to stand firmly behind the agreed strategy, which they probably had promoted in Corinth, believing it to be the only or the best way to fight Xerxes, or because they wished to uphold Sparta's position as the military leader of Greece.

From the beginning, the decision to fight at Thermopylae was a symbol of the profound differences in the Greek coalition. Sparta, on whom the entire land operation rested, supplied the smallest contribution to the land army and thereby failed to live up to their part of the agreement. By moving up to Thermopylae to meet the Persians and the decision to take a last stand against the Persian masses, Leonidas and his guard tried to save the day and diverted the attention from the fact that Sparta had not complied with the strategy its own delegates must have promoted at the conference they themselves had convened. The decision to send home the main force and stay behind was surely a courageous one, but it is another question altogether whether Sparta's sacrifice made the Athenians and the Greeks forget and forgive its modest contribution and yet another whether the act inspired the Greeks to unite and fight the Persians in a more coherent fashion only a month later at the Battle of Salamis.

Between defeat and victories

The notion that Thermopylae united the Greeks depends ultimately on two conditions. The first factor is time. The news of the Spartan sacrifice would have had to circulate and be accepted before it could have had any impact on the desperate and frustrated Athenians who had lost their city and seen the smoke from its burning temples. Secondly, there needed to be at least some sign that after the Battle at Thermopylae the allied cities were ready to compromise their own safety in defence of the alliance. Not surprisingly ancient commentators describe a desperate situation right after the loss of Thermopylae. The attempt to stop the Persian army had failed, Sparta had lost one of its kings and three hundred of its best soldiers, and the Persian breakthrough had forced the Greek fleet to abandon Artemision, allowing the Persian armada into the waters of central Greece. Besides the military crisis, Herodotus describes a political climate marked by distrust and dissolution, where the Athenians felt deserted by the Peloponnesians, who in addition to the poor engagement at Thermopylae had initiated the construction of a defensive wall across the Isthmus, sending a clear signal to their allies in central Greece that they were left to their own destiny.

> They [the Athenians] had been expecting to find every available Peloponnesian in Boeotia, waiting for the invader, but in fact they found nothing of the sort; instead they heard that the Peloponnesians were building a defensive wall across the Isthmus, since all that mattered to them was the survival of the Peloponnese. They were protecting the Peloponnese and abandoning everything else.
> (Herodotus 8.40)[27]

And Herodotus moves on to describe the spontaneous dissolution in the Greek fleet.

---

27. Translation Waterfield: *Herodotus: The Histories*.

> When news of the events of the Athenian Acropolis reached the Greeks on Salamis, they were so panic-stricken that some of the commanders did not even wait for a final decision on the proposal about what action to take, but rushed for their ships and began to hoist their sails with the intention of beating a hasty retreat.
> (Herodotus 8.56)[28]

Herodotus describes the shock felt by the crews when they learned that Athens had fallen to the Persians. Nearly half of the ships were manned by Athenians. They had left Athens to engage the Persians on the sea with the expectation that the Peloponnesian army would defend Athens and central Greece. The Peloponnesian sailors on the other hand wanted to fall back to the Peloponnese to participate in the defence of their homes.[29] Plutarch, who wrote biographies of Greek and Roman statesmen in the 1st century CE, also describes how the Spartans and the Peloponnesians abandoned their allies in central Greece.

> Although Xerxes had marched up through Doris and invaded Phocis, and was putting the Phocian Settlement to the torch, the Greeks [the Peloponnesians] did not go to their relief, despite the fact that the Athenians were begging them to take the field in Boeotia and make a stand against the enemy there in the defence of Attica, to match the way they – the Athenians – had sailed to Artemisium to help the Greek cause.
> (Plutarch Themistocles 9.3)[30]

In Plutarch's account the Peloponnesians betrayed the Greek cause by failing to assist the cities in central Greece. Also Diodorus, one of the few Ancient writers to hold the events at Thermopylae as essential to the final victory, adds to the picture of a coalition marked by panic and dissolution.

---

28. Translation Waterfield: *Herodotus: The Histories*.
29. Hignett judges that the Athenians were little impressed by the Spartan sacrifice (in *Xerxes' Invasion*, 148); Hammond: The expedition of Xerxes', 566-7; Barry Strauss: *The Battle of Salamis: The Naval Encounter That Saved Greece – and Western Civilization*, New York 2004, p. 61.
30. Translation by Waterfield in *Plutarch: Greek Lives*: Oxford World Classics 1989, Oxford 1998.

> The Hellenic land forces (the Spartan and Peloponnesian army) likewise were equally terrified by the enemy's vast armaments: the loss at Thermopylai of their most distinguished fighters utterly dismayed them, while the disasters taking place in Attica before their very eyes reduced the Greeks to a state of deep despair.
> (Diodorus 11.16.2)[31]

But having described the mayhem following the invasion of central Greece, Diodorus relates how the delegates at Corinth agreed to build the defensive wall at the Isthmus – indicating that it was not the Peloponnesian motion alone but a joint decision within the coalition to improve the defence of Peloponnese (Diodorus 11.16.3). Diodorus is not necessarily wrong, but after the loss of Boeotia and Attica the non-Peloponnesian delegates in reality had no influence on how the Peloponnesians would choose to organise their own defence.

More ships from the Peloponnese did join the navy after Thermopylae, and according to Herodotus the numbers of vessels at Salamis were higher now than before the departure to Artemision (Herodotus 8.43). This new mobilisation could indicate a sense of hope among the coalition parties and testify to a readiness to invest in a joint defence of Salamis and thereby a decision to protect the Athenians. But as noted by both Herodotus and Plutarch, the Peloponnesians showed no intention of engaging the Persian fleet at Salamis. Instead, the Peloponnesian command planned to redraw the entire Greek navy to the Peloponnese and form a new line of defence between the fleet and the army at the now fortified Isthmus. According to both writers, the Spartan navy commander Eurybiades, who held command over the entire Greek navy operation, opposed the idea of a Battle of Salamis until faced with the threat, real or not, that the Athenians would migrate to Siris in Italy – a move which in reality would dissolve the fleet and enable the Persians to land troops on the Peloponnese – if he refused to fight at Salamis (Herodotus 8.49-50; 8.60-3).[32] Faced with the prospect of a war on two fronts, the Spartan

---

31. Translation by Green in *Diodorus Siculus: Books 11-12.37.1*, 2006.
32. Hammond: The expedition of Xerxes', 571; Green: *The Greco-Persian Wars*, pp. 164-5, pp. 168-171.

command had no choice but to keep the fleet together. Diodorus tries to uphold the illusion of a tense but still united coalition. The Peloponnesian plan to fall back is mentioned but Diodorus states that the decision to fight at Salamis was unanimous, ignoring the profound disagreement between the Peloponnesians and the Spartan naval command on the one hand and the Athenians and the rest of Central Greece on the other (Diodorus 11.4.).

The disagreement over the strategy seems real enough, and very much in line with the strategy followed by Sparta and its Peloponnesian allies both before the Battle at Thermopylae and, as we shall see below, after the Battle of Salamis. In any case, there is nothing in the writing of Herodotus and Plutarch to suggest that Sparta's role at Thermopylae brought the coalition closer together in the month between the Battle at Thermopylae and the Battle of Salamis. The Peloponnesians' limited investment in the defence of Thermopylae, their inability or unwillingness to fight for central Greece and their fallback to the Isthmus, where they invested in the construction of the defensive wall, all testify to a coalition that was falling apart. The ancient writers all agree that Leonidas' defeat and the subsequent loss of Athens sent the Greeks, not least the Athenians, into a state of shock, despair and disbelief, and nothing in the writing of Herodotus and Plutarch suggests that the events at Thermopylae had any effect on Greek morale or ability to unite before the Battle of Salamis.

To use the words of Lazenby, the Thermopylae-Artemision campaign was a disaster, but the turning point, however, was just around the corner. Xerxes attacked the Greek navy at Salamis before the Peloponnesians had a chance to abandon the bay. Against all odds, the Greek coalition won a magnificent victory. Not only was the Persian fleet decimated and on the run back to Asia, but the victory delivered a decisive blow to the Persian command, forcing Xerxes to flee Greece. However, Salamis was a fundamental victory but not the end of the war. A large share of the Persian infantry and cavalry was left behind and still represented a great threat to Greece, which would require the coalition to engage in a risky ground battle to defeat the Persian army once and for all. Nevertheless, the victory created a euphoric atmosphere in Greece as it proved that despite their superior force the Persians could be defeated. The awaiting battle, on the other hand, would be dangerous and a defeat would still prove fatal to the cities involved.[33] The united Greek navy may have won Greece the initiative, but the Spartan commanded forces at the Isthmus would still have to move out from behind the wall to finish what the fleet had started.

If the rest of the coalition saw Sparta's contribution at Thermopylae as a betrayal or at least as an example of Peloponnesian unwillingness to invest fully in the defence of central Greece, the Battle of Salamis was the event which could have inspired the coalition to mobilise an army to finally defeat the Persians. It was here that Greek sailors from Athens, the island of Aegina, the Peloponnese and central Greece fought and won what would soon prove to be a decisive victory. The naval success, to which Sparta made no little claim, combined with the heroic sacrifice at Thermopylae, could have served as a source of inspiration and encouraged the hitherto reluctant and defensively minded Spartans and Peloponnesians to join the rest of Greece in the attempt to defeat the remaining Persians. The momentum, however, was, as will be argued below, lost in diplomatic manoeuvres and the hope that other states would take the lead and more importantly the risk. Characteristic for the coalition's chronic inability to unite and agree to a common strategy, the winter was not used to mobilise the necessary coherence to launce the much-needed attack on the Persian army.

Instead, the ancient commentators describe how the Persian general Mardonius offered the Athenians the leadership of Greece if they would submit to terms of the Persian king. The arrival of a Persian delegation caused Sparta to send envoys to Athens only to learn that Athens had rejected the generous offer after all. The Athenians used the opportunity to urge Sparta to engage the Persians but when Mardonius, having received the Athenian rejection, invaded Athens for the second time, the Peloponnesian army remained passive.[34] As a result, Athens reminded the Spartans that they could be forced to accept the Persian offer if Sparta chose to remain passive. Persuaded by the Athenian threat, the political class in Sparta finally agreed to lead an army of what proved to

---

33. Lazenby: *The Defence of Greece*, p. 197.
34. Herodotus 8.140-44; Plutarch Aristides, 10.3-6. Diodorus 11.18

be a joint army, including a large contingent of Athenian troops, against the Persians who were finally defeated at the city of Plataea in the spring of 479.

In his description of the battle, Diodorus relates how the Greeks took an oath swearing that they would value freedom above life before initiating the campaign (Diodorus 11.29.3). Formally, it was finally a united Greece that fought the Persians. It is, however, necessary to remember that Sparta only reluctantly led the campaign in the first place and did not commit to the tasks until threatened by the prospect of an agreement between Persia and the Athenians. Such a constellation, if indeed the negotiation between Athens and Mardonius was more than just an Athenian deal breaker, would have had severe political and military implications for the Spartans, who could hardly hope to maintain their leading position in Greece if Athens achieved political, financial and military support from Persia.

According to Herodotus, Sparta was fully aware that such an alliance would enable the enemy to land troops behind the defensive wall forcing the Peloponnesians to fight a war on two fronts while at the same time leaving their cities unprotected, which could easily have dissolved the Peloponnesian league (Herodotus 9.9).

In any case, there is, however, nothing to suggest that the events at Thermopylae the year before did anything to inspire the Greeks before the Battle at Plataea. Not even the victory at Salamis seems to have had that affect. What motivated Sparta's change of strategy was, according to the sources, the fear that the Athenians would eventually lose their patience and seek an agreement of some kind with Persia. At last the fighting had come to an end but the struggle to reconstruct what had just happened was only about to begin. All the parties involved were eager to tell their side of the story and assure that their particular contribution to the war was recognised as essential to the later victory. As a part of this process, strategies were explained; history re-written and traditions were invented to create the right reputation. It is here that the idea of a Greece united against Persia emerged.

The battle of the past

The attempt to underline the importance of Thermopylae was initiated right after the war, where not least Sparta tried to change the story of Thermopylae from the defeat that almost decided the war to the tale of brave Spartans who won a moral victory by inspiring the Greeks with their courage and self-sacrifice. This tradition survives in a number of celebratory poems and honorific inscriptions recorded in the works of later historians. One example is offered by Diodorus, who quotes the poet Simonides' celebration of the men who died at Thermopylae.

> Of those who died at Thermopylai
> renowned is the fortune, noble the fate:
> Their grave's an alter, their memorial our mourning,
> their fate our praise.
> Such a shroud neither decay
> nor all-conquering time shall destroy.
> This sepulcher of brave men has taken the high
> renown of Hellas for its fellow occupant, as witness
> Leonidas, Sparta's king who left behind a great
> memorial of valor, everlasting renown.
> (Diodorus 11.11.6)[35]

The message is clear that Greece must honour the men who fought and died for its freedom. The focus is on the deed itself not the implication of the battle. Another example is an inscription quoted by Herodotus, where the Spartans' last stand is singled out and honoured separately by the famous words "Stranger, tell the people of Lacedaemon that we who lie here obeyed their commands".[36] According to the law, Spartans were not allowed to flee or abandon their post but were expected to fight to the end. Once again it is the self-sacrifice and the readiness to give up their lives for Greece and the obedience of the Spartan life which is in

---
35. Translation by Peter Green *Diodorus Siculus: Books 11-12.37.1*.
36. Herodotus 7.228.

focus. A similar approach is found in another inscription, mentioned by Herodotus, where the Peloponnesians as a force are honoured for having fought at Thermopylae.

> Here once were three million of the foe
> Opposed by four thousand from the Peloponnese.[37]

These honorific inscriptions and poems are often used as evidence for the alleged positive influence the Battle at Thermopylae is said to have had on Greek morale, and it has been suggested that the attempt to present the battle as decisive for the later victories was in line with a general feeling among the Greeks.[38] Judging from the lyrics alone, it is far from obvious that that the inscriptions support such a claim. The Battle at Thermopylae, in particularly the last stand, was no doubt a remarkable act of bravery, which both the Spartans and their Peloponnesian allies proudly celebrated. What is, however, less obvious is why the Athenians and the other Greeks would see Sparta's performance in the pass as a vital contribution, particularly when the defeat led to the loss of Athens, the beginning of the dissolution of the fleet and a Peloponnesian attempt to protect themselves by the construction of a defensive wall at the Isthmus. Herodotus and Plutarch both mention that the Athenians expected to find the Peloponnesian army in Boeotia ready to defend Athens and describe, as did Diodorus, how Sparta failed to help the Athenians when the city was sacked the second time.[39]

Another factor to consider is the chronology. Sparta's version of the events at Thermopylae and their role in the war needed time to circulate before it would affect Greek morale. The month between the battles at Thermopylae and Salamis was insufficient even if the sacrifice of Leonidas and his men did create a sense of collectivity within the coalition. In a sense the lyrics and the honorific inscriptions represent a post-war

---

37. Herodotus 7.228. Translation by Robin Waterfield in *Herodotus: The Histories*. It is possible that Simonides wrote the text of all the epic inscriptions at Thermopylae, but this cannot be proven with certainty.
38. Bradford: *Thermopylae*, pp. 147-8; Green: *The Greco-Persian Wars*, p. 143.
39. Herodotus 8.40; Plutarch Themistocles 9.4; Diodorus 11.28-29.

sentiment, where the euphoria following the Spartan-led victories at Plataea had improved the city's reputation in parts of central Greece and encouraged the celebration of the earlier engagement at Thermopylae. In the end everything went well, Greece prevailed and it is not unreasonable to assume that many Greeks, particularly the Peloponnesians, saw Sparta, and thereby to some extent themselves, as the liberators of Greece. Herodotus' remark that in his opinion it was the Athenians who saved Greece may have been a response to a tradition celebrating the Spartans as those who ensured victory in the end (Herodotus 7.139). It is, however, important not to transfer the post-war euphoria and gratitude following the final victory to how the non-Peloponnesian members of the coalition experienced Sparta's engagement during the war.

The only ancient commentator to explicitly describe the Battle at Thermopylae as essential to the later victories is Diodorus. Having praised the men who remained behind to take the last stand for their courage he summarises the importance of the battle in the longer run.

> Moreover, anyone who argues that these men were also more responsible for achieving the freedom of the Greeks than the victors in subsequent battles against Xerxes would be in the right of it; for when the barbarians recalled their deeds, they were terror-struck, whereas the Greeks were encouraged to attempt similar acts of bravery.[40]
> (Diodorus 11.11.5)

Diodorus' opinion supports the notion that Thermopylae rallied the Greeks, inspiring them to pursue similar deeds in the coming battles. There is a consensus in modern scholarship that Diodorus' source of inspiration derives from the intellectual environment in 4th century Athens, where political thinkers and commentators argued for the need to wage war on Persia in order to put an end to the king's increasing influence on Greek politics.[41] There is a tendency in the Athenian dominated

---

40. Translation by Green in *Diodorus Siculus: Books 11-12.37.1*.
41. John Marincola: 'The Persian Wars in Fourth-Century Oratory and Historiography', in Bridges, Hall and Rhodes *Cultural Responses to the Persian Wars: Antiquity to the Third Millennium*, Oxford 2007, p. 108, pp. 111-12

sources to present the Athenians as the Greeks who suffered the most in the fight for freedom.[42] But at the same time we see a trend among the intellectuals to emphasise Thermopylae as the battle, where the Spartans stood up against the Persians and sacrificed themselves to hold back the invading force for as long as possible. The battle was still regarded as a defeat but only because the Spartans were too few in number to prevail.[43] The Athenians could afford to be generous and use Thermopylae as the event in which Sparta, on the moral level, contributed decisively to the war against Persia, and thereby as a moral victory in order to convince their fellow Athenians, other Greeks and not least the Spartans, that a new war against Persia was in the best interests of Greece and manageable if the Greeks came together, once again, to fight their mortal enemy in a new common front. This approach is particularly evident in the writing of Isocrates, who throughout most of the 4th century argued for a common front of Greek states against the Persian Empire, which still in the 4th century played a dominant role in Greek politics.[44] As such to present the Battle at Thermopylae as a moral victory that contributed to the final victory was an Athenian intellectuals' politicising attempt to include Sparta in a new war against Persia, which men such as Isocrates hoped would enable Athens to win back her former glory, while at the same time underlining that it was the Athenians who won the Persian Wars.[45]

Furthermore, the great importance attributed to the Battle at Thermopylae is tied closely to Sparta's political and military status in the beginning of the 4th century. This is also particularly evident in the writing of Isocrates, who in 380 described the Spartan contribution as vital and Spartans as important partners in a coming war against Persia. After the Battle at Leuctra in 371, where Sparta lost most of its military and political powers and thereby the ability to contribute decisively to a new campaign against the Persian king, the perception of the Spartans and their

---

42. Marincola: The Persian Wars in Fourth-Century Oratory 111-12. Isocrates Panathenaikos 49-58, Panegyricus 98.
43. Isocrates Panegyricus, 90-92; Anuschka Albertz: *Exemplarisches Heldentum: Die Rezeptionsgeschichte der Schlacht an den Thermopylen von der Antike bis zur Gegenwart*, München 2006, p. 69; Marincola: The Persian Wars in Fourth-Century Oratory, p. 112.
44. Isocrates Panegyricus 15-17, 186.
45. Marincola: The Persian Wars in Fourth-Century Oratory, p. 114

role in the Persian Wars changed from a moral victory to a plain defeat. Isocrates now saw the Macedonian king Philip II as the ideal leader of a new campaign against Persia, and in his speech Panathenaikos from 339 the Spartans are portrayed as a selfish and imperialistic people, who lost the Battle at Thermopylae.[46]

The positive attitude towards Thermopylae in the 4th century was therefore both political and ideological. To what degree Diodorus was inspired by the Athenian intellectuals is an open question. It is likely that he gained much of his material on the Persian War from the 4th century historian Ephorus, who was, as a student of Isocrates at least to some extent related to the intellectual environment in Athens. But judging from his description of the importance of the Battle at Thermopylae and his constant readiness to find a justifiable explanation for Sparta's passive attitude, Diodorus may have found some inspiration in the Spartan tradition as well. All we know is that Ephorus saw the wars on Sicily between Syracuse and Carthage, the latter a Persian ally, as the most decisive battle in the war between Persians and Greeks.[47] As a Greek from Sicily writing in the first century BCE, at a time when Greece had been under Roman rule for about a century, Diodorus may have felt inspired by the sacrifice of the three hundred Spartans who gave their lives for the freedom of Greece. Diodorus, however, offers no examples of or explanations as to how the Battle at Thermopylae inspired the Greeks to carry on their resistance. His point of view that the Battle at Thermopylae was the most important of the battles against the Persians is therefore little more than a personal opinion to which he is obviously entitled but one that cannot be sustained by what we know from the ancient accounts of the events – including Diodorus' own narrative.

Summing up, the perception among modern scholars that the Battle at Thermopylae inspired the independent Greek cities to unite and face the invading Persians rests ultimately on a Spartan tradition, which has come down to us primarily from secondary references to inscriptions set up at Thermopylae after the war had ended and after Sparta had led the Greeks to victory at Plataea; from a politicising intellectual debate in Athens aimed at convincing the Greeks to unite against a still more

---

46. Isokrates Panathenikos 183-190; Albertz: *Exemplarisches Heldentum*, pp. 73-74.
47. Marincola: The Persian Wars in Fourth-Century Oratory, p. 112.

dominant Persia; and from the personal perception of a Sicilian historian writing in a time, where Greek freedom and independence was becoming a thing of the past. But why did the Battle gain its reputation as the event that united the Greeks when ancient commentators describe the battle as a defeat, which placed the alliance under enormous pressure threatening to dissolve the coalition?

Part of the explanation may be found in the tendency to see the Persian Wars as a clash of civilisations, where a coalition of Greeks fought to defend their common culture against Persian destruction. Now this approach requires that the Greeks and their Persian enemy stood firmly against each other or at least that the leading Greek states were able to stand united against the invading forces. To uphold the idea of a united Greece, the Battle at Thermopylae, where Sparta failed its Greek allies, had to undergo a redefinition from a defeat with great military and political implications, to a courageous sacrifice for the greater good, which rallied the Greeks to continued resistance and thereby to stand as a moral victory decisive for the later victories. This interpretation is problematic because it ignores or reduces the implication of the disagreements and political instability following the defeat at Thermopylae to provide a picture of a Greek alliance which may have disagreed on the strategies, but nonetheless defended its common culture together.

Now, as this discussion has tried to show, there is little to suggest that the Battle at Thermopylae had a mobilising effect on the Greek resistance or served as an example that the other Greeks aimed to follow – neither at Salamis nor at Plataea. The Battle at Thermopylae is more convincingly seen as the symbol of a divided Greece, where each city followed its own individual strategy to protect its own interests. As such, the idea of the Persian Wars as a clash of civilisations, where a united Greece defeated the Persian Kingdom and thereby saved not only their own but also Western civilisation is a myth which has become an integral part of Western tradition.

In the Haven of Eternity? A Churchyard as a Contested Place

Martin Rheinheimer

In its commemoration of the dead, a community ensures its identity.[1] Therefore, gravestones and churchyards have a special meaning, which is emphasised by the sacred character of these places. The gravestones are an expression of collective memory,[2] and any rearrangement of the gravestones, therefore, also means a change in their meaning.

Spatial sociology distinguishes between the *place* (in German *Ort*) as a concrete geographical point and the *space* (in German *Raum*) created by the placement of objects and people as well as attributions of meaning. In this way, the same place may include several spaces. Space is not static, but dynamic and multidimensional. For example, the attributions of meaning can change and thus change the space.[3]

Spaces change over time as society changes. But what is the process like? Which conflicts arise? This issue will be explored by the example of a churchyard. My example is the rearrangement (translocation) of the seafarers' gravestones at the churchyard of Amrum, of which the as-

---

1. Cf. Jan Assmann: *Das kulturelle Gedächtnis. Schrift, Erinnerung und politische Identität in frühen Hochkulturen*, 2nd edition, München 1997, p. 63. On the significance of graves and gravestones, see also Aleida Assmann: *Erinnerungsräume. Formen und Wandlungen des kulturellen Gedächtnisses*, München 1999, pp. 322-328.
2. The collective memory forms – as defined by Mathias Berek – the "entire collection of represented images, texts, and meanings of the past ... which are held present or potentially available in the society", while "Erinnerungskultur" means "the social processes where the past is reproduced". Mathias Berek: *Kollektives Gedächtnis und die gesellschaftliche Konstruktion der Wirklichkeit. Eine Theorie der Erinnerungskulturen*, Wiesbaden 2009, p. 33.
3. Cf. Martina Löw: *Raumsoziologie*, Frankfurt a. M. 2001.

sociated conflicts will be analysed. The analysis focuses on the process of reinterpretation of the gravestones and the churchyard in the course of social change, namely the transition from a society based on seafaring towards a society based on tourism.

After looking at the churchyard and the gravestones of Amrum, we will first examine the function of the gravestones in the seafarers' community of Amrum. Then the translocations of the gravestones will be described as a background for the analysis of the changes in the meaning of the churchyard and gravestones, which is the topic of the following section. This leads to conclusions concerning the new function of the gravestones in the tourist experience economy.

The churchyard of Amrum and its gravestones

In the cemeteries of the North Sea islands, many old gravestones from the 17th, 18th, and 19th centuries have been preserved, on Terschelling some even from the 16th century. On many gravestones, representations of ships can be found as an expression of the local seafaring tradition.[4] These gravestones receive high interest. An example of this is the measures for the preservation and reorganisation of the gravestones on the island of Amrum. Along the same line, Theodor Möller and Georg Quedens have written richly illustrated books about the local churchyard and its headstones.[5] Georg Quedens's book has just been published in a third edition, now under the title "Im Hafen der Ewigkeit" (In the haven of eternity).

St. Clement's Church is and was the only church on the island of Amrum and is located in the village of Nebel, situated roughly in the middle of the island. The thatched church dates from the 13th century

---

4. Cf. Martin Rheinheimer: "Skibe for evigheden. Gravsten og regional kultur ved Nordsøkysten," in *Sjæklen 2010* (Esbjerg 2011), pp. 88-111; Norbert Fischer & Helmut Schoenfeld: "Regionale Grabmalkultur am Beispiel der Nordseeküste," in *Grabkultur in Deutschland. Geschichte der Grabmäler*, Berlin 2009, pp. 347-357.
5. Theodor Möller: *Der Kirchhof in Nebel auf Amrum und seine alten Grabsteine*, Neumünster 1928; Georg Quedens: *Im Hafen der Ewigkeit. Die alten Grabsteine auf dem Amrumer Friedhof*, 3rd edition, Amrum 2009. The book was first published under the title *Die alten Grabsteine auf dem Amrumer Friedhof* in 1984, second edition 1994.

and is surrounded by a churchyard which is bordered by a wall. Today, the church has a distinctive tower in the west, but this was only built in 1908.[6] In the churchyard, we still find about 150 old headstones from before 1900. Twenty-eight of these old gravestones and some newer ones have the image of a ship carved in the stone.[7] There are gravestones from the 17th century which were originally lying, but are now erected, as well as standing gravestones from the 18th and 19th centuries, known as stelae. Some stelae are provided with inscriptions and pictures on both sides. There are also some smaller gravestones in the form of tiles with very short and often abbreviated texts. The most beautiful gravestones have been collected by the war memorial in the north-western corner of the churchyard. We find several headstones on the inside of the western and northern walls of the churchyard, as well as on the eastern and southern exterior wall of the church. Some tiles are stored in the church loft. Only the headstones of the former pastor's family, Mechlenburg, are still located on the family grave in the north-east of the churchyard.

The old gravestones often have long inscriptions with comprehensive biographies of the deceased. Especially appealing is the headstone of Andres Finck and his wife Marret Andresen from the year 1740.

The stone is 148 cm high and 74 cm wide. On the front, the crucified Christ is shown above the family (11 people). Underneath is written:

"The blood of Jesus Christ cleanses us from all our sins / / I. N. R. I. / / Here the bones of / the blessed skipper Andres Finck / expect a joyful resurrection / born on Amrom the 20th May Ao. 1678 / entered into matrimony with Marret Tückis / there in 1705, in lasting wedlock / they begat 7 children together as 4 sons / and 3 daughters, of which 3 sons and 2 daughters / already into blessed eternity / have been received. Died the 3rd December Ao. 1738 / of his age 60 years 7 months and 13 days / as well as his wife / Marret Andresen / born the 21th July Ao.1679 / died Ao. 17 – of her age / – years – months / God be merciful to their souls."

---

6. Cf. Georg Quedens: *Kirche und Friedhöfe auf Amrum. Kirchengeschichte der St. Clemens-Kirche*, Breklum 1997.
7. Rheinheimer: "Skibe for evigheden," p. 92.

Gravestone of Andres Finck in the churchyard on Amrum, front and rear, photos: Martin Rheinheimer, 2005 and 2009.

A Wadden Sea ship moving to the right is engraved on the back. Underneath is written:

"As a skipper I have sailed / a lot of years and long time / with people, also merchant goods / on the Elbe, Weser and elsewhere / also endured / a lot of worry day and night / in the sea and on the beaches / to rest God has brought me / Andres Finck / Ao. 1740."[8]

On many gravestones the profession of the deceased is mentioned. If a ship is depicted, they were always commanders, captains, skippers (like Andres Finck) or other kinds of seafarers. The ship is thus an expression of their profession. The biographies are, particularly on Amrum and Föhr, often very specific and indicate how long and at what age the deceased went to sea, as well as from which places (e.g. Copenhagen or Amsterdam) and where to (Greenland, the East Indies, in the case of

---

8. On this gravestone, see Quedens: *Im Hafen der Ewigkeit*, pp. 60-63; Möller: *Kirchhof*, pp. 60f.

Andres Finck in the Wadden Sea to the Elbe and Weser, i.e. to Hamburg and Bremen).

The stones have often been made for couples, sometimes even for their children and other family members. Some have been used for entire families. The spouse who died first, man or woman, is listed first. In other cases, wives got their own headstones. Gravestones showing a picture of a ship which were made only for a wife were probably originally intended for her husband, too. The only example on Amrum is the gravestone of Anna Johanna Sönken († 1815). Her husband, Sönke Girres, remarried after her death and got himself another, less impressive gravestone with his second wife.[9]

Biographies and pictures on the gravestones give the impression of authenticity, but in reality they are highly stylised and their content is adapted to the purpose. On a gravestone, the deceased will always be described in a positive way. His life is reduced by fixed narrative patterns on certain conventional data and experiences: birth, marriage, number of children, occupation (and possibly career), death. Occasionally, tragedies like the death of a spouse or enslavement in Algiers were listed. Since the tragedies were allegedly overcome with God's help, they were understood as something positive. All data are usually placed in a Christian context, and thus make sense.

The pictures are not purely authentic pictures such as a concrete ship owned by the deceased – even if there are stylised indicators, such as the name of the ship. Sometimes, the ship in the picture is of a different type than the one owned by the deceased.[10] Therefore, the value of gravestones as a source is limited in terms of the actual past. The value rather lies in the interpretation of the biography and the self-image that the family wanted to communicate to contemporaries and posterity. Some gravestones and texts were already made while the person was alive, and the dates of death

---

9. Cf. Quedens: *Im Hafen der Ewigkeit*, pp. 132-135. In Emmerlev Botille Catharine Ries († 1860) got her own gravestone showing a ship beside the gravestone of her husband. – For the biographies on the gravestones on the island of Föhr, see Ines Weißenberg: "Weibliche und männliche Biographien auf Grabsteinen des 18. und 19. Jahrhunderts von der nordfriesischen Insel Föhr," in Alexandra Lutz (ed.), *Geschlechterbeziehungen in der Neuzeit. Studien aus dem norddeutschen Raum*, Neumünster 2005, pp. 155-177.
10. Cf. Rheinheimer: "Skibe for evigheden," p. 98.

were added afterwards. In these cases, the deceased ensured control over the image that posterity would have of them. Other memorials were not made until several years after the person had died. It was apparently the widow who had the gravestone for Andres Finck produced, but her own date of death was never added to the stone even though there is clearly space left for this addition after her date of birth.

The role of the gravestones in the seafaring community of Amrum

In 1787, as much as 81 per cent of the adult men on the island of Amrum were employed in seafaring. During the early part of the 19th century, the rate temporarily fell to just below 60 per cent, but in 1860 it was again at about 75 per cent.[11] The local community was at that time completely dominated by the maritime sector. The men were absent for a large part of the year while most women, children and the elderly remained on the island. Above them always hovered the threat that their providers would not return, because many seamen died by accident, shipwreck or disease.[12] However, seafaring also offered the chance to achieve prosperity. A case in point is Hark Nickelsen († 1770) whose elaborate gravestone shows a large three-master. He rose from being an orphan to being the richest man on the island. His fate illustrates both the dangers and the risks of seafaring. In his youth, he fell into the hands of Algerian corsairs and spent three years as a slave in Algiers. Later, he earned his income as a captain in the triangular trade between Denmark, Guinea and the West Indies. The former slave thus became a slave trader. On his gravestone is of course only written that he succeeded in "sailing a ship as a captain to the West Indies and the coast of Guinea",[13] i.e. a purely positive interpretation.

---

11. Cf. Martin Rheinheimer: "Eine maritime Gesellschaft im Wandel. Amrum im 19. Jahrhundert," in *Zeitschrift der Gesellschaft für Schleswig-Holsteinische Geschichte* 132 (2007), pp. 77-106, here pp. 86-91.
12. Cf. Martin Rheinheimer: "Seefahrt und Bevölkerung auf Amrum 1694-1918," in *Rundbrief des Arbeitskreises für Wirtschafts- und Sozialgeschichte Schleswig-Holsteins* 105 (2011), pp. 38-53.
13. Cf. Martin Rheinheimer: *Unter Sklaven und Piraten. Die abenteuerliche Geschichte des Amrumer Kapitäns Hark Nickelsen*, Amrum 2010.

The seafarers acted in a seamen's discourse. This discourse was carried on by the conversation on board and at home, when the seafarers told their stories, describing and exaggerating their adventures. The discourse lived at home and was manifested in the gravestones on which it was staged. Here the story of seafaring and family was jointly told and was visible for all, brought together and condensed into a monument. Because of their long biographies these headstones have been called "talking" or "speaking" stones.[14]

On the gravestones, the families from Amrum expressed their lives through biographies and pictures, for example, of ships. Thus, their subjective experience could also be known by other people – also people they had never met. This way, an *objectification*[15] took place, by which the subject itself became the object and thus created the possibility that his or her subjective experience was passed on to others and could become a part of collective memory. This possibility was strengthened by the fact that the headstones stood in the churchyard – in a special, sacred space. This assigned a special meaning to their stories.

The picture of a ship on the gravestone had not only a social significance by identifying the deceased as a seafarer, but also a symbolic and religious significance. It referred to the life journey. Unrigged or dismantled ships indicated the end of the journey. On the neighbouring island of Föhr, ships were sometimes shown lying in the harbour. This could be a specific port (e.g. Amsterdam), but also referred to the haven of eternity. At the churchyard of Boldixum, an unrigged ship lies under the heavenly Jerusalem.[16]

On the headstones narrative strategies were used for creating a story of the local maritime community, an identity. Certain families subscribed to it consciously. By looking into the history of these families, we can identify various motives for doing so.

Generally, specific families had "speaking" gravestones made. In most cases, these were old families that had already been present on the island before 1700. Before 1900, ten families (in the male line) put a ship

---

14. Cf. Walter Lüden: *"Redende Steine"*. *Grabsteine auf der Insel Föhr*, Hamburg 1984; Wolfgang Runge: *Sprechende Steine. Grabstelen im Oldenburger Land von 1600 bis 1800*, Oldenburg 1979.
15. Cf. Berek: *Kollektives Gedächtnis*, p. 58.
16. Cf. Rheinheimer: "Skibe for evigheden," p. 88, 95.

engraving on a single headstone, four families on two gravestones, and one family had three gravestones with a ship. Only one of the families immigrating to the island after 1700 represented itself with ship images, namely the family Quedens, and for this family we find as many as five gravestones with ships. Four children (three sons and one daughter), and one grandson of the immigrant Georg Hinrich Quedens had ships carved on their gravestones: Boy Quedensen († 1785), Philipp Ernst Quedens († 1797), Hinrich Quedensen († 1799), Anna Johanna Sönken († 1813), and grandson Georg H. Quedens († 1837). The daughter Anna Johanna had married Sönke Girris, a captain from an old local family – a family however without its own tradition in gravestones with ship images.

The father, Georg Hinrich Quedens, was originally a surgeon on Föhr. Later he became a customs officer and bought a house on Amrum in 1734.[17] His brother was a pastor on Föhr. His children went to sea, as was customary on Amrum, mostly on ships of their own. The family was thus new on Amrum and had no sea-going experience. Still, the children being the first generation of seafarers were very successful and had their gravestones decorated with vessels as other seafarers on Amrum did. By setting gravestones with images of ships, they marked that they had risen to the same social level as the old seafarer families and also inscribed themselves in the collective memory of the island. Through the "speaking" stones and their pictures, the churchyard became the vehicle of the collective memory. Here, the families mediated their identity.

The Quedens family was quite wealthy. In 1755, the immigrant Georg Hinrich Quedens was already the thirteenth richest of the 154 taxpayers on the island and thus belonged to the local elite.[18] Georg Hinrich Quedens did not have a ship on his gravestone, but with a long, representative inscription he already put himself in the vicinity of the rich seafaring families.[19] With the help of ship images and "speaking" stones, the Quedens family wrote itself into the history of the island and became part of the local identity – the local myth. Here, there is a link between ico-

---

17. Cf. Martin Rheinheimer: *Geschlechterreihen der Insel Amrum 1694-1918*, Amrum 2010, nr. 213.
18. *Kreisarchiv Nordfriesland A 3, Landschaft Westerlandföhr nr. 829*. The "Ummärkungsprotokolle" contain the tax schedules of Westerland Föhr and Amrum starting in 1755.
19. Cf. his gravestone in: Quedens: *Im Hafen der Ewigkeit*, p. 142f.

nography (vessel picture) and narratives (biography on the headstone). Individual and collective identities are always linked to stories and images and are constructed by them. This was the function of the gravestones. They served as self-representation of individuals and families, and were intended to clearly show their success to everybody. At the same time, they were to make any negative features of the deceased be forgotten in the face of death and eternity.

The family of Oluf Jensen produced two of the most beautiful headstones with ship images: the gravestones of Oluf Jensen († 1750) and Hark Nickelsen († 1770). The gravestone of Hark Olufs and those of the widows Marret Hark Nickelsen and Antje Harken, which are also preserved, are also appealing but they do not show a ship. Instead they depict a crown (Hark Olufs) and the Lamb of God (Marret Hark Nickelsen). The headstone of Antje Harken bears only a longer inscription.[20] This family was one of the oldest and richest. In 1755, Oluf Jensen's nephew and son-in-law Hark Nickelsen was the wealthiest taxpayer on the island, and Antje Harken, the widow of Oluf Jensen's son, Hark Olufs, was the eleventh richest. Still, this family had a need for self-representation, because Hark Olufs had been a slave in Algeria, during which time he had been promoted to the rank of general and probably had converted to Islam before he returned to Amrum as a rich man. After his death he was reported to haunt the island as a ghost.[21] Hark Nickelsen had earned his wealth, as mentioned, as a slave trader. These characteristics of the deceased were not mentioned on the headstones; these served entirely for promoting their fame.

The representation of a ship on someone's gravestone conveyed their success. The career of a seafarer included the possibility of social advancement. At sea, if you acquired or already had the necessary skills, you could move from humble beginnings to wealth.[22] The image of the ship itself and the financial capability necessary to have a ship carved on

---

20. On these gravestones, see Quedens: *Im Hafen der Ewigkeit*, pp. 36-51.
21. Cf. Martin Rheinheimer: *Der fremde Sohn. Hark Olufs' Wiederkehr aus der Sklaverei*, Neumünster 2001.
22. Cf. Jann M. Witt: "Generationen an Bord. Karrieremuster norddeutscher und nordeuropäischer Seeleute im 18. und 19. Jahrhundert," in Martin Rheinheimer (ed.), *Der Durchgang durch die Welt. Lebenslauf, Generationen und Identität in der Neuzeit*, Neumünster 2001, pp. 217-246.

the headstone served to indicate that the ascent was a success. The ship was in this way particularly suited for self-representation. Sometimes, however, people only feigned success. For instance, Andres Finck's family was among the old, but not among the rich on the island anymore. In 1755, when the tax registers (*Ummärkungsprotokolle*) start, his widow was just one of the poor taxpayers (127th of 154 taxpayers), and his eldest son Jens was also not particularly wealthy (45th of 154 taxpayers).[23] Nevertheless, this family had one of the most elaborate gravestones of the island produced. The headstone bears artistic images on both the front and the rear. This was a reminiscence of former better times and feigned a wealth, in reality no longer existing.

The gravestones had particular significance for the deceased and his or her family. The deceased wanted to tell a certain story about himself and thus achieve an intended memory within his family and the local community. With his death, the story of his life began to be transformed. In the beginning, for those left behind and later for following generations of the family and the local community, the headstone meant something other than for the deceased himself. The meaning of the contents was their individual understanding of it, even though stone and text remained the same. An explanation for this is the following: The deceased accounted for his life's story on the headstone. This story did not necessarily correspond to the truth, but was a story supporting how he wanted to be seen. There were typically other stories in circulation about the deceased. In the family and in the village stories were perhaps told about the deceased, stories which could be completely different from what was written on the gravestone. Over time, these stories were, however – if they were not put into writing – forgotten, and only the story carved in stone on the headstone was left and became history. Thereby, the deceased (or the bereaved who had the stone produced) had told the story his way, and this historically became the most powerful version, because it survived other competing stories.[24]

---

23. *Kreisarchiv Nordfriesland A 3, Landschaft Westerlandföhr nr. 829.*
24. An example is Hark Olufs who succeeded in displacing unwanted versions of his story by writing an autobiography and controlling the text on his gravestone; cf. Martin Rheinheimer: "Vom persönlichen Mythos zum lokalen Erinnerungsort. Hark Olufs und das Geschichtsbewußtsein der Amrumer," in Bea Lundt (ed.), *Nordlichter. Geschichtsbewußtsein und Geschichtsmythen nördlich der Elbe*, Köln/Weimar/Wien 2004, pp. 199-226, here pp. 211f.

Carl Ludwig Jessen's second painting of the church on Amrum, 1864. Museum Kunst der Westküste, Föhr.

The church was the central building on Amrum, and from all the villages on the island people went there – and also across the churchyard to the graves. The churchyard with its free-standing headstones was, as a painting by Carl Ludwig Jessen from 1864 shows, the meeting place of the parish, whose members promenaded among the graves after the service, and this way lived with the visible reminder of the past.

A ship is clearly visible on a headstone to the right in the painting. It seems to be the gravestone of Willem Claasen († 1792).[25] At another stone to the left, two men are discussing form or inscription.[26] The painting is evidently a conscious staging of the seafaring community. As evidence of this, the painting also displays a sailing ship in the background and seamen identified by the top hat and by the ribboned hat as a skipper

---

25. Cf. the picture in Quedens: *Im Hafen der Ewigkeit*, p. 109.
26. Cf. Ulrich Schulte-Wülwer: *Föhr, Amrum und die Halligen in der Kunst*, Heide 2003, pp. 47-49 with illustration 18. The painting can now be seen at the Museum Kunst der Westküste at Alkersum on Föhr.

and an ordinary sailor respectively. In the background, we see women in traditional island costumes, and far right, a woman praying in front of a gravestone.

Jessen had drawn his studies and sketches on Amrum in 1859. He then processed these into paintings later on when the Copenhagen Academy wished for paintings of the lives of ordinary people. For this purpose, he drew from the motives of his Frisian homeland. In his first painting from 1859, the church and churchyard of Amrum are shown without people.[27] These were added five years later. With them, myth and staging were also added. He staged a healthy community "living peacefully and carefree in a harmony of religion and traditions, past and present".[28] The real world was certainly not so harmonious.

Traditionally, people were buried in family graves. Each local family had a burial place in the churchyard, where their relatives were buried. Over time, new family members were buried and the graves of the older generations were removed. In this process the grave monuments like the headstones often disappeared.[29] This led to a silent change of meaning. Both the graves and their space have been modernised to some extent. Particularly beautiful old grave monuments (and those of persons important for family or community) have, however, often been preserved, creating continuity across generations, a kind of timeless identity. When families died out completely, the burial site was allocated to another family due to lack of burial sites. In such cases, the old headstones were perhaps removed, and the meaning of the space was changed. New families took over the place and gave their own meaning to it. This way, they created their own space. Sometimes the connection to the old families was preserved when families-in-law kept some of the ancient gravestones

---

27. This painting is located in the St. Clement's Church at Nebel on Amrum.
28. Konrad Grunsky-Peper, Klaus Lengsfeld & Ernst Schlee: *Gemaltes Nordfriesland. Carl Ludwig Jessen und seine Bilder*, Husum 1983, p. 29.
29. Sometimes the old headstones have been reused. On Föhr the text of several gravestones has been ground off, but the old image was kept. The same happened to the gravestone inside the church of Morsum on Sylt. Where wooden grave monuments were used, they had a shorter natural life span. Therefore, they have been preserved only at a few places, e.g. single monuments at Den Helder and Schaprode on Rügen. But they were much more popular because they were much cheaper than the real stones.

at the site. It is clear that the system with family graves only worked in a world where families lived for many generations at one place. Industrialisation and modern mobility have destroyed these relationships and created a new burial culture, since family graves lose their sense when all descendants have moved away from the place. As a consequence of this, more and more gravestones became "homeless". This was one of the reasons for the conscious rearrangements of the stones that later took place.

Translocations of the gravestones

In both paintings by Jessen, dating from the late seafaring period, the gravestones were in their original location around the church. The churchyard was a pasture without paths and clearly defined gravesites.[30]

The first major rearranging of the headstones in the churchyard took place in the 1880s. Ida Christine Matzen mentions this in her book "Children of Friesland", which idealises Amrum. Her account has the form of a dialogue:

> "'The architect Schmeiser, who supervises our lighthouse, has designed a map for the reorganisation of the graves. While the mounds until now have only been indicated by the side and the direction in which they lay around the church, they will now be divided into districts which are separated by crossing paths from south to north. The mounds that cross the walkways will be levelled and the grave monuments will be removed from the paths. Every house will regain its gravesite of four graves; the old houses will receive their former family gravesite, but with the provision that some of the old mounds that are on the walkways must be demolished. Some will move the beautiful gravestones from the walkways to the family grave. Where this does not happen, all residents are free to set up any monuments that they like on their hereditary grave. After a certain date the crossing paths should be cleared, and in case there are

---

30. The oldest surviving churchyard map from 1803 is, unfortunately, in such poor condition that I was not allowed to look at it. *Kirchenkreisarchiv Nordfriesland (Leck), Archiv der Kirchengemeinde Amrum St. Clemens, nr. 282.*

Church and churchyard on Amrum at the end of the 19th century, postcard. The churchyard is still a pasture without paths, and the gravestones are located at their original places.

still monuments on the paths, they will be set up by the churchyard wall. The matter will be enforced under much protest, of which I have already learned. Cornelius Martinen from Süddorf wanted to save the magnificent ancestral grave of Hark Olufs and preserve it unharmed for future generations. He urged to leave all the magnificent monuments in their original state. He did not, however, succeed in this. The double ancestral grave was cut in such a way that only Oluf Jensen's memorial remained untouched on his grave. Cornelius Martinen, the owner of Hark Olufs's house, has just enforced that no one lays a hand on Oluf Jensen's memorial. Therefore, Oluf Jensen's monument stands untouched where his son once had it set up, on his dust, but the monuments by his side, that of his son Hark Olufs, his son-in-law Hark Nickelsen and his wife Anje, have been removed.

Anje Harken's monument now stands ten steps from the gate to the right of the churchyard and as many steps further in the same direction Hark Nickelsen's; opposite him left by the path Hark Olufs's.

'Jacob, it is not in my power, if I could, I would move the monuments back to where they belong, to the ancestral grave, just as they stood, and where I often looked at them when I visited grandfather's grave holding my father's hand.

Oluf Jensen, Hark Olufs to his left, Hark Nickelsen further to the left, and finally Anje Harken, side by side, so they were, so I would like to see them again!'"³¹

Matzen's description expresses the conflict which the reorganisation triggered. Sections of the population still lived with the old graves, and the most striking headstones, such as Hark Olufs's, Oluf Jensen's and Hark Nickelsen's, enjoyed special appreciation, also outside their own family (Ida Christine Matzen was through her mother a great-granddaughter of Hark Olufs's).³² The reorganisation of the churchyard was therefore by no means uncontroversial. But at this time other interests were stronger than those of the old seafaring families.

In 1928, Theodor Möller added a map of the sites of the old gravestones which he had registered in June 1925 to his book on the churchyard in Nebel.³³ From the map, one can see that in spite of the rearrangements that took place in the 1880s, most of the old headstones were still in their original locations in 1925. A total of 32 of the old gravestones had already been set up at the edge of the war memorial. The graves in the churchyard were arranged in long rows separated by paths. This shows that there has been a complete redesign of the churchyard since Jessen did his paintings. In the same span of time, the church had twice been significantly rebuilt. In 1886, the walls of the choir had been made taller and in 1908 the dominant tower was added. Altogether, the shape of the church and the churchyard had completely changed.

In 1941, Magnus Weidemann painted a picture of the church and the churchyard in the snow, showing the church without the tower built in

---

31. Ida Christine Matzen: *Kinder Frieslands. Ein Familienbild um das Abendrot von Alt-Amrum*, Nebel 1914, pp. 260f.
32. Cf. Rheinheimer: *Geschlechterreihen*, nr. 217. 06.1.3. 8. – By the way, Cornelis Martinen, who was mentioned by Ida Matzen, used the rear of Marret Hark Nickelsen's gravestone as his own. First, the stone was used again for his wife in 1880. His own death date was carved afterwards in 1885. Font and style followed Marret's inscription with the protruding letters on the front.
33. Möller: *Kirchhof*, p. 136f.

Translocated old gravestones by the war memorial in the churchyard on Amrum before 1945, postcard.

1908.[34] Even the gravestones are still in their old order, but there seem to be more headstones than in Jessen's paintings. As in Jessen's paintings you can see the sea in the background (which is now obscured by bushes and trees). In the picture, there is thus a connection to the sea, which often plays a role in Weidemann's landscape paintings. Altogether the picture resembles the first postcards which originate from the period around 1900 and show the church, still without a tower. One wonders why Weidemann painted such an outdated motive in 1941, especially because he, during his short time as a pastor on Amrum in 1906/07, was involved in the plans to build a church tower. (His short time as a pastor can be ascribed to Ida Matzen who, with the sanctimonious group around her, quickly succeeded in enforcing a transfer of the – in their opinion – too

---

34. It is located in the Nordseemuseum – Nissenhaus (Husum), nr. 1351.

modern pastor.)³⁵ It seems absurd that he painted the church without a tower, even if he may have made sketches before the change. Rather, it might be a commissioned work for someone who intentionally wanted a painting of the state before the changes. In any case, the painting shows that there was a yearning for the past and original state.

In 1938, the churchyard was no longer sufficient, and a new, additional cemetery was situated to the north of Nebel, in an open field, so to speak.³⁶ Only gradually was it accepted by the locals, and today it looks somewhat neglected. This shows that the old graveyard in the vicinity of the church has significance as more than a burial site. Over time, the old churchyard around the church was further modified. The collection of the old headstones by the churchyard wall near the war memorial was just the first step. The war memorial was expanded and transformed after the Second World War. At this time, all the old headstones were collected on the west and north sides of the churchyard, and some were placed by and on the outer wall of the church. Only the gravestones of the Mechlenburg family³⁷ remained in their old place. None of the other old headstones can be found any more at the site of the original graves. The headstone of Hark Nickelsen was centrally situated in the middle of the place of honour in front of the war memorial, and at his side, left and right, the headstones for Hark Olufs and Oluf Jensen were placed (i.e. moved again since Ida Christine Matzen's description). The headstones for their wives were set far away by the churchyard wall.

Today, there are again plans for changes in the churchyard. Since 2009 a restoration of the lichen-infested old gravestones has been discussed, and in this context also a complete reorganisation of the cemetery.³⁸ The project description says: "The present condition does not allow a high profiled public presentation of the historic gravestones. The main objec-

---

35. On Weidemann, see Quedens: *Kirche*, pp. 75f.; Ulrich Schulte-Wülwer: *Sylt in der Malerei*, Heide 1996, pp. 140-143; Jürgen Wulf, Magnus Weidemann: *Keitum-Sylt 1880-1967*, Schleswig 1980; Manfred Wedemeyer: "'Amrum blieb mir verborgen'. Magnus Weidemann als Vikar in Nebel," in *Natur- und Landeskunde. Zeitschrift für Schleswig-Holstein, Hamburg und Mecklenburg* 110 (2003), 3/4, pp. 80-84.
36. Quedens: *Kirche*, p. 103.
37. Three members of this family had been pastors on Amrum in the 18th and 19th centuries.
38. Cf. Amrum News, 1.10.2009, 16.11.2010, 1.2.2011, 14.3.2011, 13.4.2011. http://www.amrum-news.de

tive is to set up the so-called 'talking' gravestones so that they 'talk in a way that is easier to communicate'. The planned presentation area is, with its high volume of visitors, not intended to be too much in touch with the mourning culture of the churchyard. Despite this separation of functions, the presentation area is to act as a natural part of the cemetery. The expansion of the cemetery must therefore take the character of the site into consideration." To this end, "an expansion area bordering immediately to the north of the churchyard" shall be used. Therefore, the plan includes removing the northern churchyard wall. "Brief stretches of hedge elements will break up the rigid rows of stones" as part of the vision, while granite blocks are expected to invite visitors to sit and linger. "After walking through the churchyard gate, the interested visitor gets the opportunity to enter the presentation area without detouring through the churchyard. Special gravestones with inscriptions on both sides can be staged and experienced here. The area is separated from the main churchyard area with its mourning culture by a yew hedge." The whole construction is to be adapted to accommodate the tourist visitors: "The area beyond the entrance offers space for a group of about 20 visitors who can gather here during expert guided tours. During the tours, the visitors will remain between the diagonally positioned rows of headstones." The new structure of space is clearly stressed in the concept: "Towards the old churchyard, the gravestones are to be arranged into two staggered rows in the gravel. This will also make a boundary to the churchyard area with its mourning culture." Through these rearrangements of the headstones, a tourist space will be created which will retain an artificial connection to the past: "Seen from the church, the old headstones act as a natural part of the cemetery ensemble." The museum-like character will not least be underlined by atmospheric lighting. The connection of the authentic mourning culture in the churchyard with the tourist attraction is explicitly sought: "By redesigning the exhibition area, the historic headstones can be appropriately exhibited and preserved. The museum area will act as a part of the cemetery ensemble, without the high traffic flow of visitors affecting the mourning culture in the main churchyard." The whole construction is conceived as an exhibition, and display panels will be added. "The endpoint of the pathway is – after the stones have told their stories – the rear of the presentation area, which is

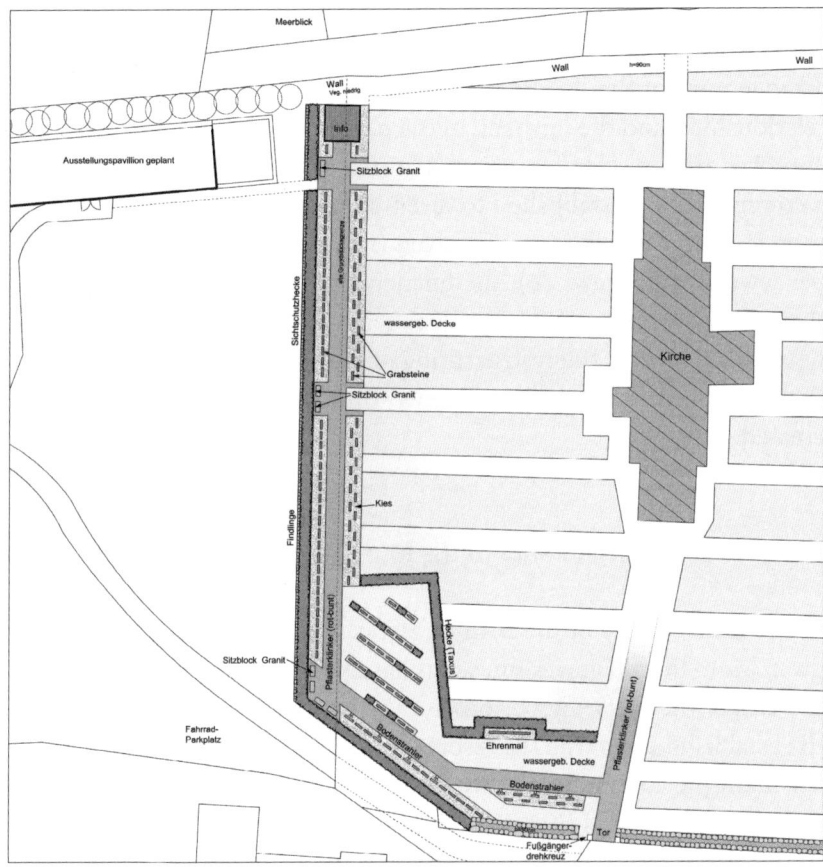

Concept for the redesign of the churchyard on Amrum, 2011. The old gravestones are now seperated from the churchyard, once more translocated, and presented to the tourists with information tables. The area at the left side has been bought to this purpose.

a steel frame in the form of a cube spanning a timber deck. Here, a wide view to the east over the Wadden Sea reveals itself to the visitors, while fixed panels provide detailed information on the exhibition."[39]

The development of the concept that will result in this change in

---

39. The project description can be found at: http://www.amrum-kirche.de/friedhoefe_historische-grabsteine.htm (July 2, 2011).

IN THE HAVEN OF ETERNITY? A CHURCHYARD AS A CONTESTED PLACE   257

the space took place in a negotiation process.⁴⁰ There was an initiative (the local historian Georg Quedens had always criticised the existing arrangement of the headstones showing no consideration for family relationships, and the husband of the pastor, an architect giving guided churchyard tours, also campaigned for restoration and rearrangement); a committee was established to discuss the approach; expert opinions were sought; the public was involved (not least via the online newspaper www.amrum-news.de); the financing of the project was organised through sponsorships for individual headstones; and finally, according to the plan, in 2013, the restructuring of the space will be completed by the rearrangement of the headstones. Thus, a new tourist space will be created.

The role of the gravestones in the tourist experience economy

In the local society of the 20th or 21st centuries, seafaring, which had given life to the old gravestones, was hardly an issue anymore. Following the end of the seafaring period and the breakthrough of tourism after the establishment of the sea resort in Wittdün from 1890, the people in the maritime communities have lived from tourism.⁴¹ Nevertheless the seafaring headstones showing images of ships have become central to the local memory – even if they express a very different society than the present one.

The change in resources and meanings led to a reconstitution of the space in form of the translocation of the headstones. In the words of Aleida Assmann, the step here is from a "site of generations", *(Generationenort)* where families live and die for generations, to a "site of memory" *(Erinnerungsort, lieu de mémoire)*, where "a certain history has not just gone on, but has been more or less abruptly cancelled".⁴² According

---

40. Cf. Löw: Raumsoziologie, p. 225.
41. Cf. Georg Quedens: *Das Seebad Amrum*, Amrum 1990; Friedrich Remde: *Amrum. Ein Beitrag zur Genese und Struktur einer Inselsiedlung*, Diss. Münster 1972, pp. 113-135.
42. Aleida Assmann: "Erinnerungsorte und Gedächtnislandschaften," in Hanno Loewy & Bernhard Moltmann (eds.), *Erlebnis – Gedächtnis – Sinn. Authentische und konstruierte Erinnerung*, Frankfurt/New York 1996, pp. 13-29, here p. 16.

to the definition of Etienne François and Hagen Schulze, such sites of memory can "be material as well as immaterial. They include some real and mythical figures and events, buildings and monuments, institutions and concepts, books and art – in today's parlance you could call them 'icons'. They are not sites of memory due to their material objectivity, but because of their symbolic function. They are durable focal points of collective memory and identity, outlasting generations, embedded in social, cultural and political customary practices, and they change in the extent to which the way of their perception, appropriation, use and transfer changes."[43] Aleida Assmann sees them as contact zones to the past.[44] Without doubt, the gravestones produce "materialisations of the reference to the past" which both the individual and the collective memory need.[45]

The old, decorative headstones have been collected at a specific location at cemeteries other than the one on Amrum. Examples can be seen in Boldixum on the neighbouring island of Föhr and in Keitum on Sylt. In some places, the most beautiful stones have even been brought into the church to protect them from the weather. This has happened on Helgoland, in Morsum on Sylt, in Sønderho on Fanø, and in Nieblum and Süderende on Föhr. Sometimes the gravestones were transferred to another cemetery when the old churchyard was closed or had disappeared (as in Hamburg, Bremen and Galmsbüll).[46] The memory preserved in the gravestones was so important for the collective identity of these local societies that they spent resources moving the gravestones to another place. Through the translocation, the character of the gravestones was fundamentally changed. They were no longer individual grave monuments keeping awake the memory of the deceased at the grave itself and

---

43. Etienne François & Hagen Schulze: *Erinnerungsorte Deutschlands*, München 2001, vol. 1, pp. 17f. On the concept of "sites of memory" (lieux de mémoire), see Pierre Nora: *Les lieux de mémoire*, 7 volumes, Paris 1986-92. – Cf. Martin Rheinheimer: "Mythos Sturmflut. Der Kampf gegen das Meer und die Suche nach Identität," in *Demokratische Geschichte 15* (2003), pp. 9-58; Rheinheimer: *Vom persönlichen Mythos*, pp. 199-226.
44. Berek: *Kollektives Gedächtnis*, p. 84. Cf. Assmann: "Erinnerungsorte und Gedächtnislandschaften," p. 25.
45. Cf. Berek: *Kollektives Gedächtnis*, p. 84.
46. Cf. Rheinheimer: "Skibe for evigheden," pp. 98-100.

offering the bereaved a place of contemplation and remembrance, but became sites of collective memory. In the case of the headstones with ship images, they became sites of memory of the maritime history of the community. They preserve the memory of the seafaring period and create a myth of seafaring,[47] the "founding myth" of the society.

With the move from communicative to cultural memory, a functional change has taken place. The function for the tourists is different from what it was for the people of Amrum in the seafaring period. The tourist is on a romantic search for something "authentic"[48] that he or she believes will be found in the gravestones. The tourists do not have any real connection to them, as the relics of the seafaring period do not existentially mean anything to them. On the headstones are sometimes exciting biographies and life stories to decipher. There will be guided cemetery tours and history can be taught narratively. This is a form of entertaining history usage[49] which has nothing in common with the existential importance of seafaring and the graves of the ancestors in the seafaring period. The headstones are only a holiday entertainment. For the people of Amrum, the meaning of the headstones has changed, too, because the focus of today is on potential earnings from tourism. The gravestones have become part of the tourist economy, which consists of entertainment and money making (even Georg Quedens's books must earn the author a living). The translocations of the headstones reflect this development: first away from the graves and to the edge of the churchyard, now to an adjacent plot of land outside of the old churchyard. This is a location outside the sacred space exclusively serving the entertainment of tourists. However, the headstones still maintain the proximity to the churchyard because the tourists then get a taste of

---

47. Cf. Klaus-Joachim Lorenzen-Schmidt: "Maritime Landschaft Unterelbe?," in Martin Rheinheimer (ed.), *Mensch und Meer in der Geschichte Schleswig-Holsteins und Süddänemarks*, Neumünster 2010, pp. 281-307. – On the role of gravestones for the group formation process cf. Reiner Sörries & Stefanie Knöll (eds.): *Creating Identities. Die Funktion von Grabmalen und öffentlichen Denkmalen in Gruppenbildungsprozessen*, Kassel 2007.
48. Cf. Orvar Löfgren: *On Holiday. A History of Vacationing*, Berkeley/Los Angeles/London 1999, pp. 97ff., 184, 261.
49. On history usage, cf. Niels Kayser Nielsen: *Historiens forvandlinger. Historiebrug fra monumenter til oplevelsesøkonomi*, Aarhus 2010.

the authentic and the existential from it, supporting the illusion which the tourist is looking for.

The headstones offer the tourists something "authentic". At least they give this impression to the tourist. The separation from the old meaning is reflected in some new gravestones, too: if individual gravestones from around the year 2000 on Ameland and Föhr show large, traditional tall ships,[50] it is not likely that the deceased sailed on them. Rather, old headstones have been copied and intentionally connected to an actually lost tradition. These stones have a nostalgic flair. They are a frozen symbol that says nothing about the real life of the deceased – except that he liked beautiful sailing ships and the old tradition, and that he wanted to create an identity as an individual different from others with the help of the stones.

The first translocation in the 1880s still caused a conflict because the surviving descendants of the old skipper families were reluctant to change and feared a loss of identity. The translocation that began in 2009 proceeded without conflict, reflecting the completion of the reinterpretation and the accomplished identity change from seafaring to tourism.

With the change in local history and the development of the maritime communities from seafaring to tourism, the local identity changed, and the gravestones gained a new meaning. They were now witnesses of a bygone era with which the present did not have much in common, except earning good money. Some of the translocations of gravestones are related to this symbolic meaning. The headstones of the skippers that were originally scattered throughout the churchyard have been preserved and gathered at a central and representative place where tourists have a good opportunity to admire them. The translocation is thus part of the marketing of the local society (which sells itself to tourists).[51] As sites of memory, the gravestones with ship images are reminders of

---

50. An example is the gravestone of Dirk Arfst Foitzik († 2002) at Nieblum on Föhr. There are similar examples at Hollum on Ameland.
51. Accordingly, old gravestones are often lost in places without tourism, as there is no (material) interest in preserving them. Thus, tourism has two sides: it leads to reinterpretation and trivialisation, but also contributes to preservation.

Guided tour by Georg Quedens to the old gravestones at the war memorial, 2002. In the foreground the backs of the gravestones of Oluf Jensen, Hark Nickelsen (in front of the stone of Andres Finck) and Hark Olufs. Photo: Martin Rheinheimer.

a, in some ways, glorious past and simulate an identity that does not exist anymore. Exactly this is their function (and perhaps the function of history in general): to establish a connection to a past, to make you believe that you are part of something that does not exist anymore. The memory of the lost is preserved and a continued existence is given to it in our memory.

The relationship is less borne by the family than by nostalgia, as many sponsors and activists are from new immigrant families. The *special* history of the island is preserved. In addition, the tourist element plays an enormous role. The headstones are the main attraction of the island and due to their long biographies unmatched in their ability to *tell* history/stories – "speak" about the past. Almost all visitors are tourists. For the local population, living directly or indirectly almost exclusively from tourism, the gravestones are mostly an attraction that contributes to the tourist success of the island. This is the major reason why people today reserve space exclusively for the headstones and spend money on them. A "floating gap"[52] is slowly growing between seafaring and tourism. Most of the people with whom you communicate on Amrum have never gone to sea; almost all live on tourism. Still, seafaring is the generally accepted origin of the local society. Two books about the churchyard of Amrum have been published. In his book, Georg Quedens not only offers photos of the gravestones and transcriptions of the inscriptions that are sometimes difficult to read, but also tells stories about the deceased and their families. This book has just been published in its third edition.

As the above has demonstrated, through spatial structure and attribution of meaning the churchyard shows the transition from one social structure (seafaring) to another (tourism).

Conclusion

In the sense of spatial sociology, the change from seafaring to tourist economy was accompanied by a restructuring of the visible spaces in the cemetery. New graves replaced the old and "took over" the churchyard, the old gravestones were translocated and became sites of memory: first around the war memorial (a special space), then by the churchyard wall, and finally outside the main churchyard area. Thus the memory moved away from the church and the churchyard and towards the periphery. A new memory space was created. This memory is still connected with the religious (church and churchyard), but the connection is slowly deteriorating, both geographically and substantively. The headstones still have a significant meaning to the island community, as the broad participation in rearrangement and restoration has shown (also financially by sponsorships), but the kind of meaning has changed. The explanation for this may be found in changes in the society. Seafaring is no longer the main source of employment in the former maritime communities. Today, tourism plays this role. This has led to a reinterpretation of the meaning of the gravestones.

At the beginning, the early tourism industry on the island contested the seafarer culture that prevailed at that time, creating conflicts. The

---

52. Cf. Assmann: *Das kulturelle Gedächtnis*, pp. 48-65.

lack of dissent regarding the present translocation shows that today the tourism industry has won the conflict and absorbed the old seafarer culture as a part of the experience economy. The skippers of Amrum have not arrived "in the haven of eternity", as Georg Quedens titles the third edition of his book on the gravestones of Amrum, even though they have been dead and buried for a long time. Rather the journey of their gravestones goes on, from one place to the next. The journey reflects the changing society and the changing significance of their past. What was once personal history and a created identity, now serves to attract and entertain tourists.

A Violently Contested Void – No Man's Land during the First World War

Bjarne Søndergaard Bendtsen

At all times, wars have brought out the utmost creativity in man to be able to conquer his enemy and thereby led to wide-ranging technological inventions. The First World War was definitely no exception, and as a by-product of the inventions instigated by this war, the phrase *no man's land* emerged and quickly evolved into an explosively productive metaphor. Initially, before the modern military usage, the phrase designated a stretch of land belonging to nobody, an uninhibited wasteland: a *terra nullius*. During the war, however, it was used about the area between two hostile trench lines: the physical centre of combat, particularly on the Western Front, contested like no other place – and yet it was nobody's. Even in the case of a breakthrough, the termination of the deadlocked trench warfare when an actual conquest of the contested area took place, no man's land simply moved to another position between the lines. Was this paradoxical status of no man's land reflected by the war literature and popular culture concerned with it? How did the soldiers' narratives treat the topic? This chapter will attempt to answer these questions, describe the character, place and geography of the no man's lands of The First World War, as well as examine the etymology of the phrase and the new metaphorical usages of it: the way it was rapidly turned into a new topos – a basic theme or motif – in literature, movies, painting and popular songs.

The dictionaries' definitions and the actual space described by the phrase

To start with the etymology, the short definition in *Oxford Advanced Learner's Dictionary* mentions two different kinds of places covered by the expression *no man's land*: it is "an area of land between the borders of two countries or between two armies and so under control of neither."[1] *Webster's Encyclopedic Unabridged Dictionary* divides the expression into three meanings, of which the first is relevant here: "a tract of land between opposing armies, over which no control has been established."[2] Even though the expression in this military sense is closely connected to the First World War, the phrase itself is much older than that. *The Oxford English Dictionary* gives this definition: "A piece of waste, or un-owned, land; in early use as the name of a plot of ground, lying outside the north wall of London, and used as a place of execution",[3] which in its own fashion is in keeping with the no man's land of the war. The earliest example of this usage dates back to 1320. Interestingly enough, in the issue of the *OED* from 1933, the modern military usage is not mentioned – at least not in the regular volume. This usage has been added in the supplement: "The terrain between the front lines of armies entrenched opposite one another."[4] The first example of this usage, however, dates back to 1908: "Here and there in that wilderness of dead bodies – the dreadful 'No-Man's-Land' between the opposing lines – deserted guns showed up singly or in groups." The next example quoted by the *OED* is from 1915, and here the inverted commas are no longer needed, indicating that the word by then was well-established. As evidence of the close connection between the phrase no man's land and the First World War, the majority of examples in a later supplement to the *OED* are about this war.[5] In the course of the war itself, the phrase furthermore became widely used

---

1. *Oxford Advanced Learner's Dictionary*, 5th edition, Oxford 1995, p. 785.
2. *Webster's Encyclopedic Unabridged Dictionary*, New York 1996, p. 970.
3. *The Oxford English Dictionary*, vol. VII, Oxford 1933, p. 183.
4. *The Oxford English Dictionary*, Supplement and Bibliography, Oxford 1933, p. 73.
5. R.W. Burchfield (ed.): *A Supplement to the Oxford English Dictionary*, vol. II, Oxford 1976, p. 1224.

in the languages of the other major belligerents and the neutrals. The phrase was either used directly (in French, the English *no man's land* was the common term[6]) or as a word-for-word translation (in German *Niemandsland*, and similarly in the Scandinavian languages, for example, *ingenmandsland* in Danish).

The first example of the modern military usage from the *OED* comes from Ole Luk-Oie's collection of short stories *The Green Curve, and other Stories* (1909), the dictionary says.[7] Ole Luk-Oie was the pseudonym used by Sir Ernest Dunlop Swinton (1868-1951) who, among other things, had fought in the Boer War and worked as the official British historian of the Russo-Japanese war of 1904-05. Swinton's short stories quite clearly predicted the character of the coming war regarding mass-scale battles with trenches and a no man's land in between, which might derive from his intense knowledge of the war in Manchuria. During the First World War, he worked as an official war correspondent on the Western Front, writing under the name *Eyewitness*, and, the thing he is most famous for, fostered the idea of the tank – to enable infantry to cross the no man's land of modern warfare, commanded by artillery barrages, machine guns and barbed wire.

Another example of this usage can be found in John Brophy and Eric Partridge's *Songs and Slang of the British Soldier: 1914-1918* (1930), where no man's land is defined as "A strangely romantic name for the area between the front line trenches of either army, held by neither but patrolled, at night, by both."[8] However romantic and strange, a modern encyclopaedia on the war defines no man's land as a "British term that was the accepted description of ground between opposing trenches by

---

6. See, for example, *Trésor de la Langue Française. Dictionnaire de la langue du XIXe et du XXe siècle (1789-1960)*, vol. 12, Paris 1986, p. 193-94.
7. In the 1976 issue, the source is changed to *Blackwell Magazine*, December 1908, p. 761. It is from the short story 'The Point of View', p. 243 in *The Green Curve, and other Stories*. For a digitalised version, see http://openlibrary.org/books/OL7143567M/The_green_curve_and_other_stories (April 9, 2012).
8. John Brophy & Eric Partridge: *Songs and Slang of the British Soldier: 1914-1918*, enlarged 3rd edition, London 1931, p. 142.

1914."[9] Furthermore, it describes the character, place and archetypal geography of it:

> On the Western Front in particular, No Man's Land was a permanent, if fluctuating, geographical feature for more than three years. Typically reduced to cratered wasteland, littered with corpses and other battle detritus, its width along the Western Front could vary between about twenty metres and almost a kilometre. Inevitably the focus of major engagements, it was often very quiet during daylight hours between actions, but was a scene of intense activity at night.

This chapter will follow suit as to the focus on the emblematic Western Front – despite the fact that no man's lands also existed and were frequently referred to by this name on the other fronts of the war. The character of no man's land, or rather the character of the trench systems that constituted the demarcation of it, has been described by the historian Tony Ashworth in his outline of the evolvement of the Western Front:

> The western front first emerged as the infantries of each deadlocked army huddled in countless hastily dug and unconnected rifle pits, then joined these together into two continuous but parallel and opposing trench lines [...] Between, and separating, the trenches of each opposing army lay no-man's-land. This was a continuous strip of ground held by neither army but patrolled at night and fired across by day by both. The length of no-man's-land was that of the western front itself; but its average width varied from 100 to 400 yards, although it narrowed, in some places, to as little as 5 to 10 yards and widened, in others, to as much as 1000 yards. The trenches of each side were roughly parallel to and stretched back from the outer boundaries of no-man's-land.[10]

---

9. Stephan Pope & Elizabeth-Anne Wheal: *The Macmillan Dictionary of The First World War*, London 1995, p. 345. 1914, however, seems to be too early for the phrase's usage. Furthermore, no man's land never became an official military term, cf. Cornelia Vismann: "Starting from Scratch: Concepts of Order in 'No Man's Land'," in Bernd Hüppauf (ed.): *War, Violence and the Modern Condition*, Berlin 1997, pp. 46-64, on p. 54.
10. Tony Ashworth: *Trench Warfare 1914-1918. The Live and Let Live System*, London 1986, p. 4.

As this passage – also – points to, no man's land emerged at random at places which the armies had accidentally occupied or where they were stopped by the enemy. At least generally so: The Germans were able to choose strategically advantageous high grounds for their trenches as their initial war of movement was halted after the first battle of the Marne, September 1914. Likewise, they planned their positions and thereby the position of no man's land after the tactical retreat to the heavily enforced Hindenburg Line in 1917.

The most predominant feature of no man's land, besides the shattered landscape and rotting bodies, was the wire:

> About 20 yards in front of the fire trench, a continuous belt of barbed wire, some 10 yards broad and 3 feet high, was staked in no-man's-land; occasionally, a second wire obstacle was built beyond the first, with its outer edge 40 or 50 yards from the trench. Soldiers had access to no-man's-land through tunnels in the parapet of the fire trench and lanes through the barbed wire defences.[11]

The soldiers' feelings for the wire were mixed: It protected their own trench against enemy assaults, and at the same time halted their attacks on the enemy, fatally slowing down their progress through no man's land, often resulting in soldiers getting stuck on the wire, helplessly exposed to enemy fire. Furthermore, the wire meant danger for the soldiers when they were ordered on nightly wiring parties – one of the main reasons for actually leaving the trenches and entering no man's land. Otherwise, the only kind of human life in this barren zone were saps and listening posts: "Sometimes a sap trench jutted into no-man's-land for 20 or 30 yards and served as an observation or advanced warning post."[12] And all activity took place underground during daylight.

As opposed to the dictionaries' older definitions of the land's undesirable character, the no man's lands of the First World War were fought over and seemingly incomparably desirable. Or so it seems, at least from a naïve perspective – why else would both sides be willing to risk the lives

---

11. Ashworth: *Trench Warfare*, p. 4.
12. Ashworth: *Trench Warfare*, p. 5.

of so many men to conquer it? Despite this status, it was an unstable kind of land, which changed to somebody's possession in the moment it was actually won by one side or the other.

No Man's Land as a literary and popular cultural topos

No man's land played and still plays a central role in the memories and mythologies of the First World War, as a powerful symbol, especially of the futility of this war with the stalemate, mud and madness in the trenches of the Western Front, but also as the place where daredevils went exploring and hunting. It was used in the titles of fictional and autobiographical literature that came out of the war. Johannes Reiff for instance, a Danish-speaking soldier in the German army, used both no man's land and the wire as central symbols of his war experiences in his two minor collections of war poems *Sangen fra Ingenmandsland* (1926) and *Nye Sange fra Ingenmandsland* (1930) (The Song from No Man's Land and New Songs from No Man's Land). In a stanza used as the motto for the first collection and in the final poem of it, his rather old-fashioned and romantic use of the war materiel as poetry is evident: "My lyre has rusty strings / from a Flanders barbed wire fence / and in my songs / the rain of the trench nights sings."[13]

Already during the war, a book using no man's land as its title and – to some degree – subject matter appeared: "Sapper"s (the pseudonym of Herman Cyril McNeile) *No Man's Land* (1917). In this book, the typical British high-spirited approach to the war is evident, depicting the war in many theatre and entertainment similes and metaphors, but not containing much about the actual no man's land. As part of the war book boom of the late 1920s, R.C. Sherriff's successful play *Journey's End* (1928) is set in a front-line dugout the night before the big German offensive 21 March 1918; Erich Maria Remarque's bestseller *All Quiet on the Western Front* (1929) takes place among front soldiers but interestingly enough

---

13. Johannes Reiff: *Sangen fra Ingenmandsland*, Copenhagen 1926, p. 28: "Min Lyre har rustne Strenge / fra et flandersk Pigtraadshegn, / og i mine Sange synger / Skyttegravsnætternes Regn."

without using the word *Niemandsland*; and in the memoirs of the British war poets Blunden, Graves and Sassoon, who all fought in the infantry and thus in the front lines, no man's land plays a significant part. This was also the case in Vernon Bartlett's novel simply entitled *No Man's Land* (1930).[14] The title was so popular that Thomas Dinesen, a Danish volunteer with the Canadians and brother of the famous author Karen Blixen, probably felt he had to change his *No Man's Land. En Dansker med Canadierne* (1929) to *Merry Hell! A Dane with the Canadians* in his own 1930 English translation. Even in scholarly literature the phrase has been widely used, most importantly here in Eric J. Leed's *No Man's Land. Combat & Identity in World War I* (1979), but also as an unsurprising theme in gender studies, for example in Sandra M. Gilbert and Susan Gubar's three-volume *No Man's Land. The Place of the Woman Writer in the Twentieth Century* (1988-94).

There were movies dealing extensively with the topic or even using it as a title, most famously Lewis Milestone's Oscar-winning adaption of Remarque's *All Quiet on the Western Front* (1930), or German movies like G.W. Pabst's *Westfront 1918* (1930) and Viktor Trivas's *Niemandsland* (1931), which in the English version was called *Hell on Earth*. In Trivas's movie, five men accidently meet in a cellar under a ruin in no man's land – a German, an Englishman, a Frenchman, a Russian Jew and a black American vaudevillian – and decide to fight "their common enemy – WAR" instead of each other, as the overtly pacifist caption at the end of the movie states.[15]

No man's land was also a prominent subject in painting, especially among the more elitist modernist artists. A well-known example is Paul Nash (1889-1946), who fought in the trenches on the Western Front from February 1917, until he was appointed an official war artist later that year. His paintings of the war ironically reflect the apocalyptical

---

14. In the American version it was, however, called *The Unknown Soldier*. Bartlett furthermore co-wrote the novel version of Sherriff's *Journey's End*.
15. An incomplete English version of the film can be found at http://archive.org/details/Hell-OnEarth (April 9, 2012). There were also movies during the war using the phrase in the title, e.g. John H. Collins' *The Flower of No Man's Land* (1916), which, however, does not seem to have anything to do with the war, cf. http://www.answers.com/topic/flower-of-no-man-s-land (April 9, 2012).

hopes for a new world emerging out of the war, as in *We are Making a New World* (1918), where the sun rises on the devastated, desolate landscape of a present or former no man's land. Or, in more direct ways, they express bitter comments on the futile, industrial destruction of lives and landscape, as in *Void* (1918), with its thematic equation with the emptiness and nothingness of no man's land evident in the title, and *The Menin Road* (1919), which is all shell holes and mud and no road in sight.[16] Thus, no man's land was used as the visual sign and emblem of the madness of war in both wartime painting and the pacifist films of the early 1930s.

However, no man's land played its most prominent role as a theme in popular songs – the number of songs employing the phrase in different fashions is truly striking. One of the earliest was by the American soldier, actor and pulp fiction writer Arthur Guy Empey (1883-1963), 'Your Lips Are No Man's Land But Mine' from 1917 – "A real romantic war ballad", as the dramatic cover of the music sheets states. The romantic character of the song is evident in the chorus, with its interesting doubling of the topos as the real war's topographical stretch of land *and* a metaphorical love token or rather domineering demarcation of one's territory: "I'm coming back some day when the fray is over, my darling. / I know you'll be true, dear, so I'll never be blue, dear. /Across the foam in No-Man's land I'll soon be fighting. / But I know your lips are no-man's land but mine."[17] Empey had served in the US Navy and Cavalry for some years before the war, and, after the sinking of the *Lusitania*, he volunteered for the British forces, serving in a Royal Fusiliers machine gun company and participating in the early stages of the Battle of the Somme, in which he was wounded and as a consequence discharged.[18]

Like Empey's, the majority of these songs seem to have been Ameri-

---

16. http://www.iwm.org.uk/collections/item/object/20087 (August 2, 2012).
17. http://www.militarysheetmusic.com/your-lips-are-no-mans-land-but-mine.htm (May 5, 2012).
18. See Arthur Guy Empey: *Over the Top*, London 1917, and his short biographical sketch in the *Wyoming Tribune*, 15 January 1918, p. 4, http://wiki.wyomingauthors.org/w/page/27124071/ Arthur%20Guy%20Empey (April 8, 2012). In the latter, however, he does not mention the *Lusitania* as the reason for joining the British, but a German on Broadway passing the remark that the Americans were too proud to fight.

can: Al Jolson's sentimental song 'Hello, Central! Give me No Man's Land' (c.1918) is one example, naïvely narrated from the perspective of a child not understanding that her father has been killed in the war *over there*: "Hello, Central! Give me No Man's Land, / My daddy's there, my mamma told me [...]"[19]; Bernie Grossmann and Ray Lawrence's 'Just a Baby's Letter. Found in No Man's Land' (1918) is another: "[t]o a soldier daddy over there, / Filled with crosses at the ending, / Meaning kisses baby's sending".[20] There were also fairly racist songs, though typical for the time. Will E. Skidmore and Marshall Walker's 'When I Gets Out in No Man's Land (I Can't Be Bother'd with No Mule)' (1918) is about an old Uncle Tom type African American riding his mule into no man's land with a six shooter in his hand and a rum bottle sticking out of his pocket – German soldiers shouting "Kamerad!" and surrendering at the mere sight of him. Or is it the ragged mule's braying that scares them?[21]

Songs written by women and narrated from a female perspective were rarer, but one example is Jessie Spies's 'While You're over there in No-Man's Land (I'M OVER HERE IN LONESOME LAND)' (1918), with its lonely but faithful girl somewhere in the States, keeping "the home fires bright."[22] This song plays out almost all the contemporary propaganda clichés with the girl being proud of her sweetheart *doing his bil*, and thus urging those not doing theirs to get *over there*, another US cliché – while she keeps the *home fires bright*.

As is evident from the examples, these songs all use the topos of no man's land as a central metaphor for the war, and to different degrees in maudlin, sentimental ways. An instance of no man's land used as a sentimental setting for a classical First World War figure, namely the nurse, can be seen in Jack Caddigan and James A. Brennan's 'The Rose of "No Man's Land"' (1918). Naturally, the song's rose is placed in a strictly metaphorical no man's land, since the nurses did not enter the real one: "It's the one red rose the soldier knows, / It's the work of the Master's hand;

---

19. http://www.firstworldwar.com/audio/hellocentral.htm (May 15, 2012).
20. https://jscholarship.library.jhu.edu/handle/1774.2/20021 (April 8, 2012).
21. https://jscholarship.library.jhu.edu/handle/1774.2/29919 (May 15, 2012).
22. https://jscholarship.library.jhu.edu/handle/1774.2/13633 (May 15, 2012).

/ 'Mid the War's great curse stands the Red Cross Nurse, / She's the rose of "No Man's Land"."[23]

The phrase no man's land was used in an aggressively propagandistic manner as a regular threat against the enemy in J.E. Dempsey and Tom Kennedy's 'Germany you'll soon be no man's land', published in Australia, probably towards the end of the war.[24] After the armistice, the transformation of no man's land when peace followed war was treated in Harry Carlton and Jay Whidden's post-war song 'Good-bye No Man's Land! (You'll be Some Man's Land Someday)' (1919).[25] As this song's title indicates, no man's land would ultimately *have* to become somebody's after the war. The song's rather unbiased approach might derive from the fact that it is Australian, and thus less directly involved in the European dogfight over territories – which, however, the first of these Australian songs strongly contradicts. The same theme about winning no man's land, with additional boastful pride, was used by the black American lieutenant James Reese Europe (1881-1919), leader of the 369th U.S. Infantry "Hell Fighters" Band and participant in the war, who in March 1919 recorded a title written by him and Noble Sissle, 'All Of No Man's Land Is Ours'.[26] Europe furthermore wrote and recorded a rather rare song that deals with the actual no man's land as seen from the soldier's point of view: 'On Patrol in No Man's Land' (1919), with fantastic sound effects of *Minenwerfers*, hand grenades, machinegun fire, and sirens and bells warning about gas, performed by the band.[27]

During the early post-war years, the topos became a central part of

---

23. http://library.duke.edu/rubenstein/scriptorium/sheetmusic/a/a12/a1238/a1238-1-72dpi.html (May 16, 2012), and for a performance of the song: http://www.firstworldwar.com/audio/roseofnomansland.htm (April 9, 2012). The song also exists in a French version: 'La Rose sous le Boulets'.
24. There is no year on the sheet music, cf. http://nla.gov.au/nla.mus-an12885278 (April 9, 2012).
25. Cf. http://nla.gov.au/nla.mus-vn4601751 (March 16, 2012). The song was performed by Claude Hansen, who served with the 3rd Australian Auxiliary Hospital, was wounded at Gallipoli and eventually promoted to staff sergeant serving in Britain. See also: http://ozvta.files.wordpress.com/2011/01/17-appendix-c-1920-1935-bibliography1.pdf (May 15, 2012), p. 518.
26. See Tim Gracyk's article "Lieutenant James Reese Europe. Songs Brought Back from the Battlefield", http://www.worldwar1.com/sfjre.htm (May 15, 2012).
27. For Europe, see R. Reid Badger: *Life in Ragtime. A Biography of James Reese Europe*, Oxford 1995.

the bitter comment on the demobilised soldiers' situation in the anonymous song 'Stony Broke in No Man's Land', also referred to as 'The British Soldier's Discharge Song', with its resigned criticism of the broken promises to the citizen soldiers: "In 1914 a hundred years ago it seems / When first the world was awakened from its peaceful dream / The bugle called I went away / They said I was a man then / But ah what can I do today". The promise that his job would be there for him when he came back, which was intensely used in the recruitment propaganda, proved to be a lie – as the song says, "When we crossed shell-swept No Man's Land / Through poison gas attacks / This promise heard: / "If you are scared you'll get the old job back!""[28]

Finally, to leave the popular songs, metaphorical no man's lands can be found in a couple of books by female authors. In Gladys Browyn Stern's (1890-1973) novel *Children of No Man's Land* (1919) the phrase is used about national identities caught between the belligerents, i.e. about neutral foreigners in Britain during the war who were suspected of being pro-German. And in Mary Borden's (1886-1968) collection of sketches and poems *The Forbidden Zone* (1929), partly about her "four years of hospital work with the French Army",[29] an interesting example appears in the story 'Rosa'. An unconscious wounded soldier, big and strong like a bull, is described in this way: "His spirit – brother spirit of the ox and bullock and all beasts of the field – was deep asleep, in that sleep which is the No Man's Land of the soul, and from which men seldom come back."[30] Thus, no man's land could also be used about a state of consciousness near death.

The no man's lands in soldiers' memoirs and letters

The enormous interest and curiosity regarding the mythological no man's land, reflected by its widespread metaphorical use and by its prominence

---

28. A version performed by Frank Miller in 1921 can be heard at: http://www.firstworldwar.com/audio/stonybrokeinnomansland.htm (March 16, 2012).
29. Mary Borden: *The Forbidden Zone*, London 1929, n.p.
30. Borden: *Forbidden Zone*, p. 94.

in popular cultural products, was also found among the soldiers fighting in the actual no man's land. In their memoirs and letters, there are numerous descriptions of no man's land. These descriptions often contain accounts of fresh recruits arriving in the trenches, scared senseless but still fascinated by finally having reached the centre of things: the place where the belligerents' immense forces collided, and where the ultimate test of manhood was performed.

The soldiers' experience with this unknown land would mostly be connected with extreme danger and anxiety, such as in the case of nightly patrols, wiring parties, and especially when the entrance was part of large scale attacks. Going over the top,[31] as was the contemporary phrase for this action, would be the climax of heavy bombardments and intense fear in the hours and minutes leading up to the attack. As the bloodiest example, the first day of the Battle of the Somme, 1 July 1916, cost the British nearly 60,000 casualties.

The curiosity about no man's land can even be found in some of the few Danish war books: the aforementioned volunteer with the Canadians, Thomas Dinesen (1892-1979), who won the Victoria Cross for bravery, wrote about his first time in the front line trenches at Avion, 24 March 1918:

> I am standing on a piece of board stuck like a step into the wall of the trench, and gaze across the parapet over the desolate No Man's Land. Immediately in front of me is a big heap of *débris* and masonry – all that is left of a tall house, whilst a little to the left the roof of another house is lying as if it had just slid down, and whenever a star-shell lights up the scenery I can see the rafters protruding like the ribs of some huge animal.[32]

Later on, at Liévin, 20 April, he describes the view towards the German trenches in this way: "During the day there is no sign of life to be seen among the gravel-heaps over there. The whole waste-land looks grey

---

31. Quite reasonably connected to the meaning of something being "to an exaggerated or excessive degree", cf. *Oxford Advanced Learners Dictionary*.
32. Thomas Dinesen: *Merry Hell! A Dane with the Canadians*, London 1930, pp. 111-12.

and forgotten, like a landscape on the moon."³³ And, in more detail, the same place at night:

> A hundred yards east of us, a similar embankment runs across the valley, parallel with ours; behind it, the Germans are lying, they say, watching us just as we watch them, though of course we can't see anything of them. Every now and then a star-shell shoots high into the air from Fritz's outposts [...], and the desolate waste of No Man's Land, with its shell-holes and barbed-wire entanglements, lies sharply outlined in black and white; whilst the dazzling rocket sinks slowly to earth and dies in the mud with a hiss.³⁴

As opposed to the boldness of fire-eater Dinesen, the Northern Schleswiger Johann H. Petersen highlights the fear and high-strung nerves evoked by the baptism of fire in his autobiographical war novel *Yngste Reserve* (1930, The Youngest Reserve). When he, or his fictional character, arrives at the front trench and is ordered to stand on guard at night, his nerves are so feverish that he imagines all sorts of movements in no man's land, fires round after round at ghosts, and eventually nearly faints from the paralysing fear.³⁵ His fear is, however, not quite groundless: No man's land could only be entered after dark or in extremely foggy conditions, and therefore patrols and raiding parties were sent out under cover of darkness, for instance to take prisoners for intelligence purposes. Both sides also used nightfall to improve trenches and wire entanglements, and to bring in wounded and dead soldiers, which was no direct threat to the enemy soldier standing on guard. These actions, however, could easily be interpreted as preparations for dangerous raids by the nervous guard. Hence, danger was lurking everywhere after nightfall, and grown men seemed suddenly to have become afraid of the dark, provoked by the caveman-like conditions of atavistic violence in the trenches.

One of the famous – and famously stoic – British war poets, Robert Graves (1895-1985), who fought with the Royal Welch Fusiliers and was

---

33. Dinesen: *Merry Hell!*, p. 143.
34. Dinesen: *Merry Hell!*, p. 145.
35. Johann H. Petersen: *Yngste Reserve*, Copenhagen 1930, pp. 77-78.

seriously wounded during the Battle of the Somme, wrote in his autobiography *Good-bye to All That* (1929) about the first time he faced no man's land:

> The German front line was about three hundred yards beyond them [British listening-posts in no man's land]. From berths hollowed in the sides of the trench and curtained with sandbags came the grunt of sleeping men.
> I jumped up on the fire-step beside the sentry and cautiously raising my head stared over the parapet. I could see nothing except the wooden pickets supporting our protecting barbed-wire entanglements, and a dark patch or two of bushes beyond. The darkness seemed to move and shake about as I looked at it; the bushes started travelling, singly at first, then both together. The pickets were doing the same. I was glad of the sentry beside me; his name, he told me, was Beaumont. 'They're quiet to-night, sir,' he said, 'a relief going on; I think so, surely.' I said: 'It's funny how those bushes seem to move.' 'Aye, they do play queer tricks. Is this your first spell in trenches, sir?' A German flare shot up, broke into bright flame, dropped slowly and went hissing into the grass just behind our trench, showing up the bushes and pickets. Instinctively I moved. 'It's bad to do that, sir,' he said, as a rifle bullet cracked and seemed to pass right between us. 'Keep still, sir, and they can't spot you. Not but what a flare is a bad thing to have fall on you. I've seen them burn a hole in a man.'[36]

Similar descriptions of flares and no man's land at night can be found in Arthur Guy Empey's autobiography *Over the Top* (1917), with the additional title: "by an American soldier who went, Arthur Guy Empey, machine gunner, serving in France":

> About every twenty minutes the sentry in the next traverse would fire a star shell from his flare pistol. The "plop" would give me a start of fright. I never got used to this noise during my service in the trenches. I would watch the arc described by the star shell, and then stare into No Man's Land waiting for it to burst. In its lurid light the barbed wire

---

36. Robert Graves: *Good-bye to All That*, Oxford 1995, pp. 99-100.

and stakes would be silhouetted against its light like a latticed window. Then darkness.[37]

And later on in his book:

The real work in the fire trench commences at sundown. Tommy is like a burglar, he works at night. Just as it begins to get dark the word "stand to" is passed from traverse to traverse, and the men get busy. The first relief, consisting of two men to a traverse, mount the fire step, one man looking over the top, while the other sits at his feet, ready to carry messages or to inform the platoon officer of any report made by the sentry as to his observations in No Man's Land. The sentry is not allowed to relax his watch for a second. If he is questioned from the trench or asked his orders, he replies without turning around or taking his eyes from the expanse of dirt in front of him. The remainder of the occupants of his traverse either sit on the fire step, with bayonets fixed, ready for any emergency, or if lucky, and a dugout happens to be in the near vicinity of the traverse, and if the night is quiet, they are permitted to go to same and try and snatch a few winks of sleep. Little sleeping is done; generally the men sit around, smoking fags and seeing who can tell the biggest lie. [...] If a man should manage to doze off, likely as not he would wake with a start as the clammy, cold feet of a rat passed over his face, or the next relief stepped on his stomach while stumbling on their way to relieve the sentries in the trench.[38]

An enemy attack under gas is described in this way:

Our eighteen-pounders were bursting in No Man's Land, in an effort, by the artillery, to disperse the gas clouds. The fire step was lined with crouching men, bayonets fixed, and bombs near at hand to repel the expected attack. [...] I trained my machine gun on their trench and its bullets were raking the parapet. Then over they came, bayonets glistening. In their respirators, which have a large snout in front, they looked like some horrible nightmare. All along our trench, rifles and machine guns

---

37. Empey: *Over the Top*, pp. 36-37.
38. Empey: *Over the Top*, pp. 63-64.

spoke, our shrapnel was bursting over their heads. They went down in heaps, but new ones took the place of the fallen. Nothing could stop that mad rush. The Germans reached our barbed wire, which had previously been demolished by their shells, then it was bomb against bomb, and the devil for all.[39]

As an appendix to the book, Empey has compiled a "Tommy's Dictionary of the Trenches". Here, no man's land is defined in this rather jocular way: "The space between the hostile trenches called "No Man's Land" because no one owns it and no one wants to. In France you could not give it away."[40] This definition could seem to contradict my initial assumptions as to no mans' land being sought after, but the sharp irony of it is probably due to the perspective offered by the low-ranking Tommies in the trenches, paying the price for attacking the enemy. Or to the humorous and often sarcastic tone of his "so-called dictionary", as he calls it.[41] Empey's autobiography was made into a film in 1918, in which he acted as himself, and later, in 1928, he co-directed the film *Into No Man's Land*. None of these unfortunately seem to exist anymore but still exemplify the use of the topos in popular culture.

When actually going over the top and attacking the enemy in the open, trying to cross that mythical no man's land and attempting to make it your own, the attacker paradoxically became more vulnerable than the attacked: "The victimized crowd of attackers in no man's land [...] has become one of the supreme images of the war. Attackers moved forward usually without seeking cover and were mowed down in rows, with the mechanical efficiency of a scythe, like so many blades of grass."[42]

Descriptions of entering no man's land during attacks quite understandably take up central parts in memoirs of veterans lucky enough to survive. In Edmund Blunden's (1896-1970) *Undertones of War* (1928), his battalion going over the top at Passchendaele, 31 July 1917, is described this

---

39. Empey: *Over the Top*, pp. 190-191.
40. Empey: *Over the Top*, p. 301.
41. Empey: *Over the Top*, p. 281.
42. Modris Eksteins: *Rites of Spring. The Great War and the Birth of the Modern Age*, London 1990, p. 145.

way: "We rose, scrambled ahead, found No Man's Land a comparatively good surface, were amazed at the puny tags and rags of once multiplicative German wire, and blundered over the once feared trench behind them without seeing that it was a trench."[43] The quote shows the attackers' lack of knowledge of the conditions in no man's land, and their experience is described as amazement and confusion.

To return to the descriptions of no man's land, the poet Wilfred Owen (1893-1918), who was killed during the last week of the war, wrote about propaganda and no man's land in sarcastic terms in a letter to his mother, 19 January 1917:

> They want to call No Man's Land 'England' because we keep supremacy there. It is like the eternal place of gnashing of teeth; the Slough of Despond could be contained in one of its crater-holes; the fires of Sodom and Gomorrah could not light a candle to it – to find the way to Babylon the Fallen. It is pock-marked like a body of foulest disease and its odour is the breath of cancer. I have not seen any dead. I have done worse. In the dank air I have perceived it, and in the darkness, felt. Those 'Somme Pictures' are the laughing stock of the army – like the trenches on exhibition in Kensington. No Man's Land under snow is like the face of the moon chaotic, crater-ridden, uninhabitable, awful, the abode of madness. To call it 'England'![44]

It is not quite clear to whom Owen refers by 'they': the army in France or, more likely, the war correspondents and propaganda authorities back home in Britain. But the biblically cursed character of no man's land and, in particular, the metaphors of disease clearly point to his feelings for this stretch of land. Likewise, Owen's sarcasm regarding the immensely popular "Somme Pictures" is striking – the documentary *The Battle of the Somme* (1916) sold more than 20 million tickets in Great Britain during the first two months after its release, 17 August 1916. The movie's battle

---

43. Edmund Blunden: *Undertones of War*, London 1928, p. 214.
44. Quoted from Wilfred Owen: *Collected Letters*, Harold Owen & John Bell (eds.), London 1967, p. 429, Owen's underlining. See also http://www.oucs.ox.ac.uk/ww1lit/collections/document/5234?REC=9 (April 6, 2012).

scenes were as authentic as the unrealistic, clean and dry trenches dug in Kensington Gardens to show the home front how splendid were the conditions for the boys in Flanders and France.[45]

Similar descriptions of no man's land's desolate lunar character can be found in many participants' reminiscences, for instance those of painter and writer Wyndham Lewis (1882-1957), who was the leader of the aggressive British avant-garde movement Vorticism. When he replaced his art war with the real one as second lieutenant in the Royal Artillery, serving as a gunner on a howitzer battery during the Third Battle of Ypres or the Battle of Passchendaele, July-November 1917, his first impression of the barren war zone was that of a lunar landscape or an African desert. After going through the British lines, up to the front, passing wounded field artillerists and debris of war, he writes in the autobiography *Blasting & Bombardiering* (1937):

> But at this point civilization ended. At least so far, we [Lewis and his commanding officer] could be sure of our bearings. Beyond this battery was a short stretch of shell-pitted nothingness – for we had entered upon that arid and blistering vacuum; the lunar landscape, so often described in the war-novels and represented by dozens of painters and draughtsmen, myself among them, but the particular quality of which it is so difficult to convey. Those grinning skeletons in field-grey, the skull still protected by the metal helmet: those festoons of mud-caked wire, those miniature mountain-ranges of saffron earth, and trees like gibbets – these were the properties only of those titanic casts of dying and shell-shocked actors, who charged this stage with a romantic electricity.[46]

Upon his immediate arrival at the front, and thus having had limited time to polish his impressions, Lewis described the landscape of modern war in a letter to his fellow Vorticist Ezra Pound, 14 June 1917:

---

45. For the Kensington trenches, see e.g. Paul Fussell: *The Great War and Modern Memory*, Oxford 2000, pp. 43-44.
46. Wyndham Lewis: *Blasting & Bombardiering*, London 1982, pp. 131-132.

Imagine a stretch of land one mile in depth sloping up from the old German first-line to the top of a ridge, & stretching to right & left as far as you can see. It looks very large, never-ending and empty. There are only occasional little groups of men round a bomb-dump, or building a light railway: two men pushing a small truck on which a man is being brought back, lying on his stomach, his head hanging over the side. The edge of the ridge is where you are bound for, at the corner of a demolished wood. The place is either loathsomely hot, or chilly according to the time of day at which you cross it. It is a reddish colour, and all pits, ditches & chasms, & black stakes, several hundred, here & there, marking the map-position of a wood. Shells never seem to do more than shave the trees down to these ultimate black stakes, except in a few cases when they tear them up, or a mine swallows them.

The moment you get in this stretch of land you feel the change from the positions you have come from. A watchfulness, fatigue and silence penetrates everything in it. You meet a small party of infantry slowly going up or coming back. Their faces are all dull, their eyes turned inwards in sallow thought or savage resignation; you would say revulsed, if it were not too definite a word. There is no regular system of communication trenches yet; this is the bad tract, the narrow and terrible wilderness. As a matter of fact it only becomes clearly unsafe as you approach the ridge.[47]

Despite the precise description of the ruined landscape of the Western Front, this is clearly not the contested place between the lines: it is a former no man's land, now conquered by the British.

Regarding the change of status that no man's land underwent in the process of battle, or in the following example as a consequence of winning the entire war, lieutenant-colonel Theodore Roosevelt (1887-1944) – son of the former president and *Rough Rider* during the Spanish-American war of 1898 – wrote in his memoirs *Average Americans* (1919): "We passed the barren zone that had been No Man's Land for four years and was now again France."[48] As the latter part of the quotation indicates, no man's

---

47. Timothy Materer (ed.): *Pound/Lewis, the correspondence of Ezra Pound and Wyndham Lewis*, New York 1985, pp. 75-76.
48. Theodore Roosevelt: *Average Americans*, London 1919, p. 202.

land comprised a de-nationalised zone, something that was obviously neither German, since the German soldiers had not been able to conquer it, nor French anymore, since the French had not maintained control of it – and otherwise it would not have become France *again*. Later on, as Roosevelt's regiment led the way into Germany, occupying the left Rhine bank, the area around Verdun is described as an extended no man's land. It consisted of the large strip of land that had been so ferociously fought over since February 1916, "the uninhibited zone", and of its hinterland, where not all the inhabitants had fled: the "freed French villages",[49] as they are called. In this zone, much to Roosevelt's chagrin it seems, the inhabitants did not welcome their liberators with any kind of enthusiasm but rather watched their coming with apathetic scepticism. Hence, this area can be seen as a mental no man's land as well, its inhabitants taking up a psychological position somewhere between the belligerents, not daring to feel for either side.

Conclusive remarks: Good-bye No Man's Land?

As shown above, the different usages of the phrase "no man's land" primarily varied within the metaphorical field of cultural products, while the descriptions of the actual battlefield zone had a more homogenous character. Nevertheless, there was some variation of the use of no man's land in veterans' memoirs and letters. Some even refrained from using this phrase, for instance Roosevelt in the latter passage quoted above or Lewis in most of *Blasting & Bombardiering*. In Roosevelt's case, quite reasonably as the war was over at the time of his passage through the no man's land of Verdun – adding proof to the narrow definition of the phrase: that a no man's land requires two opposing armies, and that it vanishes the moment the one retreats or wins the war. In Lewis' case, the more distant and observant approach of the artillery officer to the strip of land between the frontlines can be seen as an explanation of his metaphorical universes – especially the lunar ones. The artillerist did not fight in no man's land; he fought distantly by means of coordinates and

---

49. Roosevelt: *Average Americans*, p. 218.

mathematical formulas, whereas the infantryman had to enter the eerie void between the lines during attacks. Lewis does, however, use no man's land to describe the war zone, but in a rather special way, adding to the definitions. The gunner's indirect way of fighting and Lewis's definition of no man's land are described thus:

> As a battery officer at the Front my main duties were to mouch [sic] about the battery, and to go up before daybreak with a party of signallers to an observation post. This was usually just behind the Front Line trench – in the No Man's Land just behind it. For there were blanks behind as before.[50]

This definition has not become the prevailing one, whereas the one deriving from the more direct experience of the infantryman has – as exemplified by the famous British war poets Blunden, Graves and Owen, and the less well-known Danish veterans Reiff, Petersen and Dinesen. Yet, the instable character of no man's land, the way it changed into someone's the moment an attack succeeded, is not reflected by the material examined here.

There seem to be blanks and contested places also in the metaphorical use of no man's land. The soldiers and civilians looked at the concept and the brutal, bleak reality of no man's land in highly different terms. Still, the phrase was immensely productive in a variety of metaphorical meanings, as well as in the descriptions of the actual landscape of the war. In the popular memory of the First World War, and in the literature about it, no man's land has become an emblem of a futile, deadlocked war, from which no one returned as winners. Despite its rapid departure as a popular cultural topos after the armistice, it was, however, not a goodbye to the phrase. Metaphorical no man's lands still exist to this day, describing so diverse activities as social relations between people, psychological conditions and, in tennis, the area between the service line and the baseline, where a player is most vulnerable.

---

50. Lewis: *Blasting & Bombardiering*, p. 127.

Contributors

Rune Andersen, born 1974, is a Ph.D. External Lecturer at Centre for Contemporary Middle East Studies, University of Southern Denmark, Odense. Among recent publications are: *Turisme – morfologi og manifestation: Ekskursioner i turismens idégrundlag med særligt henblik på britisk guidebogslitteratur om Egypten i det 19. århundrede*, PhD thesis, University of Southern Denmark, 2012. *Mødet med den systematiserede fremmedhed – En undersøgelse af guidebøgernes og museets gensidige formidlingsstruktur i den victorianske periode*, Academic Quarter, Volume 4 – Journeys, p. 28-41, Spring 2012.

Bjarne Søndergaard Bendtsen, born 1970, is External Lecturer in History, Aarhus University. His doctoral thesis, 'Mellem Fronterne. Studier i Første Verdenskrigs virkning på og udtryk i dansk kultur, 1914-1939' (Between the lines: the First World War and Danish culture) (University of Southern Denmark, 2011), analyses the impact of the First World War on Danish culture.

Jørn Brøndal, born 1961, is Associate Professor of American Studies, University of Southern Denmark. Among recent publications are "The Ethnic and Racial Side of Robert M. La Follette, Sr., *Journal of the Gilded Age and Progressive Era*, 10, 3 (July 2011), 340-353; "Danes and Danish Americans, to 1870;" "Danes and Danish Americans, 1870-1940;" "Danes and Danish Americans, 1940-Present," in Elliott Robert Barkan, ed., *Immigrants in American History: Arrival, Adaptation, and Integration* (4 vols.), Santa Barbara, California: ABC-Clio, 2013: vol. 1, 51-58 and 323-331; vol. 2, 871-880.

Michael Bregnsbo, born 1962, Associate Professor of modern history, University of Southern Denmark. Among major publications are *Til venstre* hånd. *Danske kongers elskerinder* (2010) and *Det danske imperium. Storhed og fald* (2004) (with Kurt Villads Jensen).

Christian Høgel, born 1964, is Associate Professor of Classical Studies, University of Southern Denmark, and senior researcher at the Centre for Medieval Studies (Danish National Research Foundation, at York & Odense). Among recent publications are "An early anonymous Greek translation of the Qurʾān: The fragments from Niketas Byzantios' *Refutatio* and the anonymous *Abjuratio*," *Collectanea Christiana Orientalia* 7 (2010), and *The Martyrdom of St Athanasius of Klysma*, (2012, together with J.P. Monferrer Salas & V. Christides).

Kurt Villads Jensen, born 1957, is Associate Professor of medieval history at the Department for History. Among his recent publications are *Jerusalem in the North. Denmark and the Baltic Crusades, 1100-1522* (2012) and 'Bigger and Better. Arms Race and Change in War Technology in the Baltic in the Early Thirteenth Century', in *Crusading and Chronicle Writing on the Medieval Baltic Frontier. A Companion to the Chronicle of Henry of Livonia*, ed. Marek Tamm, Linda Kaljundi, and Carsten Selch Jensen (2011).

Jesper Majbom Madsen, born 1973, is Associate Professor of Greek and Roman History, University of Southern Denmark. Among recent publications are *Eager to Be Roman: Greek Response to Roman Rule in Pontus and Bithynia* (2009) and "Provincialisation of Rome" in D. Hoyos, *A Companion to Roman Imperialism* (2011).

Anne Magnussen, born 1964, is Associate Professor of Spanish Studies, University of Southern Denmark. Among recent publications are "*Mara* and *Paracuellos* – Interpretations of Spanish Politics from the Perspective of the Comics", *Scandinavian Journal of Comic Art (SJoCA)*, 1:1 (Spring 2012), pp. 26-44, and "New People, New Historical Narratives. When the Mexican-Americans Came to Gonzales, Texas, at the Turn of the Twentieth Century."*Diálogos Latinoamericanos* 16 (2009), pp. 16-34.

Per Grau Møller, born 1955, is Associate Professor of cultural historical cartography, University of Southern Denmark. Among recent publications are "Post-medieval rural heritage: Research and management – some reflections", in Harnow, Henrik, David Cranstone, Paul Belford & Lene Høst-Madsen (eds), *Across the North Sea: Later historical archaeology in Britain and Denmark, c. 1500-2000 AD* (2012), pp. 119-29, and "Denmark" in Fairclough, Graham & Per Grau Møller (editors). *Landscape as Heritage: The Management and Protection of Landscape in Europe, a summary by the COST A27 project "LANDMARKS"* (2008), pp. 45-59.

David Edwin Nye, born 1946, is Professor of American Studies, University of Southern Denmark. The most recent of his 12 books are *When the Lights Went Out* (2010) and *America's Assembly Line* (2013), both published by MIT Press.

Martin Rheinheimer, born 1960, is Professor of maritime and regional history, University of Southern Denmark. Among recent publications are *Der Kojenmann. Mensch und Natur im Wattenmeer 1860-1900* (2007) and *Der fremde Sohn. Hark Olufs' Wiederkehr aus der Sklaverei* (2001, 3rd ed. 2007).

Peter Seeberg, born 1952, is Associate Professor and Director of Studies at Centre for Contemporary Middle East Studies, University of Southern Denmark. Among recent publications are "European Neighbourhood Policy, Post-normativity, and Pragmatism". *European Foreign Affairs Review*, 2011, and *The European Union's Democratization Agenda in the Mediterranean* (edited with Michelle Pace), Routledge, 2010.

Kirstine Sinclair, born 1976, is Assistant Professor at the Centre for Contemporary Middle East Studies, Institute for History, University of Southern Denmark. Among recent publications are: "Hizbut-Tahrir i Danmark og Storbritannien: Samtidige transnationale og nationale tendenser", *Tidsskrift for Islamforskning*, Nr. 1, 2012, s. 337-53, and *Lived Space: Reconsidering Transnationalism among Muslim Minorities*, Peter Lang, 2011.

Peter Thaler is Associate Professor of History at the University of Southern Denmark. His central publications on national and ethnic identities include *Of Mind and Matter: The Duality of National Identity in the German-Danish Borderlands* (2009) and *The Ambivalence of Identity: The Austrian Experience of Nation-Building in a Modern Society* (2001).